1973

**DATE DUE**

| | | | |
|---|---|---|---|
| DE 06 '9 | MY 13 '97 | | |
| DE 15 '9 | E 12 '97 | | |
| MY 1 7 '96 | MR 17 '98 | | |
| JY 23 '96 | SE 23 '98 | | |
| E 19 '9 | OC 07 '98 | | |
| OC 29 '96 | 26 '98 | | |
| NO 1 2 '96 | E 7 '9 | | |
| DE 1 3 '96 | | | |
| FE 01 '97 | | | |

DEMCO 25-380

pg.
98

1983

# ABORTION

# ABORTION

## *A Case Study in Law and Morals*

## *FRED M. FROHOCK*

Contributions in Political Science, Number 102

GREENWOOD PRESS
WESTPORT, CONNECTICUT • LONDON, ENGLAND

**Library of Congress Cataloging in Publication Data**

Frohock, Fred M.
   Abortion.

   (Contributions in political science, ISSN 0147-1066 ;
no. 102)
   Bibliography: p.
   Includes index.
   1. Abortion—United States—Moral and ethical aspects.
2. Abortion—Law and legislation—United States.
I. Title. II. Series.
HQ767.5.U5F76   1983      363.4'6      83-5614
ISBN 0-313-23953-3

Library of Congress Catalog Card Number: 83-5614
ISBN: 0-313-23953-3

First published in 1983

Greenwood Press
A division of Congressional Information Service, Inc.
88 Post Road West
Westport, Connecticut 06881

Printed in the United States of America

10 9 8 7 6 5 4 3 2 1

# CONTENTS

# INTRODUCTION

Abortion, seen from a distance, is an issue offering a variety of intellectual prizes. Any discussion of abortion can, and frequently does, touch on the origins of human life, theories of social justice, any number of competing rights (to life, to one's body, to privacy), and—especially—the role of the state in enforcing morals. No one can explore abortion issues without entering some of the deep and lasting areas of human thought.

Abortion, however, cannot be kept at a distance. It is a practical issue of the greatest importance, possibly the most volatile problem in American society today. The intensity with which views on abortion are held always impresses. Conversations with either pro-life or pro-choice groups rapidly disclose a depth of commitment that seems to have no limits, certainly little ambiguity or qualification. Fidelity to cause is a refreshing discovery for academics. But it is also disturbing to encounter a core of beliefs absolutely unflinching in the face of rational argument. The saying in my university is sad and to the point: do not have both pro-life and pro-choice on the same platform if you seek an understanding of abortion. In one famous encounter on my campus, the first question from the audience asked the pro-choice proponent why he was in favor of killing babies. Students frequently end a discussion of pro-life arguments with this aside: "The arguments may favor pro-life, but I will always personally favor pro-choice." So much for the Socratic hope that reflection can change basic beliefs.

The rock-hard character of abortion beliefs helps explain the high emotional levels at which public disputes over abortion occur. The disputants believe in what they say, and believe it with unshakable faith and little charity towards those who take an opposite view. The uninterrupted seriousness of abortion encounters suggests the form and standards for any inquiry into the issue. A book on abortion must find a way to wrap the theoretical and the practical in a single package, and to exhibit the deep structure of beliefs held with a private clarity almost impossible to translate into ordinary prose.

The narrative theme of this book is regulation—in particular, under what conditions the state is justified in enforcing morals. The delicate balance—some would say outright hostility—between social regulation and private choice is the organizing principle for the discussion that is to follow. But the substance of the book—the topic which gives content to the theme—is the moral and political status of abortion. One of the many remarkable features of abortion is the ease with which the issue bends the narrative theme to its needs. For example, it will be shown very quickly that abortion is not easily treated with standard tests for deciding between regulation and private choice. Innovative treatment is required, measures deriving from the features of abortion rather than from the accumulated wisdom of political theory. The result is that the content of the book—abortion—finally controls theory. The issue itself dominates current models of political regulation.

The dominance of abortion over theory can be demonstrated easily enough. Two models of state regulation currently occupy most of the field of political theory. One is the libertarian, or minimalist, state deployed recently by (among others) Robert Nozick. The main idea of this model is that the state is a conflict-management institution, primarily designed (as John Stuart Mill saw) to protect individuals from physical attack. The second model justifies a liberal state. Here the thought is that the state can redistribute assets and resources if individuals can agree on the principles of distribution. This second model has been famously elaborated by John Rawls.

Now there is much to say on behalf of each of these models. Adjudication between them is exceedingly complex, involving many fine arguments. But abortion requires even finer arguments and better models. A conflict-management theory of the state assumes as settled precisely what is at issue in abortion—the existence of separate individuals. The pro-life perspective believes that the fetus is a person, thus requiring protection from the state against assault by others. The pro-choice perspective mainly believes that the embryo is not a person, thus not requiring state protection. Settling this disagreement between the two sides is impossible on the premises of the libertarian model. The liberal model is more helpful because (in its Rawlsian form) it starts at an earlier point, with collective individuals in hypothetical conditions of choice. Thus one can ask a more imaginative question—what would a rational person choose as a political resolution of abortion problems not knowing whether he would be an embryonic or an actual person? (It is interesting that the hypothetical part of Rawls's theory—one of its most criticized features—is precisely what is more useful in approaching abortion problems.) But this model also fails, for the dispute over membership criteria for a human being—the main issue in abortion—carries over to the original position unresolved by the liberal model of rational choice.

The transforming effects of abortion issues on political theory are not disturbing. We are, after all, committed to induction. (Does anyone still believe that political theory can be deduced from metaphysical principles?) But the dominance of issue over theory stresses the importance of understanding abortion as fact, as actual event. Hence, two out of the six chapters are devoted to summaries of the legal, political, and experiential (who gets abortions, what are the frequencies of abortion, etc.) features of abortion. The political resolution proposed in the last two chapters must be understood in terms of what is developed and presented in the first four chapters (including, especially, the tragedy of unmarried pregnant minors).

Textual discussion, however, does not capture the partisan qualities of abortion issues, no matter how lively the text. One has to turn to the activists to see abortion as an issue in political and moral life. During the summer and fall of 1981 I interviewed a number of individuals who have been active for either pro-life and pro-choice. Selections from some of these interviews are integrated into the textual material. There is no grand or innovative methodological point to be made in this manner of presenting material (except for displaying my greater affinity for Studs Terkel than for survey research). I want only to introduce the vivid comments of activists to the more arid prose of theory and data, perhaps reminding the reader (as the author has been reminded) that intensity is still best found among those for whom issues really matter. One unusual feature of my use of interview material is the length of the quoted material. There are two explanations for this. One is that I found the views of activists truly fascinating, even when I disagreed with what they said (which was most of the time for most of the respondents). Second, abortion is an issue on which activists and philosophers have much to say, but rarely to each other. I want the textual material to proceed as if the author's arguments are part of a conversation with abortion activists. Of course, as author I have the advantage of the first and (almost always) last words. The activists have the middle words, though quite a few of them in the pages to follow.

If a single statement on method were selected to describe the efforts in this book, it would be drawn from Aristotle's *Politics* rather than from recent empirical techniques: " . . . a compound should be analyzed until we reach its simple and uncompounded elements. . . . " (Barker transl, p. 2.) The aim of this discussion is to break down the arguments of pro-life and pro-choice to more basic components and then examine these components in the context of actual statements by activists. It should be clear to anyone familiar with survey design that the interview material is not introduced as a representative sample (however defined) of abortion attitudes. The interviews are rather used here as an informal device to exhibit beliefs that are discussed extensively in philosophical literatures.

The bond in abortion issues between partisan and philosophical discussion provides two advantages. First, it illuminates the deeper logic of partisan beliefs, and, by doing so, identifies areas where pro-life and pro-choice may converge. Isolating components in competing positions is standard in negotiation and bargaining; for disentangling issues and reducing them to more elementary particles can disclose areas of agreement often obscured at macro levels of expression. Second, it demonstrates the importance of philosophical and, especially, moral discourse in understanding abortion as a practical political issue. Since abortion is a dispute that is conducted in moral terms by partisans, moral philosophy is needed to understand the issue. Notice that this use of moral philosophy says nothing about tiresome disagreements over facts *vs.* values, the cognitive status of moral statements, or value-free inquiry. Nor does the observation depend on the important evaluative functions of morality in ranking social conventions or actions. The point is more rudimentary and, one would think, indisputable: that an issue framed in terms of moral rhetoric is unintelligible in the absence of moral concepts. Or, put less delicately, understanding abortion without morality would be roughly equivalent to explaining the actions of the Federal Reserve Board without any use of economics. The method for developing the discussion proceeds on these modest assumptions—that juxtaposing partisan views on abortion with philosophical arguments illuminates the core logic of partisan argument and may expose areas of compromise between the two positions; and that moral language is a vital instrument to render abortion intelligible as a political issue.

The nine individuals whose interviews are represented in the pages to follow are: Reverend Jeremy Jackson of the Syracuse Christian Action Council; Rita Kisil, president (at the time) of the Syracuse chapter of the Right to Life Foundation; Sol Gordon, Professor of Human Development at Syracuse University; Kathy Hughes, who has served as a local counselor for the Syracuse chapter of Planned Parenthood (and also, at the time of the interview, a graduate student in anthropology at Syracuse University); John Willke, president of the national Right to Life Foundation; Bill Baird, director of three abortion clinics on Long Island, New York, and an individual long active in liberalization of abortion laws (and who was interviewed by my research assistant, Wendy O'Brien); Karen DeCrow, a Syracuse attorney who is past national president of the National Organization of Women; U.S. Congressman Henry Hyde, author of the Hyde Amendment that cut off federal funding for abortions; and one of the women who related in confidence to me their abortion experiences (the "respondent" interview concluding the text). In addition to these nine individuals, I also want to thank the following for talking with me, sometimes at considerable length and always with great patience: Dr. Carolyn Gerster, past president of the National Right to Life Committee and (at this writing) Vice-President in Charge of International Affairs of NRLC; Mary McGahn, president of Birthright in Syracuse; Marilyn Lyman, Community Services Coordinator of Planned Parenthood in Syracuse; Norma Harris, a counselor at Planned Parenthood; Deborah Vogel and Ann Tierney, at the time representing the New York State Abortion Rights League; Mildred Jefferson, current national president of the Crusade for Life, who took part in a debate with Sol Gordon on campus that will be remembered forever by those in witness thereof; Ann Buerkle; the Reverend Graham Hodges; and those of my students who debated abortion issues with me in a series of seminars, including especially Ron Mohar. Also, I am pleased to record my substantial debt to Guido Calabresi, Sterling Professor of Law at Yale University, whose lectures at Syracuse University in the spring of 1982, "Ideal Beliefs and the Law," changed my thinking on abortion. The suggestion in Chapter 3 that *Roe* could have been developed on the equal-protection clauses in the Fourteenth Amendment I have taken from several of Professor Calabresi's remarks in his last lecture in the series. But I do not have any reason to think that he would agree with the thoughts I express there or in any other place in the text. I am also grateful to Sam Donnelly of the Syracuse University Law School, who read all of the manuscript and made many helpful comments, especially on the *Roe* decision, and Kent Rissmiller, a graduate student in the political science department here at Syracuse University who assisted in the research and clarified my thoughts on many points of law, and my wife, Val, for typing the final draft of the manuscript and providing helpful advice at several stages of the work. Finally, my thanks to an anonymous reader (contracted by Greenwood Press) for many detailed suggestions for improvements. Naturally I assume full responsibility for what I have said and do not in any way suggest that the individuals whose thoughts are expressed here in the interviews agree with my arguments or conclusions.

The certitude of those active in the abortion conflict has eluded me, in spite of (or perhaps because of) the many conversations I have had with activists. I find no truths written in stone on this issue, but instead difficult and painful options, and many different types of victims. Uncertainty may be a congenital defect in my makeup. But I still am grateful to those who tried to convince me of the rightness of their views. Ironically, the most forceful of all those I spoke with is the one with whom I finally disagreed most strongly — Jeremy Jackson. What lesson is to be found in that experience I do not know. But let the record show that all of these individuals (and many others) patiently explained and defended their views to an individual chronically outside the minds of those who see truth as pure and uncomplicated.

# ABORTION

# 1
# ENFORCING MORALS

**1**

Abortion is a Rashomon story. It has many tellings, and the narrators see different truths. Listen to Bill Baird describe how he became involved in abortion politics.

. . . . In New York City, I heard a woman scream going into a hospital. . . . I ran into the hallway and saw this woman, who looked to be about 30 years of age, literally staggering. I was still pretty fast back then and I ran after her and I caught her. As I held her for a moment, I let her slide to the ground and I noticed the lower part of her body was totally covered with blood and she had an eight-inch piece of wire coathanger sticking in the uterus with which she had obviously tried to abort herself when she found she was pregnant for the ninth time, on welfare, but single and in those days, you could not get birth control pills if you were single. That was the law of New York. So the woman died right before me and she was so worried about her kids, what would happen to them and now the whole family was totally split apart after her death and I was outraged that a society could say to a woman, not only could you not have an abortion, but you could not even have birth control. And the ironic part was that we could fly that same woman to India or to Pakistan, you and I, the taxpayer would pay for birth control overseas. But in New York and many other states, we couldn't. I thought that was foolish and that's when I decided to do something.

Baird, as any student of constitutional law knows, became an advocate for pro-choice and helped liberalize laws on birth control and abortion. Now listen to Rita Kisil, who became active on the pro-life side.

. . . . Probably I knew way back in my subconscious that abortion was killing. My first real idea of what an abortion is really is that movie they made on the book *The Cardinal.* I was a very young woman. I was married, but I was a very young woman, and I came out of that, I'll never forget that movie. After I thought about the baby being killed, I felt bad about the family situation, if people had kept their mouths shut, it would never have come to that, and the girl—the trauma that she went through—and then when Rockefeller started bringing up, came out with the abortion thing, my girl in the seventh grade said, "You've got to write to Rockefeller so he won't pass that abortion law." She said, "You have to get involved." I kept resisting. I had never written to a government. I guess I just didn't realize what was happening at that point. I wasn't involved actively and I kind of thought—I know I didn't have any picture of what it would be if we had it today. So anyway I finally did write and then I did go to a meeting where I realized what was involved with the abortion issue. I think I was probably unique in comparing myself to some people actively involved in the pro-life movement in that I can honestly say I feel equally as sorry for the woman as for the baby, or maybe even more so because of the deception. It isn't just the killing of a newly created life but the rip-off of the woman. I feel bad that women who jump on the ERA band—all the things they promote up front—we're all in it for many of the things the ERA stands for. But again the woman is being manipulated to get on the bandwagon for something that appears to be good, when underneath the woman again is getting a rip-off. I really am in it for equal rights for women because I believe women should have equal rights. The state did come into being and should always remain as a state to protect the weak. Once we allow society to accept the killing of any part of humanity, we have been intimidated—all of us. If their life is going to be unprotected, then we are all in jeopardy. Because if they can kill the unborn, and it has led to infanticide, and they are bringing us euthanasia faster. You see, the abortion [thing] took about forty years, at least forty years. And the people were the kinds of people who wanted abortion. It didn't really start ten or twelve years ago. It took a long time before the average person knew about it. Euthanasia is going at greater speed. We will see more of it in our lifetime.

The reader is asked (by the author) to ponder the implications of these remarks. They are typical of the responses made by pro-choice and pro-life activists to questions designed to draw out the deeper values partisans hold on abortion issues. Both Baird and Kisil explain themselves in moral terms; and both are concerned with the woman who is pregnant. The difference between them is, mainly, this: Baird is exclusively concerned with the woman's well-being, while Kisil believes that abortion is the murder of an innocent human being.

The intensity with which abortion activists explain their moral views can be sensed as soon as conversations begin. It spills over to touch every facet of abortion organizations. Every Friday, for example, a small group of middle-aged to elderly women pickets the Planned Parenthood center in Syracuse, New York — one of many such demonstrations across the country. Encounters with such groups are always a learning experience. On a recent Friday afternoon, for example, your author parked his car on the street and started to cross the picket line to interview a Planned Parenthood counselor inside the building. He had to pass by the group. The women were unlikely figures for a demonstration. They were dressed not in Koch-type gingham (too obvious), but in fashionable department store dresses and blouses. They held placards.

"Abortion is murder, sin. Do you agree with that?" (Nothing like starting with the basic beliefs.)

"I have complicated views on abortion," the author responded.

"Leave him alone, Mildred. He's one of them."

"Why do you say that?" the author responded. "Just because I don't agree with you wholeheartedly right now?"

"Because you're going in there [Planned Parenthood]. And because if you're with us, then you wouldn't have to think about saying so."

"Do you think this is right?" another asked. She held up a poster showing a mutilated fetus in a trash can.

Mutilated fetuses are important displays for pro-life groups. One more anecdote helps fill out the picture. The author began several years ago inviting representatives from pro-life and pro-choice to join his seminar on "Ethics and Politics." The students would spend several weeks reading the philosophical, legal, historical, and empirical studies of abortion. Then abortion activists would address the class. The author (or, in this case, teacher) first called the local chapters of Right to Life and Planned Parenthood at the start of his own odyssey into abortion issues some years ago. Right to Life responded with alacrity, arranging almost immediately to have a speaker address the class. Planned Parenthood was more wary.

Who was the pro-life speaker to be? The author told them. A Mrs. Ann Buerkle. Right, well, we'll get back to you.

Several days later the education director of Planned Parenthood, Marilyn Lyman, called.

"We can't get a speaker for you," she told the author.

"Why not?"

"No one will appear with the slides that will be shown."

"What slides?"

The author phones Ann Buerkle and arranges to see the slide show privately in the seminar room of the University library. The show begins with color photographs of *in utero* fetal development. The slides are beautiful in the artificial way that *Life* magazine photographs are beautiful. (Indeed, many of these slides *are Life* photographs from some years back.) Then, while the slide projector clicks to each change of scene, the photographs begin to show dead fetuses, mutilated fetuses after abortions, some with limbs and torsos severed, chopped up, organs mangled by suction abortions and thrown on the floor or in trash receptacles. One photograph shows a human hand holding two tiny (presumably severed) feet, said to be taken from a 10-week-old fetus. The scenes are unlike any the author has seen and remind him of war photographs from Viet Nam.

After the display is over, the author has no difficulty making a decision. "You can't show these photographs to my class." The rationale is easy to state—that the students are a captive audience, that they are young and impressionable, that college courses are reflective rather than emotional experiences. He is not sure of the truth of any of these arguments except the one he doesn't state: that if these slides are shown, the pro-choice side will be blown away, and—for better or worse—the author aims to make both sides, all sides, of the abortion controversy accessible to the students.

Mrs. Buerkle reluctantly accepts the condition. She is, by the way, a very attractive and intelligent young woman who was, at the time of the seminar presentation, about 30 months pregnant (or so it seemed to the author).

The class turns out to be an emotionally charged success which fails every test of rational inquiry. The students play devil's advocate with both sides, though they link up emotionally with Ann

Buerkle. Marilyn Lyman, who joins her side's presentation, is vexed and puzzled that the issue of life for the fetus even comes up for discussion. The two sides of activists end up shouting at each other after four hours of seminar discussion that ranges over law and morality, rights to life and rights to control one's body. The author goes home and romps with his children (an activity that never fails to restore his sanity). The next day word reaches him that Planned Parenthood has had it with campus presentations.

In future seminars, abortion guests come in sequence to the author's seminars, separated from each other by time as well as by the values they endorse.

## 2

Are these just personal or random experiences? Hardly. The formal literature distributed by pro-choice and pro-life is replete with intense appeals. No content analysis is needed to appreciate messages like those found in daily communications from pro-choice and pro-life.

Katharine Hepburn, for example, sends a regular yearly letter to your author (and to millions of other people as well) in which she says "that a minority [pro-life] is using whatever political power they can muster to force their point of view on you and me." Faye Wattleton, president of national Planned Parenthood, warns — on the *envelope* of her nationally distributed letter, that: "The New Right doesn't like what you're doing in your bedroom, so they're going to amend the Constitution to make it illegal. Don't laugh. They're sure they'll succeed."

The pro-life literature describes abortion as murder, simple and direct. In a Knights of Columbus flyer, a Diary of an Unborn Child describes (in the fetus' own imaginary words) the beginnings of existence on October 5 ("Today my life began. . . . I shall have blond hair and blue eyes. . . .") to the abortion on December 28 ("Today my mother killed me.") The Right to Life Foundation mails literature in an envelope that has a picture of an adult human hand reaching out to a child's hand (like the hand of God about to touch Adam's hand on the ceiling of the Sistine Chapel). Inside the envelopes are the latest warnings against abortions and — the natural concomitant for pro-lifers — euthanasia.

Communication is not easy between groups that regard each other as totalitarian threats, on the one side, and baby murderers, on the other side. Is it possible to tell the story of abortion without the Rashomon effect? Can we cut through the intense, and often hysterical, charges and counter-charges to see abortion as it may look without the deep and deepening layers of emotion?

There are four parts to the abortion story. Listen to only one of them and you are bound to misunderstand abortion. Listen even to only the first two or three and you receive a distorted account of abortion; for the fourth installment is the one that discloses how to connect the other three parts to each other. Imagine a puzzle with four parts and one of the parts is the key that tells if the three other parts are fitted together correctly. The fourth installment of the abortion story is like the puzzle key, casting the other parts in an intelligible whole.

Here are the parts of the story.

The first is the moral part. Pro-lifers see this as the only important part, the one that controls all other features of abortion. They believe, irrevocably, absolutely, that abortion is the murder of an innocent human being. All else in pro-life follows from this basic claim. Pro-choice has a more complex moral view. They do not see abortion as assimilable to homicide. They disagree on when life begins, and even what the issue means. They generally attach moral value to the woman's right to control her own body against state or social interference.

The second is the legal part. The law has changed several times on abortion in recent history. Abortion is now legal. The *Roe v. Wade* (1973) decision by the United States Supreme Court overturned all state statutes prohibiting abortion. From the late 19th century until 1973, state law generally prohibited abortion. In the first half of the 19th century, and earlier in the common law, early abortions were legal. This part of the abortion story, however, is not told by rendering an account of where the law has been on abortion, or even where it is now. It is told by describing law on the issues emerging from *Roe*—family consent to abortions, whether some abortions are homicides, and public financing of abortions—and by describing the connections between the moral and legal dimensions of such abortion issues.

The third part is the reality of abortion. Who gets abortions? What are the rates of abortion across demographic and social lines? What is the pathology of abortion? And what do the politics of abortion look like now in American life? It may seem odd to include as only one part of the abortion story the realities of abortion practices. But it is precisely these realities that have been distorted by the moral and legal values infusing abortion currently. No reading of abortion is complete or accurate without an unbiased account of abortion facts.

The fourth, and organizing, part of the story is how morals and the law can be fitted together to represent a rational abortion practice. This part of the story is the hardest to tell, for it requires innovative thought that goes far beyond the current mood on abortion. Abortion is today one of the most difficult and divisive issues in American society. What in part makes the issue so intractable is that the moral and legal parts of the story do not fit the realities of abortion. Both sides know this, and have drawn up their own versions of the abortion story in the political arena. For all the parts to fit together, an account of morals and law must take current practices out of partisan politics and into the domain of rational discourse.

### 3

The narrative theme of the abortion controversy is regulation *vs.* conscience — how the state sometimes tells us what to do, and sometimes does not. Let the fourth part of the story make an early and noncommittal appearance in answer to this question: Does the political system, or the state, enforce morals?

*Case 1.* Jean Harris, a distraught 57-year-old headmistress of an exclusive Virginia boarding school, drives across three states one March day in 1980 and shoots and kills her lover, Dr. Herman Tarnower, in the bedroom of his home in Westchester County, New York. Mrs. Harris is later convicted by a jury of second-degree murder.

*Case 2.* William Miller, an enterprising salesman, is convicted in California under the state obscenity law for mass mailing five unsolicited advertising brochures for illustrated "adult" books. In 1973, the United States Supreme Court (*Miller v. California*) reviews the case and (a) "reaffirm[s] the *Roth* holding that obscene material is not protected by the First Amendment, (b) hold[s] that such material can be regulated by the States (subject to certain safeguards) without (a) showing that the material is 'utterly without redeeming social value,' and (c) hold[s] that obscenity is to be determined by applying 'contemporary community standards,' not 'national standards.' " Miller's conviction stands.

*Case 3.* Lillian and William Gobitis (ages twelve and ten) are expelled from the public schools of Minersville, Pennsylvania, for refusing to salute the flag. The Gobitis family are Jehovah's Witnesses and believe that scripture forbids any gesture of respect for a flag. The United States Supreme Court allows the expulsion to stand (*Minersville School District v. Gobitis,* 1940). In 1943, the Court reverses itself. In *West Virginia State Bd. of Education v. Barnette* (1943), the Court holds that compelling a flag salute by public school children whose religious scruples forbid it violates the First Amendment.

Each of these cases represents the enforcement of morals. Some are less obvious than others. Homicide, for example, is a state crime that prohibits conduct which causes the death of a person. Depending on the circumstances, such conduct is either murder or manslaughter. But rules against killing are among the oldest of moral precepts, found in centuries of Judaic-Christian moral codes. The jury in the Harris case was deliberating guilt or innocence on an action covered by almost all moral practices past and present.

The second case is at once more straightforward and more controversial than the first. It is, clearly, a case of moral enforcement. But it is also unlikely to have the range of support normally given to homicide statutes. Many thoughtful people (and some who are not so thoughtful) argue that sexual conduct, and even the dissemination of sexual material, should be a matter of individual discretion and protected by the First Amendment from governmental regulation. Others object. Some jurists have argued for state enforcement of moral codes on sexual conduct. Others (like the U.S. Supreme Court justices) oppose the distribution of obscene materials. It seems that enforcement itself is a morally divisive issue on sexual morality (as it is not on homicide).

The third case represents a moral issue on which the Court reversed itself in a remarkably short period of time. The issue is whether some moral issues — in this case, religious in origin — shield individuals from social control in public institutions (like schools). First the Court said no (*Minersville*) — secular authority can override matters of conscience when social cohesion is the goal. Then the Court said yes (*West Virginia*) — religious conscience cannot be restricted by the state.

Since 1943, the Court has expanded the separation between church and state. Laws favoring some religions over others (through financial aid) have been ruled unconstitutional. Prayer in the public schools has been ruled out. Generally, the religious freedoms set forth and implied by the First Amendment have been zealously protected. Since the First Amendment forbids only the establishment of a state religion, the zeal of the Court to mark off a zone of religious freedoms is remarkable. But certainly the issues of religious freedom communicate the news that some moral issues are matters of individual discretion, not to be regulated by the government.

These three cases represent a spectrum from enforcement to individual discretion. They tell us that whether the state enforces morals depends on the moral issue at stake. Few would maintain that Jean Harris had discretionary authority to kill Herman Tarnower if her conscience required it. Few would argue that religious convictions ought to be regulated by the state. In between these two extremes are numerous controversies and concepts. To make sense of how Mrs. Harris and the Jehovah's Witnesses differ on the authority of conscience is also to go some small way toward understanding abortion problems. If abortion is homicide, then of course the state overrides individual conscience. But if abortion is a moral issue falling under the same, or a similar, rule that protects religious freedoms, then individual conscience controls abortion. These are the far ends defining abortion solutions — unless some mediate ground can be found where enforcement and conscience are complements rather than opposites.

## 4

The frustrating part of trying to find a mediate ground to resolve abortion problems is that none of the justifications commonly accepted for the enforcement of morals seems to work very well on any issue, and they work least well on abortion.

Six tests mark out the range of justification for state enforcement of morals. Let's look at them one at a time in terms of well-rehearsed elaborations and critiques.

*Test 1 — Consensus.* Liberals sometimes say that sectarian doctrine is a proper test of political opinion only in homogeneous societies — where, in the words of Bill Moyers (in 1980) on the Public Broadcasting System, "all are alike in thought and root and intent." Patrick Devlin (1970) suggests that consensus on moral values is needed in every society; and this consensual core both justifies enforcement of morals and identifies which moral values society ought to enforce. Justice Frankfurter, in *Minersville,* observed that "the ultimate foundation of a free society is the binding tie of cohesive sentiment."

The use of "consensus" as a test for enforcing morals is helpful in two ways. First, it neatly accommodates both liberals and conservatives. Since America is obviously pluralistic on many moral values, liberals can champion individual freedoms with a clear conscience. Conservatives, on the other hand, are provided at least with a clear test and even a goal (social agreement) for the legitimate enforcement of the right moral codes. Second, consensus is a democratic test. Secular moral principles originate in voluntary agreement. If all agree on a moral code, freely and rationally, enforcement seems not to violate the democratic agreement and even appears consistent with voluntary action. The noncontroversial enforcement of the no-killing rules is in large part explained by the fact that people widely agree on the wrongness of homicide.

But is consensus the only right test for the enforcement of morals? Hypothetical scenario: the Cain Witnesses, a new religious group on the block, believes that all individuals have an obligation to kill one other human being (but no more than one) as proof of moral strength and in order to liberate one's deeper spiritual powers. Initiation rites require consummating this belief. The popularity of the Cain Witnesses begins to spread. Many are convinced that this religion is the key to salvation. Does the resulting division in public opinion on the morality of homicide provide a reason to change the homicide statutes?

A moment's reflection yields commonplace distinctions between consensual, institutional, and critical morality. A society in which the vast multitude of members expresses affection for homicide rites may be at odds with both its own deeper values and the values in basic concepts of morality. A reconstruction of Western institutional traditions would demonstrate with little controversy that ceremonial murders offend the rules and practices governing social actions. That public opinion can stray from its own legacies is nowhere seriously doubted. But the critical features of morality may yet condemn ceremonial murders even when social traditions endorse them. The acceptance of core concepts of human dignity and autonomy in general traditions of moral law and theory do not tolerate Cain Witnesses, no matter how high the threshold of popular support.

The list of values that have represented social agreement is a mixed bag. Slavery, racial segregation, Nazism—all at one time commanded near majority support. Even if social unanimity were found on such items, reason demands moral opposition to the value, not its enforcement. Consensus can be an adequate test to enforcing morals only if we believe that social agreement is always morally correct. The Cain Witnesses hypothetically demonstrate that it is not. Any glance at social history can provide more realistic denials.

*Test 2—Society's Rights.* Doesn't society have any rights? Even to utter this (deceptively complex) question is to strike a familiar chord. Assume that any society is a community of like-minded citizens, in agreement at least on basic ideas of good and evil. Assume further that without this common core of moral ideas the society would fly apart, disintegrate. Then, on this view of moral consensus, immorality always has centrifugal effects, threatening the cohesive unity expressed by moral agreement. On the additional assumption that society has the right at least to preserve its own existence, then enforcement of moral codes is an exercise in integrity, a maintenance of basic values needed for the survival of social practices.

At the center of this test is the thought that the criminal law has two functions: the protection of individuals and the protection of society. But talk of society's rights, of protecting society, is a bit mysterious. What is "society"? Lawyers use words like "corpora-tion" to designate fictitious persons. A second look at language, however, will quickly reveal that collective terms are collections of individuals when the language of rights is assigned. Having a right means (basically) that no one can legitimately prevent me from do-ing what the right permits. Thus if I have a right to free speech, it is wrong to prevent me from speaking freely (especially by the gov-ernment, against which most rights historically have been directed). If society has a right to something, then—on the reasonable assumption that fictitious persons act only in fiction—this must mean that some set of individuals has that right. If the set is the whole, then no competition among individuals occurs (all have an unchallenged right). But if society is exercising its right to protect itself against those who challenge the values to be preserved, then it is a case of one group of citizens against another.

Look again at the obscenity cases (*Miller, et al.*). Where is the society that has the right to be preserved? On the one hand is a col-lection of centrist individuals who feel (on good and bad reasons) that sexual license is evil; and by virtue of the role of sex in family stability, procreation, and moral well-being, that such license is a threat to the stability of society. On the other hand are individuals who view sex in entirely different ways. They see sexual freedom as the fulfillment of individual liberty, and separate the pleasures of sex from its procreative functions. The idea of society's rights to maintain and protect itself is not easily applied here; for the society is split on the basic values at issue.

The obscenity issues also tell us that an agreement on basic values may not be needed to sustain a society. No doubt a threat to estab-lished values is perceived by those threatened as an attack on soci-ety itself. But social change, even when evil by all established values, does not always mean that a society is going out of business. It may be just changing. The world of Hugh Hefner is far removed from that of the Moral Majority. But if Hefner's world replaces more traditional values, American society will go on existing (though with different practices).

The question of whether any society, or even any practice, has a right to self-preservation is itself a moral issue. Does a fascist soci-ety have a right to maintain itself? Anyone can produce examples (real and hypothetical) of societies so morally repugnant that their values ought to go out of existence as soon as possible. Jerry Falwell feels this way about Hefner's world. Hefner no doubt feels as little charity toward the Moral Majority. Adjudicating the conflict between Falwell and Hefner would be an interesting undertaking. But applying a "society's rights to preserve itself" argument isn't going to get very far. The opening question would be which set of values is to be preserved through enforcement.

*Test 3 — Harm-to-Another.* The libertarian test for enforcement is whether the action in question harms another human being. John Stuart Mill originated the test in modern form. Imagine a society of free and separate individuals. They live and work without substantially affecting one another's well-being. In the libertarian scheme of things, no regulation by the greater society can be justified so long as each individual is not harmfully affecting any other. The starting premise in libertarian thought is that individuals have natural rights to liberty — to set and pursue their own values freely. But if these atomistic individuals collide with one another — if (without the billiard ball metaphor) they harm one another — then their actions are to be socially regulated.

The libertarian model of society is wonderful in several ways. It is internally consistent. Premise: All individuals have a right to liberty. Conclusion: No regulation is justified so long as individuals leave each other alone. Condition: Suppose individuals harm one another. Conclusion-from-condition: Then social regulation is warranted on the starting premise — that the liberty of those harmed is violated and regulation is needed to reestablish the social reality of the starting premise. The model is also intuitively appealing. It is comfortable to think that all individuals have a right to liberty. (Anything else is almost unthinkable.) And the model makes sense of many of our laws. Homicide statutes proscribe that most grievous of harms, taking another's life. Enforcing morals seems eminently reasonable on the harm test.

The harm test fails our high hopes, however, when its premises and working logic are inspected more closely. The model must assume, first, that harming human beings is morally wrong. This assumption is easy enough for most people. But in a society of masochists or sadists who celebrate (in different ways) the virtue of harm, Mill's test cannot be used. The model, second, must also assume that individuals share an understanding of what harm means. The test, however, anticipates pluralism, not consensus, on basic values. Think of a society of individuals who agree on all values. Public regulation would not be a substantial issue in this society, certainly not worth the intellectual effort Mill makes. No important deviance would occur, and only inconveniences would be regulated. Mill's theory carefully sets out liberties of consciousness, thought, expression; of tastes and pursuits, and life-plans; and of association. A theory so concerned with the value of individual liberty is telling us that individuals will have different life-plans; and that differences in values ought to be respected, not regulated by the state. In the language of our day, each ought to be able to do his thing as long as he harms no one else.

When pluralism is a reality, however, the consensus needed to make Mill's model work is jeopardized. The modern question must be raised and answered — what is "harm"? Easy cases abound. Herman Tarnower was certainly harmed by Jean Harris when she shot and killed him. Was Jean Harris harmed by Tarnower when he (allegedly) dismissed her in favor of a younger mistress, Lynne Tryforos? Yes. Enough to justify social regulation of Tarnower's amorous activities? No (though with less certainty here already). Even homicide does not always easily fit the harm thesis. Mercy killings, for example: A totally paralyzed accident victim begs to be killed. He finds living more painful than death. Is he "harmed" when his wishes are carried out? Yes. No. Juries are quick to sense the differences between mercy killings and more standard types of homicide. The American Medical Association's legal department reports (*New York Times,* December 10, 1981) that juries typically fail to convict mercy-killers and judges are likely to grant probation when conviction occurs.

Mill reserved "harm" to actions affecting interests which should be considered rights. He also had a view of government that limits regulation even without the harm thesis — that the evils of regulation far outweigh the errors made by an individual as final judge of his actions, that public regulation is likely to be in error when addressing purely personal conduct, that the individual will be punished (through social censure) for his wrongdoing without the intervention of law. There are familiar arguments employed today to limit governments. But the centerpiece of Mill's theory is the harm thesis. And this thesis depends on a shared understanding of "harm."

Even the meaning of basic interests is disputable in pluralistic societies. There are individuals who believe that sexual license is an evil worse than physical harm, others who see sexual freedom as a basic right. How is the harm thesis to adjudicate this difference in belief? If there is a core dispute over the meaning of harm, then problems occur beyond the expectations of Mill's thesis. Regulation itself, for example, can have harmful effects. The jail sentence given to Jean Harris, while justified legally on the harm thesis, affected her (grown) children harmfully. Sometimes harm is in equilibrium. Full employment occurs today with inflation. Those needing jobs (the young especially) are helped by efforts to reduce unemployment. But those on fixed or limited income suffer with inflation. Reducing inflation at the cost of increased unemployment shifts harm in the other direction. The absence of regulation can even cause harm. Requiring seatbelts in automobiles is not, on the surface, justified by the harm thesis. (Choosing not to have seatbelts jeopardizes no one but oneself.) But in the absence of social regulations mandating seatbelts, the items may be so expensive (as a special order) that many who would want them cannot afford them. Such individuals are harmed when seatbelts are voluntary instead of mandatory.

A satisfactory definition of "harm" is so elusive in pluralist societies that one begins to suspect the libertarian premises. Finding a real-world correlate of any model of free and separate individuals is a practical nightmare. Individuals affect one another in numerous ways. The paradigmatic instance of an isolated figure is the solitary drunk who, in the parlance of the day, harms no one but himself with his drinking habits. But of course he harms a network of family, friends, colleagues. Is any action ever without effects on others? Society is not a seamless web. There are effects and effects. The solitary drunk is one step removed from the belligerent drunk who inflicts violence on bystanders as well as intimates. But lives are so interwoven on a daily basis that it is typically impossible to say where the individual's actions end and another's begin.

The general problems are (a) the meaning of "harm" can be settled only by reference to a set of moral concepts, and the moral ideas we work with are notoriously vague on some famous issues. Among these issues are mercy killings, the differences between offensive and harmful actions, and whether economic loss counts as harm. And (b) the interactive nature of social life suggests that harm from another is so ordinary an experience (broken hearts, disappointments in work, etc.) that its presence can hardly justify even candidates for social intervention without ushering in extensive and undesirable regulations. These two problems are reflected in law. Obscenity statutes endlessly circle offensive actions (*Playboy* covers, lascivious billboards) without settling what constitutes harm. And homicide statutes do not stop with harm tests: murder-by-consent is still illegal even if the victim agrees that no harm occurs.

Still, in spite of the difficulties, the harm thesis does suggest some beginning rules for enforcing morals. Those violations of moral codes that result in acknowledged harm to another (murder without the victim's consent) are strong candidates for regulation. Conversely, immoral conduct without clear and present harm for another (that 1950's euphemism "sex between consenting adults"?) are brought into the zone of regulated actions with more difficulty. Of course those who view all immorality as harmful to society will not be persuaded to modify their ideas so long as "harm" is so ambiguous a notion.

*Test 4 — Paternalism.* The easy response when "harm-to-another" breaks down as a test is to say that morals are enforceable in the interests of the individuals whose actions are being regulated. Paternalistic regulation is sometimes successful where children are its recipients. On the assumption that at least very young children are not yet capable of making moral or rational decisions, parents enforce morals with only one justification: that it is in the best interest of the child. The strong instructional feature of such moral enforcement makes the paternalistic justification eminently reasonable.

The problem with paternalistic justifications is that they are restricted to childlike creatures. One standard assumption in all moral systems is that individuals are responsible for their actions. (Otherwise moral blame could not be assigned; moral credit could not be granted.) If an authority enforces morals because he knows best, then responsibility has shifted from the individual to the authority. Imagine a political system that enforces all morals paternalistically. The citizens are then childlike, a state of affairs at once insulting and (paradoxically) without generalized moral responsibility.

There is one exception to the problem of paternalism. A long tradition of political thought has claimed a distinction between real and perceived interests. The distinction has mundane applications. When I go through a divorce proceeding on one understanding of the law, then later find out that I was mistaken in my reading of the law, what I perceived was my interest in agreeing to a property settlement may turn out in retrospect not to have been my *real* interest at the time. More generally, social conditions can influence perception of interests; and a change in conditions can change those perceptions. Whether successive changes in how interests are perceived are progressive — so that an approximation to real interest is achieved — is of course what academics call a debatable item. (Each change in conditions may simply occasion a different perceived interest.) But *if* real interests exist, and *if* the enforcement of real-interest morals raises the consciousness (or perceptual levels) of those whose actions are being regulated, then paternalistic enforcement can be justified as an instrument to achieve a deeper sense of moral responsibility (for one's real interests) than no-enforcement can achieve.

But the *ifs* have to turn out to be true statements.

*Test 5 — Social Utility.* A strong justification for the enforcement of morals is that it is often socially useful to do so. Even laws that do have a moral component — like homicide statutes — are expressions of social interests. One important goal of any society is security for its citizens against physical attack. Similarly, shielding religion from state regulation is a useful feature of society. The longest modern tradition in social thought — utilitarianism — weighs all actions on a scale of social utility. Those working in this tradition would have no problems in evaluating state regulation of any issue in terms of social usefulness.

The logics of social utility and moral rights, however, may conflict with each other. Social utility is goal-oriented. Public measures are useful if they contribute to some sense of aggregate well-being. Rights are, in general, more stable, valid even when in conflict with social goals. Whether to pursue full employment or reduce inflation rates, for example, will change with the goals society sets for itself. But Sixth Amendment rights to a fair trial are insulated against changes in either means or goals. That it is more useful to deny due process does not in and of itself justify the denial of the process. Many heroic efforts have been made to make utility and moral rights compatible. But, in the language of the day, rights are in general trumps against utility (though some extreme welfare thresholds — e.g., survival — override all but the highest of rights).

What is socially useful is also not clear or settled. Increased economic growth is useful. A contracting economy with increased emphasis on spiritual needs is useful. Which statement is true? Even on a single dimension social utility can conflict with itself. Free trade is useful for consumers in setting quality and costs of goods. Protective trade policies are useful for domestic industries. Anyone purchasing a Japanese automobile can attest to the truth of the first proposition. Anyone working in mercantile industries can support the second. And automobile workers and mercantile consumers take (respectively) opposite stands. The meaning of social utility, exactly what is useful and why, is easily a moral issue concerned with the proper form of human life. Or, the enforcement of morals on a test of social utility anoints the prior *moral* settlement of utility.

*Test 6 — True Morality.* If all else fails, society can enforce that moral code which is true. Experts are easy to find throughout history. Plato developed the *Republic* on the truth of the higher forms. The problem, then and now, is what to do if there are several competing claims for true moralities. Plato put his trust in the educational system to set things right. Other figures may prefer to read dissenters out of the area of salvation. But those cast out by moral majorities may have their own true moralities. In any reasonably pluralistic society, a political authority committed to enforcing true morality will have to choose which true morality to enforce. Since competing true moralities also compete on how to settle truth, the choice is often impossible to make.

It is also not clear that even a perfectly true morality ought to be enforced simply because it is true. Suppose that it is true beyond reasonable doubt that truth-telling is a valid or true moral rule—that people ought always (*ceteris paribus*) to tell the truth. It does not follow that because people *ought* to tell the truth that the state ought to *get* people to tell the truth. If truth is embedded in certain institutions, like legal contracts, then state enforcement is less controversial. But a true morality may otherwise be best served by allowing people to make up their own minds on the moral code. In this way, individuals become moral or immoral from their own actions, not through external coercion.

## 5

Abortion introduces yet additional problems for any of the standard tests for enforcing morals. First, those who dispute abortion do not all agree that it is a moral issue, or, if moral, in what way morality attaches to the issue. Pro-lifers see abortion as profoundly moral, the most important issue in American politics. Pro-choicers, however, viewing the embryo as (roughly) analogous to a benign tumor or unnecessary appendage, see free choice as the only moral issue in abortion—and this only because of the pro-life assaults on choice. Second, the dispute over abortion is primarily due to differences in beliefs about the nature and status of the embryo or fetus. The normative conclusions on abortion follow from conceptual claims on the meaning and interpretation of physical data—put roughly, the significance of the biological states of human gestation. Or, individuals disagree over the morality of abortion because they disagree over the assignment of concepts to fetal life.

None of the standard tests for enforcing morals fares well when applied to such disputes. (1) Even if a social consensus could be reached on abortion, dissenters could still legitimately resist enforcement. The resistance, moreover, could take the strong form of civil disobedience to an immoral law. Paul Ramsey (1974) has testified that the people as a whole, not the judiciary, should determine the outer limits of the human community. But the poverty of this approach can be quickly demonstrated by changing the issues. Would any be sanguine if the people as a whole decided today to keep women and blacks outside the human community? Abortion, like most moral issues, is not resolvable through consensual formulae.

Neither (2) the rights of society nor (3) harm-to-another are intelligible guides in negotiating enforcement practices on abortion. The rights of society against individuals are not relevant to abortion disputes. The conflicting and conditional relationships of rights-to-life and rights-to-control-one's-body are at the center of abortion issues. Harm-to-another cannot be used as a test for enforcement on abortion until other questions have been answered. Mill's libertarian test assumes as settled exactly what is at issue in abortion—the "other" who is harmed. Similar objectives set aside (4) paternalism as a test. Whose interests are being met by any approach to abortion depends on how the set of respondents is defined (two persons: woman-offspring *vs.* one person: woman-embryo).

The test of (5) social utility is, at the least, limited. Again, the appropriateness of the test depends on a prior moral settlement. It is unlikely (though conceivable) that social utility would be endorsed if fetal rights-to-life are recognized (equivalent to infant children being killed or protected only if social utility demands it). Even more telling, however, is that pro-choice cannot tolerate social utility tests. If a woman has a right to control her own body, this right does not vary with changes in social utility. If, for example, abortion is permitted as a method of population control, then, if population declines and society requires higher birth rates, abortion must be restricted. An expansion and contraction of rights on social utility (whether the rights are to life or to control of one's body) does not meet the moral tests set up by either pro-life or pro-choice.

Finally, the test of (6) true morality is the least likely justification of enforcement practices on abortion. Each of the several sides in abortion disputes affirms a set of truths. Pro-life holds as true that

(a) human life begins at conception and (b) the right to life overrides all other rights and interests. The pro-choice view maintains that (a) human life begins at a later stage and (b) the right to control one's body overrides all remaining rights and interests given that the right to life has been set aside (as irrelevant). These truths in each case are supported by evidence and noncontroversial inference rules. There are variations. Pro-lifers are more likely to introduce transcendent authority (e.g., scripture). Pro-choicers incline toward pragmatic tests. But each side offers a coherent program of truth. Unless there is some overarching truth that can adjudicate the two sets of conflicting claims, any rule bidding us to enforce the true morality is not going to work as a political resolution.

One hope for resolving abortion problems is that the issue will provide different relationships between law and morality than the six tests provide. Note this: the surface features of abortion seem to demand that the state endorse one or another of the points of view on abortion. Abortion is not, like sex, an act that can be consummated in private. Abortions are carried out, for good medical reasons, in hospitals or clinics. Third parties are necessarily involved. Public moneys can be, and are, at issue. The public character of abortion seems to make a public resolution of abortion problems unavoidable. And the resolution would seem to follow from the status of the fetus. Pro-life is ever prone to point out that once blacks were recognized as human in the abolitionist movement, no one could say, "Let the slave owner decide whether to have slaves or not." Slavery had to be outlawed by the state. On the other hand, if the fetus has no right to life, then individual choice resolves the issue.

The problem is that the moral part of the abortion story cannot fit the other parts together in a coherent whole. Neither side accepts the views of the other on the life-status of the fetus. And, as we shall see, nothing about the arguments or evidence on either side can compel anyone to accept the opposition's values. Those hoping to resolve abortion conflicts are going to have to look elsewhere for success. Perhaps a deeper look at abortion problems will dissolve the surface need for state regulation of abortion practices and establish more subtle and interesting connections between law and morality.

The incomplete and contradictory sides of the abortion story are represented in current abortion law in the United States. The legal status of abortion is stated in *Roe v. Wade* (1973). By a 7-2 vote, the United States Supreme Court ruled (a) a state cannot bar any woman from obtaining an abortion from a licensed physician during the first three months of pregnancy; (b) in the second trimester, the state can regulate abortions only where the regulation is related to the preservation or protection of the mother's health; and (c) in the last trimester, the state can regulate or even prohibit abortions except those necessary "in appropriate medical judgment to protect the woman's life and health." The main legislative items on abortion are the Hyde Amendments, which have denied Medicaid money for abortion except on narrow conditions — primarily a threat to the woman's life from pregnancy, though other conditions (rape, incest) have also been allowed at various times. Though states and localities have different policies toward abortion, the Hyde Amendments, since the passage of the initial version in 1977, have effectively cut off federal funding for abortions. From 1977 to 1979, federally financed abortions dropped from 295,000 to 2,400. Let it be noted, however, that the elimination of Medicaid funds for abortion has had little effect on the number of legal abortions obtained by poor women. About 94 percent of the nearly 300,000 Medicaid-eligible women wanting an abortion in the year after the Hyde Amendment took effect were able to get one. State Medicaid funds paid for about 65 percent of these abortions, while 29 percent of the women used other sources of financing, including private funds, clinic subsidies and philanthropic donations (Cates, 1981).

These two measures — the *Roe* decision and the Hyde Amendments — represent a portion of the social conflict today over abortion. The Court decision affirms individual discretion in the first trimesters. But notice that abortion is still legal throughout pregnancy if a physician certifies certain conditions ("life and health" in the last trimester). The discretionary authority of the woman is limited only by a physician's judgment, not by the state. The Hyde Amendments, by contrast, represent a pro-life perspective. On the assumption that abortion is immoral, supporters of the amendments argue that public funds — which are revenues taken generally from all citizens — should not be used to support the practice.

Society is saying, in a way, that abortion is moral *and* that abortion is immoral. A measure of schizophrenia in public attitudes toward abortion should not be surprising. The issue is not addressed in a rational manner in current practices. We will try here, author and reader, to fit the complex pieces of abortion together in at least an intelligible, if not sane, arrangement, while listening as we proceed to the views of pro-life and pro-choice activists on abortion.

**For Further Reading**

Cates, Willard. "The Hyde Amendment in Action," *Journal of the American Medical Association* 246 (September 4, 1981): 1109-12.

Devlin, Patrick. *The Enforcement of Morals* (Oxford: Oxford University Press, 1965).

Dworkin, Ronald. *Taking Rights Seriously* (Cambridge, Mass.: Harvard University, 1978), pp. 240-58.

Feinberg, Joel. "Moral Enforcement and the Harm Principle." Tom Beauchamp, ed. *Ethics and Public Policy* (Englewood Cliffs, N.J.: Prentice-Hall, 1975), pp. 283-96.

Hart, H.L.A. *Law, Liberty, and Morality* (New York: Vintage Books, 1963).

Mill, John Stuart. *On Liberty.* David Spitz, ed. (New York: W. W. Norton, 1975).

Nagel, Ernest. "The Enforcement of Morals," *The Humanist* 28, No. 3 (May/June, 1968): 20-27.

Ramsey, Paul. "Protecting the Unborn," *Commonweal* 50 (1974): 308-14.

# 2
# MORAL ARGUMENTS

---

## 1

Both pro-choice and pro-life often start their moral arguments from hard (loosely defined here as "extreme") cases. Here are three hard cases which lead people to favor legal abortion.

(1) A 14-year-old is raped by her mother's boyfriend. The assault on the girl is so severe she suffers a hairline skull fracture and a broken arm. She undergoes therapy with a psychiatrist to restore her mental stability. Upon finding out that she is pregnant, she immediately requests and receives an abortion. She says later that "I would have gone under with a baby. I had to forget the whole thing to stay sane."

(2) A woman married seven years discovers she has multiple sclerosis. She stops using birth control pills because they aggravate the illness. In spite of reasonable precautions, she becomes pregnant. She has an abortion, explaining that "I cannot care for a child, and my husband cannot bear the burden alone." Both the woman and her husband are relieved and have no regrets.

(3) A forty-one-year-old woman with three grown children accidentally becomes pregnant. After some discussion, she and her husband accept their renewed responsibility. She undergoes an amniocentesis test at the request of her doctor. The test indicates that the unborn child has Tay-Sachs disease. The woman decides to have an abortion, explaining that "My husband and I could not bear to allow a child of ours to suffer for several years and then die."

The appeal of cases like these is unmistakable and widespread. Public opinion polls (discussed in the fourth chapter) show that most Americans favor abortion in cases where (a) the pregnancy is the result of rape or incest, (b) the woman is physically handicapped, (c) the fetus suffers from a severe genetic defect, (d) the woman's health is jeopardized by the pregnancy, or (e) if the woman is a pregnant, unmarried teenager. Whether these beliefs are morally valid will be explored in a moment. But the cases do incline most people to a pro-choice conclusion.

Now look at some hard cases that favor pro-life.

(1) A woman married for six years with two children in school accidentally becomes pregnant. She and her husband are in critical stages of their careers — he about to change jobs, and she just getting established as a real estate broker. They are financially secure, but the prospect of starting over with diapers and nursery school is appalling to them. They both decide that she should have an abortion to keep intact the style of life they are living.

(2) A young married woman wants to have a baby with her husband, even though he is uncertain about taking on parental responsibility at this time in his life. To her delight and his surprise, she becomes pregnant. He argues with her at length and convincingly that the time is not right for them to start a family. Even though she willingly conceived, she reluctantly agrees to have an abortion.

(3) A thirty-eight-year-old woman becomes pregnant with her lover of several years. He is pleased and starts making long-term plans for their relationship, including marriage. She is not sure she wants to make the relationship permanent. She wavers over an abortion for several months, hoping that the amniocentesis test will demonstrate a fetal defect justifying an abortion. Instead, the test indicates that no problems exist with the fetus. In her sixth month of term, she finally decides to have an abortion and finds a doctor who will perform one on her.

These three cases are hard for pro-choice to use as a basis for their arguments. Though no opinion polls have asked such questions, the reasons for aborting in these three cases do not meet the tests widely accepted for legitimate abortions. Abortions performed (1) for convenience, (2) after consenting to pregnancy when no important impediments will interrupt carrying to term, (3) on the wishes of another (husband, lover, parents, etc.) instead of the woman, or (4) late in term when no overriding reasons of health or life exist, are not the stuff on which to build pro-choice arguments. Such abortions are cases that are more effectively used to support the pro-life point of view.

Those active in abortion politics are not usually moral philosophers. This fact may be classified in the benefit, not the loss, column by those responsible for counseling women contemplating abortion. Michael Herr in *Dispatches* describes a brief glance into the eyes of a long-range recon patroller as "looking at the floor of an ocean." Anyone who has studied moral philosophy in depth could not quarrel with this description as a metaphor for morality: visually rich, constantly refracted. Indeed, as we shall see very shortly, moral argument will not resolve the main disputes over abortion. But it is also fact that any exploration of abortion takes the inquirer very quickly into the language of moral discourse. The cases listed above, if read aloud to any attentive listener, will begin a discussion of abortion. Pregnancies from rape must place abortion decisions with the victim. Abortions on convenience are indefensible. Why (in both cases)? Because—and here the rules and evidence of moral argument take over.

Among the gloomier discoveries made by the author in his inquiries is that morality almost never enters the counseling given by pro-choice organizations unless raised by the woman; and that the moral considerations pressed on the women by pro-life organizations are rigid principles drawn from the dogma of absolute fetal rights to life. If abortion is a moral issue (as it surely is), then an inspection of moral philosophy is bound to be helpful in arranging (without dogmatic rigidity) the complex and often conflicting principles in abortion arguments. Among the more modest goals might be some illumination into our intuitions on the hard cases often introduced to abortion disputes without any reflection on why they are hard cases.

Any student of moral philosophy can report that moral reasoning is not an axiomatic science. Reasonable people can differ on the conclusions of moral deliberation even when following the same rules and looking at the same evidence. But courses of action can also be narrowed, alternatives ruled out, rational (not axiomatic) conclusions reached if moral arguments are framed with care. An inspection of moral arguments over abortion may allow us to adjudicate between pro-life and pro-choice — to see which of the sides is the greater persuasive force.

The moral arguments available in abortion issues are many and varied. The initial priority is language. The terms used to describe abortion and its referents are evaluatively rich. Those opposed to abortion often use "fetus," a word derived from Latin for "offspring" (and which is neutral between animal or human), though the pro-life movement much prefers the more evaluative phrase "pre-born child" (for obvious reasons). Those favoring individual discretion on abortion lean toward "embryo," from the Greek word meaning "to swell inside." The term "conceptus" is more neutral (though exceedingly abstract). It effectively covers fetus, embryo, and the less frequently used terms "zygote" (a cell formed from the union of two gametes — a mature sperm and an ovum) and "blastula" (an early embryonic form). The strategy here will be to use *fetus* when discussing pro-life and *embryo* when discussing pro-choice — if possible. In this way, an acceptable language will be used within each point of view. Abortion, the act itself, means no more and no less than the failure of any process to attain full development.

Language clarification is only a preliminary, however. The second, and major, step in moral argument is to organize the relevant considerations in such a way that a rational conclusion can be drawn telling the affected parties what ought to be done. Suppose that we exhibit the underlying structure of moral reasoning in terms of principles and rules that must be interpreted and applied to human experience. The dominant principle in abortion is respect for the value of human life. It generates a widely held rule: "One ought not to kill human beings." This rule (as with all rules) may be established in a variety of ways — discovered in natural laws or the word of God, chosen by individuals on rational grounds. But whatever the origin of the rule, it must be interpreted as to meaning and extension. What does "kill" mean? What is a "human being?" Applications of the rule to particular situations must be settled. Such settlement requires determining whether exceptions or defeats occur, these by combining description and additional rules. Self-defense, for example, will normally free persons from their obligation not to kill—at least for the particular circumstances of saving their own lives. When the primary rule is interpreted, and when no exceptions or defeats occur, then a directive (recommendation, imperative) can be drawn (deduced, inferred) from the rule prohibiting killing, in this case, most appropriately, "Do not kill" (here and now).

No actual case of moral reasoning need ever exactly fit this simple outline. The outline may even be entertained as a metaphor, depicting our thoughts as we move from deeper rules and principles to practical cases of moral action. But the outline is still helpful in arranging various moral arguments for and against abortion. Both sides on the abortion issue, for example, respect human life and accept rules prohibiting the killing of human beings. (Were this not so, abortion would be easier to resolve and less interesting an issue—one side could simply be labeled as killers *and* the label would be accepted by both sides). The disagreements over abortion occur on minor premises and the role of such premises in deriving either a pro-choice or anti-abortion conclusion.

Start with the opposition to abortion. The major rule is accepted—"One ought not to kill human beings." Then two moves occur as minor premises. First, the issue of relevance is settled by an acceptance that the fetus is a human being and has a right to life. Second, very few defeating conditions are allowed. Some (not many) pro-lifers will not even accept self-defense as a justification for abortion, even when the fetus threatens the woman's own safety or physical well-being. On these two determinations (relevance, no defeats), it is then a straightforward matter to end with the moral imperative, "Do not abort," since it resembles a standard "Do not kill" imperative.

The pro-choice conclusion follows in logically similar ways. Again, the major rule is accepted. But then two different minor premises are introduced. First, and primarily, the embryo is not accepted as a human being, or the acceptance includes no right to life. Second, as an alternative, some defeat is accepted. For example, self-defense may be claimed. If the embryo poses a physical threat to the woman (causing renal deficiency, for example), then, though the embryo does not intend to harm the woman, a case for aborting is accepted sometimes even by those who accept the fetus as human. Either premise permits abortions by denying the moral imperative routinely accepted by pro-life.

These two patterns of reasoning are skeletal forms. The logic dominating each form, however, is clearly expressed. The pro-life argument extends the no-killing rule from start to finish. The right to life of the fetus sustains the rule through to the conclusion. The pro-choice argument prevents the no-killing rule from yielding a moral imperative. Two tests halt the derivation. Either no human being is present or justifiable killing is demonstrated.

Each point of view — pro-choice, pro-life — is usually fleshed out with additional rules and principles. One helpful way to understand these rules and principles is to imagine oneself in the position of either a pro-life or pro-choice supporter. Then, within the skeletal form of moral reasoning, one searches for those things that will extend and elaborate one's basic convictions.

Start with the pro-life view. One important rule is the doctrine of double-effect. Stated succinctly, it is a rule prescribing that (1) bad effects not be intended either as a means or an end, and (2) the good effects which are intended should outweigh the unintended bad effects.

*Example 1:* Penicillin is a powerful drug that can adversely affect the fetus. If, however, a pregnant woman is ill with a serious strep infection, the objective of curing the woman is important enough to warrant use of the drug. The intended good effect — combating the strep infection — outweighs the unintended side effects of the drug on the fetus.

*Example 2* (adapted from Dinello, 1971): Jones cannot live more than two weeks without a heart transplant. Smith cannot live more than two months without a kidney transplant. Each is the only possible donor for the other. When Jones dies, Smith gets Jones' kidney. If Smith is killed, Jones gets Smith's heart. A moral end to this story must consist of Smith getting the transplant.

Notice the differences brought out by these two examples. In example 1, a good effect outweighs unintended bad effects. Use of the drug is justified with the doctrine of double-effect. In example 2, a bad effect would be intended with surgical (or other) intervention. Thus the passive response is justified. Though each possible action in 2 — do nothing *vs.* kill Smith — leads to the certain death of one of the donor pairs and the salvation of the other, killing Smith is obviously wrong. It intends a bad effect — killing a human being. Letting circumstances take their course is morally right. Even if Jones is the better person, or the needier of the two (with more dependents, say), or the more vital to society (an important scientist), no moral or legal code would sanction an active intervention to save Jones by sacrificing Smith. The doctrine of double-effect explains why these intuitively sound examples are also theoretically valid.

The extension of the doctrine of double-effect to abortion is unimpeded. Abortion is wrong because, on the acceptance of the fetus as a human being, it intends (for all practical purposes, especially in the early stages of term) a bad effect — the death of a human being. One particularly controversial implication of the double-effect doctrine for abortion is that medical intervention is not justified even to save the mother's life. Like the Smith-Jones example, only the natural outcome of pregnancy is acceptable unless the lives of both mother and offspring are in jeopardy. (Then a greater good — saving one life — is preferable to a passive response that allows both individuals to die.)

The key to all moral principles used in the pro-life position is the starting point for human life. The pro-life position is firmly committed to the view that life begins at conception. Two arguments support this view. One rests on a theory of *being.* All that any individual has genetically is present at conception. Therefore, in the sense of genetic endowment, a zygote is human. The second argument rests on a theory of *becoming.* A human conceptus develops into a human being, not anything else. Like acorns becoming oak trees, the process is natural. (Only an external intervention or a deficiency within the process prevents the teleological end-state from being reached.) Thus any effort to abort such a process is, ipso facto, the termination of the end-state (the fully developed sentient being). In one sense, these two arguments are different — one relies on what is, the other on what will be. But in another sense they are not. The fact that a full genetic endowment is present in the zygote is what makes the potentiality argument valid.

The pro-life belief that life begins at conception is supported by the natural continuum of gestation. One famous device used by pro-life supporters is the "slippery slope" argument. The argument is employed against any attempt to mark a stage in pregnancy before which pro-choice is valid, after which abortion is regulated or denied (as in *Roe v. Wade*). The strategy is this: pick any point in the development of a fetus from conception to birth. Now if this point is to be a divider between permissible and impermissible abortions, I will choose a point a few hours or days earlier. You must then tell me how your point differs in a morally relevant way from mine. Obviously the "slippery slope" argument is effective because the slope between conception and birth is continuous, without natural demarcations. (Even "trimesters" is an arbitrary division of time.) The developmental nature of pregnancy provides a rebuttal to any assignment of human life to some stages of pregnancy while denying the assignment to others. But the "slippery slope" argument is ineffective toward those who maintain that life begins at birth (or later).

The pro-choice position, as might be expected, is elaborated with different rules and principles. Pro-choice proponents also interpret some of the same rules and principles differently when they extend across both positions. The fundamental moral principle for pro-choice is the right to control one's own body against social regulation. This right is deeply embedded in Western traditions. John Locke stated that "every man [woman] has a property in his [her] own person. . . ." Authority over one's body is a right of privacy, in the most intimate sense. Though many laws prohibit suicide, the right to one's own body is at the center of what is minimally meant by individual liberty. The pro-choice position again and again comes to rest on this right.

But, since rights to privacy (however conceived) do not override rights to life, the pro-choice position also develops several theories on killing, letting die, and the beginning of life. One powerful, though limited, principle in defeating no-killing rules is a consideration of the interests of others.

*Example 1* (adapted from Thomson, 1971): An individual is asked to give periodic blood transfusions to a close relative, his aunt. The aunt has a rare and fatal disease. She will die unless she receives bimonthly transfusions. Only her nephew has the right blood type for such sustained therapy. His own health will be jeopardized by this arrangement, the welfare of his life considerably reduced.

*Example 2:* A human being attacks another for no good reason, threatening his life. The only way in which the victim can save himself is by killing the attacker.

Both examples expose a general truth sometimes ignored in abortion issues. The right to life is conditional, not absolute. The nephew is under no overriding obligation to begin the blood transfusions simply because of the aunt's right to life. She does not have a right to maintain her life no matter what the costs of doing so are to others. If the right to life can be realized only at the expense of others' lives or basic welfare, at least the question is open whether the right ought to be exercised. Example 2 makes the same point in more dramatic fashion. A right to life means only a right not to be killed unjustifiably. Self-defense is justifiable homicide. Or, as Thomson (1971) establishes more exactly, (a) a right to life, and (b) a right to have those conditions necessary to life, are two quite different rights. And (b) does not follow necessarily from (a). Type (b) rights are, in the parlance of the day, morally negotiable. The main effect of distinguishing (a) and (b) type rights is that abortion can then be justified even when the fetus is granted a right to life.

Three conditions are often introduced as restrictions on a right to life. One, the narrowest and least controversial, is self-defense. Few disagree with the view that a woman has a right to maintain her own life when threatened by continued pregnancy. Some conditions of pregnancy, like ectopic pregnancies, cancer of the uterus, and a severely traumatized uterus, can only be treated by therapies that usually result in termination of the pregnancy. Even the pro-life movement — for example in the Human Life Amendment — generally favors abortion in such conditions. (Though not unanimously — Notre Dame law professor Charles Wright has urged that no exceptions allowing abortions be introduced to the Human Life Amendment.) Maintaining the mother's life is the sole criterion agreed on by friends and foes in battles over federal funding of abortions. Abortions are almost always accepted when self-defense is demonstrable.

The abortions justified by self-defense are few in number, however. Threats to the woman's life are unusual experiences today, becoming increasingly less likely with improvements in medical techniques. Federally funded abortions were reduced to miniscule levels when rape, incest, and threats to the woman's life were allowed as the only legitimate reasons for a publicly financed abortion. Also, self-defense is a public justification, subject to approval by medical and perhaps political authorities. Since the pro-choice movement believes that authority to end pregnancies should be solely with the woman, self-defense is at best a fringe issue in the pro-choice movement.

A second condition restricting rights to life is euthanasia. It is also confined to a limited number of abortions. But it is an extremely controversial restriction. Let euthanasia stand here for any termination of life on the judgment that the life is not worth living. Applying this test to fetal life is very difficult. There is first the problem of consent. If an individual makes a judgment that his own life is not worth living, this is one type of moral problem. Many, though not all, would grant individuals the right to end their own lives on a variety of conditions (severe and endless pain, terminal illness, extreme physical debilitation, etc.). But a fetus cannot speak, cannot make such a judgment. Someone else must make the judgment on behalf of the embryo or fetus. Deciding for others that their lives are not worth living is more controversial, since what one person may judge as intolerable may be the very inspiration for another to accomplish admirable things. (The stories of severely handicapped individuals who lead full lives are numerous and well known.)

A second problem compounds the first. The defects of life are multiple and difficult to evaluate. A range of genetic and other defects can now be discovered through prenatal testing. Amniocentesis (the withdrawal of fluid from the amniotic sac by insertion of a needle into the mother's abdomen) can disclose the presence of several fetal problems — Down's syndrome, Tay-Sachs disease, sickle-cell anemia, and many more. Which of these problems (if any) warrants an abortion? Tay-Sachs disease is a terrible affliction, limiting infants to a brief and painful existence. It is one of the stronger justifications for abortion. But Down's syndrome? Here children lead a relatively short, painless, and — at lower mental levels—pleasurable existence. Do others have the right to say that such an existence is not worth living? Then there are defects whose main effects occur later in life, like sickle-cell anemia. Terminating such a life by abortion is impossible to justify from the perspective of someone other than the victim of the disease.

A third restricting condition on rights to life is consent. This condition comes closer to the pro-choice position than the first two. It justifies abortion in terms of the woman's acceptance of pregnancy. Assumption: the main condition required by a fetus for life-maintenance is access to another's body. Argument: this access must be granted, not compelled. Suppose that a pregnancy results from force (rape) or accident. The woman shares no responsibility for her condition. A pro-choice proponent would allow the woman individual discretion to abort even conceding a right to life to the fetus. The central idea here is that a woman is obligated to continue pregnancy only on a contractual basis. Coercion and accidents that are authentic (where one really took all reasonable precautions) are without consent; and in the absence of consent, no obligation occurs for the use of one's body. At least one court case supports this general view. A Pennsylvania judge in 1978 refused to issue an order requiring an individual to donate his bone marrow to a cousin suffering from aplastic anemia. The court ruled that an individual cannot be legally required to provide use of his body against his consent, though the judge found the donor's refusal "morally indefensible." (Story in *Newsweek*, August 7, 1978.)

The main strategy pursued by pro-choice supporters on defining life is to concentrate on development instead of being. The teleological process of emerging human-ness cannot be denied. The issue is what moral implications follow from the earlier stages in this process. The pro-choice position is that potential features are not actual features; and that there are few if any moral constraints flowing from potential states of affairs. Birth control, for example, is a practice designed to prevent the development of a human being. It stops a process from beginning, denying the potential outcome of uniting two gametes. And it is (depending perhaps on its form) morally innocuous.

A principle of moral symmetry is sometimes advanced as an argument against the use of potentiality in pro-life perspectives. Imagine (adapted from Tooley, 1972) a chemical which, when given to a golden retriever, renders the dog as intelligent as an average human being in the space of six months. Suppose the chemical is administered and then, two weeks later, the owner has a change of heart. An antidote is given that nullifies the effects of the chemical. Pro-choice people are inclined to see no morally relevant difference between (a) deciding not to give the chemical and (b) administering the antidote. The fact that the dog would become as intelligent as a human at the end of a process is not a consideration before it matures. In pro-choice perspectives, what *is* here and now counts, not what is there only potentially (as a future state of affairs). Abortion, though not exactly like birth control because of its costs and effects on individuals, is morally equivalent to birth control on the principle of moral symmetry—the one preventing a process from beginning, the other stopping the process before it realizes its end.

Moral and life-conceiving rules/principles tailor neatly to arguments on abortion. Pro-life arguments deny abortion on the assumption that a fetus is human and has a right to life. This basic argument is enriched with strong condemnations of direct killing and a belief in the continuity of being from conception forward. Pro-choice arguments allow individual discretion on the belief that an embryo is not human and has no right to life, or that the conditions needed to maintain life can on occasion be justifiably withdrawn (as in self-defense, euthanasia, or the absence of consent to the pregnancy). A concern with actual as opposed to potential features of an embryo characterizes many pro-choice arguments.

## 2

Activists in abortion politics are not usually aware of the range of philosophical argument available on abortion issues. But they are uniformly consistent on the basic principles informing their positions. The pro-life advocates, for example, have no doubts about the priorities established by fetal rights to life.

*Frohock:* Are there any prenatal defects that will to your mind justify abortion?

*Kisil:* No.

*Frohock:* Tay-Sachs disease?

*Kisil:* No, because when you open the door to allow for one kind of disease it's easier to open it for other diseases to follow. This is not to say that these areas are not tremendously sensitive areas. . . . But you can't allow a doctor to have a license to kill, because when he has a license to kill, the state will eventually mandate who he shall kill.

*Frohock:* So, a child with Tay-Sachs disease—

*Kisil:* Deserves to be born.

---

*Frohock:* There is a distinction in moral theory between having the right to life and having the right to those conditions needed to maintain life. Now, if I understand you correctly, you would say that the fetus or unborn child, having a right to life, then, under the [Human Life] amendment, is guaranteed use of the woman's body which is necessary to maintain that life.

*Dr. Willke:* Yes.

*Frohock:* So that right to life overrides the right of a woman to control her own body.

*Dr. Willke:* No question about it.

*Mrs. Willke:* She has the right to control, but the control comes prior to conception. Once she has engaged in that action, just like once you drive a car, you are responsible for your action, and I think what we're seeing in our culture today is, no one wants to be responsible for their actions. Everyone wants a way to get out of everything. If you have an accident, you want to know where you can go to get it taken care of. Everybody thinks they don't have to be responsible. As members of a human family, we are responsible to each other and unless we share that responsibility and do what we're supposed to do, the more [like a] jungle it becomes.

Pro-choice activists, as expected, do not accept fetal rights to life or do not view such rights as overriding all other values. As a consequence, they tend to see abortion as primarily or exclusively a political issue, or they locate the morality of abortion in the rights of women to control their own lives and, especially, their bodies.

*Frohock:* Is abortion a moral issue to you?

*Hughes:* Yes, in a way. I think that I have a strong belief in each person being able to have as much control over his or her own life as possible. We're given a potential to control our environment and to have control over our life, and an obligation almost to maximize your life. You're only here for 70 years and I don't believe if you have a choice that you should do something that's going to be harmful or self-destructive or that will frustrate your potential to have a good life.

---

*Frohock:* So you see abortion as primarily a political issue? Is this correct?

*Gordon:* I see it primarily and preeminently as a political issue. I don't see it as a moral issue at all, because I haven't noticed that the people who are pro-life are particularly moral, or who are people, generally speaking, whose views I respect. They are my political enemies, in every sense. And it's another matter, as I say, there are a large number of people whose views are different from mine whom I respect, but they also respect mine, and so they're not actively campaigning to make abortion illegal. They work by moral persuasion, in the same way that I work. I'm not requiring anybody who has an unwanted pregnancy to have an abortion. My views are clear: If you don't want to have an abortion, don't have one. If you don't want your daughter, your wife . . . There's just too many hypocrites in this field. We know of too many situations, we know intimately a lot of abortion clinics where wives and daughters of well known personalities who are anti-abortion, whose daughters, wives, relatives have had abortions. The famous case in [the] Pennsylvania State Legislature where the leading anti-abortion person had to resign when his mistress made it known that she had had an abortion and this State Legislator had paid for it. So this is not an unusual situation. There's a tremendous number of hypocrites in this.

### 3

Individuals looking for guidance in moral arguments on abortion will be struck by several things. The first is that ideas on abortion are frequently introduced by fanciful examples. Sometimes the cases are effective and colorful. Thomson (1971) asks us to imagine a city with people-seed floating about like pollen. The citizens place fine mesh screens over their windows, screens guaranteed effective (at 97 percent) to keep the people-seed out. But sometimes the seed gets in and begins growing on the carpet. Does the occupant of the house have an obligation to permit the growing persons access to the house?

An example like this is striking. It provides insights into the role of prior consent in obligations to the unborn life. But imaginative examples can also limit understanding. There is no theory of abortion (on rights—whether for the fetus or woman; on social utility; etc.) in such examples. There are just the insights. The examples (as with most examples) are also easily cancelled with counter-examples. The illustrations of killing *vs.* letting die show this. The transplant example of Jones and Smith (heart *vs.* kidney) supports a strong distinction between killing and letting die. But consider this example (adapted from Thomson, 1973): Imagine a husband intent on divorcing his wife. She has a heart condition. One evening he comes upon her gasping for breath, needing her nitroglycerin tablets. An enterprising chap, he sees a way to avoid alimony payments. He does nothing while she dies in front of his eyes. Most students of this scene will see little moral relevance in the distinction between letting the wife die and actively killing her. Which example—the transplant example or this one—best illustrates the distinction between killing and letting die?

The use of examples in a field of study often represents the state of the art. Abortion is a complex and controversial topic. No single moral theory on abortion can enlist general support. Examples seem the only reasonable substitutes for theory. They function as analogs to clarify and adjudicate claims—roughly, as representations of beliefs that might not be clearly understood in the absence of the examples. The use of examples, however, is helpful only to the degree that an issue is represented accurately. Then the terms of the example can be held constant or varied (much as we do with premises in theory), and conclusions drawn for abortion issues. Unfortunately, the absence of a generally accepted moral theory on abortion makes the connection between example and issues itself disputable.

Also, it is not clear what the examples tell us to do in resolving a moral problem. What does any individual decide after studying an inventory of such abortion discussions? It is hard to avoid concluding that the literature on abortion is simply not decisive in helping to make a practical moral decision.

The most illuminating feature of the arguments is that they are all organized around the same question. Is the fetus a human life? This question is important for both pro-life and pro-choice. The right to life cannot be assigned to an entity unless it exists as a life form appropriate for the assignment. Human beings have a right to life. Amoebas (presumably) do not. All of the pro-life arguments depend on accepting a fetus as a form of human being. Even the doctrine of double-effect is relevant to abortion only on the assumption that there is some entity there, unborn, that can be harmed directly or indirectly. The main pro-choice arguments depend on a denial of human status for an embryo. If the fetal state has a right to life, then self-defense, euthanasia, the absence of consent must be demonstrated — individual discretion on abortion cannot be permitted. Such demonstration is not what pro-choice advocates have in mind when they argue for free (unregulated) choice. The main line of pro-choice arguments must assume that an embryo is not a human being in any form at all.

The preliminary moral: those hoping to draw practical conclusions on abortion had best explore what form of life a fetus or embryo is. Activists are split in the expected ways on this issue (pro-life firm in their belief that the fetus has the moral status of a human being, pro-choice holding to the conviction that human being-ness comes about later in time). But pro-life advocates are as one in their beliefs about the origin of life, while pro-choice people disagree on the point of origin and are also inclined to dismiss the question as not vital to their own position. Think of the differences between a military formation and a group of strollers. Pro-lifers march in step with each other on the bottom-line view that human life begins at conception. Pro-choicers agree that a human being is not present at conception, but their views are scattered on when human status is achieved and where morality enters abortion decisions. The drum orchestrating pro-choice is this one: that the woman must be free to decide whether to continue or discontinue her pregnancy.

## 4

The author asked all of the activists interviewed this question: "When does human life begin, on your view?" The discussion below represents the types of responses.

*Kisil:* My view? I agree with the scientists. It begins at conception. I probably feel more strongly about that than I did maybe ten years ago when I got into the Right-to-Life Movement. . . .

*Frohock:* How is it that people believe that life does *not* begin at conception?

*Kisil:* I disagree that they believe that. I disagree with that. Let me give you an example. I can only go by what practical experience I've had. O.K. Linda Oken of Planned Parenthood, I work with her, she comes to my office for visits. I'm going to visit with her this week. I mean, we respect each other as people. Now, she's so entrenched in Planned Parenthood. I wouldn't dream of ever converting her. Neither would she dream of ever converting me. So we just don't talk about it. We rib each other once in awhile; we dig in once in a while. It's nothing distasteful, O.K.? But I remember where Linda was coming from about five years ago where we ended up at a debate. Well, it wasn't really a debate. We were both presenting, we were both on a panel, at Morrisville College to a great big group of kids. Since I was originally invited and she wasn't, and she heard about it and got on the bandwagon, at least I had the favor of going last. So, she said, "Now Rita is going to talk to you about the right to life." She said, "If you believe that there is life there, it's not really the issue here. Because the real issue is, does that fetus have right over your life?" And that was the truth coming out. It says exactly where they are. They don't really believe it isn't life. They have some place erroneously formed their conscience that because we are bigger, and we're born, and we have a mouth on us, and we have an organization behind us, that we have more rights than the newly created life. And they *know* there's life there. They don't *care*.

---

*Gordon:* I don't think there's any question that human life begins at conception. There is no argument there. In just the same way the sperm is alive, but that doesn't make the sperm a person. The fact that life begins with conception doesn't make that life a person. That's the argument, not whether there's life there. Of course there's life there.

*Frohock:* When does a person, personhood, begin?

*Gordon:* I suspect the best definition of "personhood" is when a person is born. I could go along with the idea of visibility, and I generally support the notion of the Supreme Court decision which suggests that abortion could be controlled in . . . of viability, even though we're uncertain about just precisely what's going on.

---

*Frohock:* So your own view is that the beginning of human life is at fertilization?

*Dr. Willke:* No question. Please understand—the biologic, scientific measure is absolute. There is no disagreement.

*Mrs. Willke:* You can't deny reality.

---

*Baird:* Why should that question be paramount? Why not the other way around? What is the right test to force a woman to go through pregnancy against her will? Why concentrate on the embryo? Why not concentrate more on can you force the woman against her will to become a parent?

---

*Hughes:* I think that is such an irrelevant question. It's such an arbitrary thing. I came across an article entitled "Do Infants Think?" "New experiments suggest that the cognitive or hypothesis-forming development begins at the age of nine months." Okay, on what basis are you going to define human life? Is it going to be when a heartbeat starts? Is it going to be when brain activity starts? Is it going to be when autonomy starts — well then it's age 21, or it can be 30. It's absolutely arbitrary. Life is development, it's a developmental sequence. It's a continuum, and some people go on it faster than others. We could determine that life begins at 21, when a person has achieved independent functioning, full adult human functioning. You could say it begins at conception. If you want to talk about life, every cell in my body is alive, that's life.

*Frohock:* Who then is to make the determination, this decision? It could be at conception, it could be at birth, it could be at any place in gestation, it could be at nine months when certain cognitive functioning starts, it could be at 21 — I suppose you might become a human being when you vote or whatever. But who is to make that determination? Is it an individual decision or ought society as a whole to make it?

*Hughes:* I don't see any need to decide it. Maybe when death occurs is a more relevant question, and if that's defined then maybe some of the same criteria could be applied to life, in terms of brain functioning or whatever. When you're dealing with pregnancy you're dealing not with life and death but with life versus life. All life is not equal — an acorn is not an oak tree. My life is more valuable to me than my left eye; it's more valuable to me than my right arm; it's more valuable to me than a fertilized egg, or an unfertilized egg; it's more valuable to me than a pregnancy of six months' gestation. I'm not sure where I would draw the line. I don't think these lines can or should be drawn by society because of technology being what it is — we have so many choices now that we didn't have before and so much more information, and it's overwhelming I think. Most people do not have all the information about fetal development. I have more questions about a premature baby being born. There was mention of one on the news the other night — I think it weighed a pound or something like that, and the parents didn't have the money to give it the necessary intensive care that it was going to need. I think close to a million dollars were spent keeping that fetus alive. That was a hard decision to make, those kinds of decisions are really hard. Now if I was the mother of that fetus and it was an unwanted pregnancy, I don't know — would I spend my last penny in order to save it or would I say, "It's a loss." It would be horrible. But I wouldn't decide for that woman whether or not her baby should be saved.

---

*Dr. Willke:* Ask the question, is this fertilized ovum alive? Yes, by any dimension of that word, this fertilized ovum is alive, growing, replacing, multiplying cells, life. Is this fertilized ovum human? How can you tell a human from a rabbit, from a carrot? Genetic chromosomes. Take a look,

46 human chromosomes, this is a member of the human species. This is human, growing, intact, programmed from within, moving forward in a self-controlled ongoing process of maturation, development, sexed male or female, replacement of his or her own dying cells, within ten days taking control of the host body that this little being grows within, controlling physiologically the host body for the balance of that gestation time, enlarging her breasts, softening her pelvic bones, setting his own birthday, all of this controlled by the developing baby, this is alive, human and sexed. That's the biologic measurement. Total intactness from a single cell. You're 40 million million cells, but every single cell is the identical replication, genetically speaking, of the first one. Nothing was added to that single cell, who you once were, nothing but nutrition. Biologically, there isn't a perception, there isn't an opinion, biological, it's absolute. . . . What are the other yardsticks? They all fall into a category that can be described as philosophic theories. This is not human until an exchange of love, until a certain degree of consciousness, until a certain degree of maturation, until a certain degree of independence, liability, until birth, until, until, until, until, certain IQ, whatever. Now, all of those are used as yardsticks to define the word "human life" or if you please, "person." Now the question is, what do they all have in common? Not one is subject to natural science and proof. They all are beliefs or theories. People of good will differ diametrically upon these and if you put six such people in the room, you might get six different answers. We believe the yardsticks of philosophic measurement of the word "human life" should be subject to the same political judgment as the religious beliefs on human life and just as we should not impose a religious faith, belief upon our neighbors through force of law, so we should not impose a philosophic theory upon our neighbors through force of law. That's exactly what the pro-slavery people did. . . . we would go back to the one area that we cannot disagree on, that is the biologic judgment, and we would say that the first question, is this human life, should be answered scientifically. Period, end of paragraph. . . .

---

*Hughes:* As long as that fetus cannot survive outside the woman's body it's not the same situation. We're talking about the fetus as being more important than the mother, as having more rights. I think it becomes a ridiculous, ludicrous situation. There was a court case that pointed this out, where the mother was incarcerated for an offense that she had committed and where the attorney submitted a writ of habeus corpus to release the fetus because the fetus hadn't done anything. You can't do that, you can't separate them, they are one. At that point there is only one individual, there is only one—that duality to me doesn't exist.

5

Defining life is both a biological and a moral exercise. The biological exercise, as might be expected, is more straightforward. Some rudimentary definitions clarify the task. Inanimate matter is a composition of neutrons, protons, and electrons. All living organisms on the earth contain amino acids and nucleotides. These molecules (according to best evidence) filled the atmosphere of the planet Earth in its early stages. The connecting link between the physical universe and the life-world, occupying a place somewhere on the line dividing the two, is believed to be the virus.

Every living creature on the earth, from bacteria to human being, contains the same nucleotides and amino acids. The amino acids are linked together in every living cell to form proteins. All proteins — in every form of life — are constructed out of the same basic set of 20 amino acids. The assemblage of proteins is controlled by the DNA molecule. Each individual organism (except identical twins) has a special set of DNA molecules. Since the protein determines the structure (walls of the cell, hair, muscles, bone) of the organism and its chemical reactions, the DNA molecules insure that each individual is different from every other, though all share the same molecules of life.

The theory of evolution (for which there is massive evidence all over the face of the earth) tells us that all life developed out of inert matter, and that all later forms of life developed out of earlier forms. Though the exact lineage is not determined, it is safe to assume that human beings evolved from tree-dwelling primates who began to flourish 70 million years ago when the dinosaurs died out. Through natural selection operating by means of the laws of physics and acting on chance variations, the large and complex brain of modern human beings developed.

The evolutionary view of man provides no sharp demarcation between the pre-human and the human. The oldest known primate with human-like traits evolved in India and Africa in the middle Cenozoic stage, about 10 million years ago. The closest primate ancestor to human beings, Australopithecus, appeared in Africa between 3 and 4 million years ago. The first true man, Homo erectus, emerged in the East Indies and Africa over 1 million years ago. But no anthropological evidence can in and of itself establish a boundary between the human and near-human. Indeed, the logic of evolutionary theory mandates a continuum, an unbroken series of transitions from inanimate matter through the lower and higher forms of life.

The development of a human embryo (a more appropriate term now) is also continuous. At conception—the successful union of sperm and ovum—the full complement of genotypic traits is present (roughly, the genetic endowment, which consists of 23 chromosomes and approximately 15,000 genes from each of the two parent cells). Photos of the developing human embryo 30 days after conception show that the embryo has characteristic human parts, though looking more reptilian than human at this early stage. It is half the size of a pea, with rudimentary eyes, ears, mouth, brain, and internal organs. Four days later, however, the facial features are more clearly formed. Hands and feet have started to develop. At 44 days, the embryo has all of its adult features and organs. It is now less than one inch long. Beginning fingers, toes, eyelids, teeth, and tongue are visible. Bone cells soon replace cartilage and the fetal stage begins. The fetus is completely formed by the 150th day. The remaining four months consist primarily of growth. (Bellairs, *Developmental Processes,* 1971, p. 114.) Birth is the separation of the fetus from the mother's body. Development continues after birth until the death of the organism.

The basic question in abortion issues—when does human life begin—has several meanings. Historically, human life has no clear beginning. Neither available evidence nor the dominant theory of origins (evolution) can provide an answer to the question. In contemporary terms, the question cannot be answered without further refinement. Human life consists of a collection of cells. Each individual cell is alive. Some are distinctive of the human species. But though each cell is thus a form of human life, it does not follow that no human cell can be killed. The question, properly interpreted is: At what point does a human being come into existence?

Here a theory of definition is required to organize the data. Distinctions between human and non-human individuals can be clearly drawn today on biological grounds. Though (again) all life shares both common chemical properties and (it is generally accepted) common origins, current distinctions among species are indisputable. Human chromosomes, for example, are not found in other species. The issue in abortion is, when in the development of the human organism (from embryo to mature form) does the individual count as a human being? And what type of definition will settle the issue?

Two types of definitions can be used in determining the "humanness" of an organism. One is membership. Another is metamorphosis.

*Membership.* The first model defines a human being as any entity that satisifies some single criterion or set of criteria that qualify anything for membership in the human community. Six tests have been traditionally used to establish membership. (1) The earliest starting point for the assignment of life is *conception,* the point of union between sperm and ovum. (2) *Mediate animation* — the assumption of human form (between 30 and 44 days in term) — was favored by Aristotle. (3) *Quickening* — the independent movement of the conceptus — was a commonly used starting point for life in the early 19th century in America. (4) *Viability* — the ability to live outside the womb — has been more recently used in *Roe v. Wade.* (5) *Consciousness* is sometimes used to identify the point at which human status is achieved in gestation. (6) And, finally, *birth* itself is a starting point used by many.

Each of these criteria is a test for membership. Before the criterion is indicated, no human being is said to exist. Each criterion establishes a distinction, or demarcation, between pre-human and human entities in the gestation of the fetus (and, in the case of conception, at the origin of this gestation). Sometimes clusters of criteria are used to determine membership. For example, a human being might be a creature who is conscious, is self-motivated, has concepts of a self, can communicate with others, and so on. But whether single or multiple, the tests of a membership definition establish who is in and who (or what) is out.

Membership tests suffer from a number of notorious defects. The first is that many are vague. At what point a fetus looks human is a judgment that can vary with the observer. Independent movement can be tested in numerous ways. The traditional method of placing a hand on the abdomen may easily miss movement picked up by more sensitive instruments. Recent medical research suggests that the embryo swims vigorously in the amniotic fluid at two months into term, though most mothers do not feel movement until the fourth or fifth month. Indeed, the fertilized ovum, on its own efforts in the first 3 or 4 days, journeys down the fallopian tube to enter the uterus. Which of these movements counts as quickening? The ability to live outside the womb can differ from one organism to another, and depend on whether, and what type of, resuscitation methods are administered. Consciousness is even less clear. The fetus can hear and recognize its mother's voice near the end of the second trimester. Is it conscious? Is a newborn infant conscious in the absence of memory or self-awareness? The only clear starting points seem to be conception and birth, where, in each case, an event occurs that is distinct from its predecessors. And these two points lead to radically opposed views on the morality of abortion.

A second, more general, problem with membership tests is that they chronically lead to counter-intuitive outcomes. The use of intuition in science is controversial. Many of the greatest scientific discoveries are, or were, counter-intuitive (X-rays, quasars, evolution, Heisenberg's indeterminacy, the relationship of time and velocity in Einstein's physics). But moral theory is both discovery and clarification. An outcome of moral reasoning that is contrary to important moral intuitions is suspect, not welcome. It is reason to rethink the moral tests one is employing, and not necessarily a reason to abandon a moral intuition.

Think, for example, of some hard cases that the tests do not cover. A badly deformed infant, or a severely disfigured accident victim, may not resemble a human being at all. Totally paralyzed paraplegics cannot move independently. Those who have experienced disabling diseases like polio may have to be sustained by artificial means (like respirators). Temporarily comatose patients are not conscious. Are these individuals human? Our intuitions tell us that they are. The law enforces these intuitions in codified form. Even conception and birth fail to cover some hard cases (though much more imagination is needed to conceive of the cases). Suppose that humans are successfully cloned at some point in the future. (No conception occurs.) Are such creatures human? Or suppose that *in vitro* fertilization is followed by *in vitro* gestation—complete development of the human embryo and fetus in laboratory equipment. (No birth occurs.) Are such creatures human?

Students of the law often point out that hard cases make bad law. Certainly no one wants to discard a criterion for human-ness simply because it does not cover extreme possibilities or hypothetical changes in medical technology. The problem is that many of the single-valued tests for life exclude precisely what is real and important: accident victims, defectives, the ill and crippled. At least the possibility of alternative ways of defining should be explored as such exclusions become evident.

One important refinement of membership tests is the use of covering laws. Since the union of sperm and egg begins a process that extends through birth, personhood, and death, the laws covering that process can be usefully employed to define a human being. Version one (forward looking): a human being is any entity that is in a law-like relationship with the development of a human person. Version two (backward looking): a human being is an entity that was at one time a human person. Version one sets conception as the dividing line in human-ness. Version two uses the law-like process of development to include hard cases in the definition. No change in the appearance or structure of a mature human being could, on the use of version two, affect his/her status as human. (Comatose persons were once conscious, etc.) The use of covering laws in defining human beings extends the status of human from conception to death. Their main advantage is the recognition of separate law-like relationships in different species. Since human embryos grow up normally to be mature human beings, not cats or dogs, we have a reason to regard these embryos as human.

A covering law type of definition does not establish membership in the human species by virtue of having or not having some feature. Human-ness is established by some set of features plus the covering law. The standard objection to the use of covering laws in this context is that such entities as sperm and unfertilized ovums are in a probability relationship to embryos, and thus to mature human beings. The standard response to this objection is that the development from zygote to human being is progressive unless interrupted, while the union of sperm and ovum is probabilistic even when intended. The objection and response are both more complicated than they appear. Each seems to need a clearer understanding of the types of persons at issue before and after fertilization (something to be taken up in Chapter 5). For now, note that covering law definitions avoid at least some of the hard cases encountered in membership tests.

*Metamorphosis.* The second model rejects any membership category. Instead, a process is used in which an organism becomes human at some (unclear) point. Between the non-human and human is an area in which the organism cannot be categorized as one or the other.

Suppose (Becker, 1975) that the entry process for being human is both biological and social. Then it is reasonable to think that the biological part of the process is a necessary condition for completion of the entry process. Biological development is the transformation of a set of cells into a multi-cellular organism. The metamorphic phase of development for any organism is complete when the basic gross anatomical form and the inventory of differentiated organisms are both fully present. The social development of the human species goes on beyond this point (and perhaps does not end until death). But Becker (1975) argues that the boundary between becoming and being human is no earlier than the completion of the metamorphic phase of generative development.

The substitution of metamorphic for membership tests expresses more realistically the ongoing character of human development and its ambiguous stages. It also permits a separation between the biological and the higher forms of human identification (the capacity to reason, to speak, to assign values). Many of the hard-case problems of membership tests are avoided by the soft edges of metamorphosis. Hard cases need not be viewed as nonmembers of the human race, but only as individuals located on the boundary of being human. They can even be counted as human if they have successfully passed through some metamorphic stages. A human being would unambiguously *be,* in this second definition, sometime between the fourth and fifth months of gestation.

Is there anything to be said in choosing one of these two types of defining over the other? Each organizes the knowledge available on human life. Each is properly developmental (though membership only with covering laws) and consistent with a wide range of biological data. Both provide at least some assistance in accommodating hard cases. Beyond this, there is no biological mandate for one definition over the other. A natural scientist, in fact, might decide between the two on purely pragmatic grounds. If it is helpful to view human being-ness in membership terms, fine. If it is better for research to view entities as human whenever they are in various metamorphic stages, fine also. A natural scientist might even have no difficulty in shifting definitions as research needs demand it, much as light used to be viewed in physics as either a wave or a particle according to the investigative context.

At this point, however, the moral exercise becomes relevant. Since metamorphosis favors at least individual discretion on early abortions and some membership tests complement the pro-life position, moral arguments marshalled by each side will vehemently align with one or the other type of definition. Notice, however, that definitions of life, occurring as they do in two different forms of defining, cannot resolve the moral dispute. The basic issue in abortion may be the issue of when human being-ness occurs. But biology cannot settle this issue with decisive tests. The moral need must be met with moral, not biological, determinations.

The authoritative status of morality in defining human life should not come as a surprise. Defining a human being has historically been at one with the moral determination of the outer limits of the human community. These limits, in general, have been expanded in recent Western history. Aristotle excluded non-Greeks and women from the class of human persons. More recently, blacks were defined in Western cultures as sub-human as late as the 19th century. In all of these determinations, a moral predicate was assigned to certain physical states of affairs — male-ness, white-ness — and denied to others. The physical state did not, cannot, yield the moral predicate. That skin color, head size, cultural origin no longer count as morally relevant in determining the human community speaks for changes in our moral temperament. But the physical states themselves do not arbitrate the permanence or truth of the moral determinations.

We are, in a sense, back full circle to the beginning. Moral arguments reveal the need for a clear and firm statement on the starting point for human life. Explorations of human origins tell us that the human status of a fetus or embryo is a moral issue.

**6**

When reasoning is circular, there will always be someone who proposes breaking the circle with a rational decision. Unfortunately, decision theory does not provide a solution to abortion disputes. We can start with the thought that a rational decision on any issue requires the selection of a rational decision-rule. Which rule to choose, in turn, will vary with the conditions in which decisions are made. It would be rational, for example, to maximize aggregate utility in a menagerie, but human societies may require decision-rules that are more sensitive to individual rights and needs.

The literature in decision theory marks off three broad types of conditions in which decision rules vary: certainty, uncertainty, risk. Conditions of certainty are those in which alternatives are sure to lead to known outcomes. For example, if I spend $1.35 at the pharmacy for a *New York Times,* I am sure (a) to get my newspaper, and (b) have my disposable outcome reduced by that amount. Conditions of uncertainty are those in which the outcomes of choice are not in any known relationship with available alternatives. Choosing a husband or wife, for example, is viewed by some as this type of blind (double-blind?) decision making—if rational at all. Conditions of risk are somewhere between certainty and uncertainty. Here the probability relationships between alternatives and outcomes are known. Crap shooting, weather forecasting, betting on horse racing, fiscal and monetary policies—our world is filled with decision making in conditions of risk.

These three different conditions of choice demand different decision-rules. Conditions of certainty present the simplest demands. Here rationality requires only that the outcomes be correctly balanced to achieve a desirable mix. Economists use indifference curves to represent an optimum balance between supplies of two items. Risk and uncertainty are more complicated. The dominant decision-rule in conditions of risk is Bayesian—roughly, combine probabilities and expected utility to identify the highest ranked alternatives, and then choose that alternative. For example, if deciding between the movies and the theatre, I might construct the following matrix: the probability of the movie being good is .8, of being bad is .2; the probability of the play being good is .3, of being bad is .7. If I attach a value of 10 to a good movie, 5 to a bad movie, 20 to a good play (I really love the theatre) and 1 to a bad play (few things are worse than great love going sour), then

$$\text{\it the movies vs. the theatre}$$
$$(.8)\ (10)\ +\ (.2)\ (5)\ \text{\it vs.}\ (.3)\ (20)\ +\ (.7)\ (1)$$
$$8\ +\ 1\ \text{\it vs.}\ 6\ +\ .7$$
$$9\ \text{\it vs.}\ 6.7$$

and, since $9 > 6.7$, it is rational to go to the movies. Choosing alternatives in conditions of uncertainty is less clear. The decision-rules include (a) maximin—choosing the alternative with a possible worst outcome that is better than the worst outcome of any other alternative, and (b) maximax—choosing the alternative with a possible best outcome that is better than the best outcome of any other alternative. It can also be rational to guess at probabilities and use the Bayesian rules that are rational in conditions of risk.

Do any of these rules help in deciding whether an individual ought to have an abortion or not? Suppose that a pregnant woman undergoes amniocentesis. The results show a high probability that her child will be born with Tay-Sachs disease. Let .9 represent this probability. Suppose also that 10 is the integer standing for the value of aborting a fetus stricken with Tay-Sachs disease. The value of 20 represents a healthy birth. Then, on Bayesian calculations:

$$\text{\it abortion vs. birth}$$
$$(.9)\ (10)\ \text{\it vs.}\ (.1)\ (20)$$
$$9\ \text{\it vs.}\ 2$$

and, since $9 > 2$, the woman decides to have an abortion.

What is wrong with these calculations? Mainly, that the values assigned to the respective experiences—abortion *vs.* birth—are, if not exactly arbitrary, extremely subjective. Again, the point made earlier: who is to say what value to assign a life afflicted with birth defects? And on what criteria? No general scale of integers, however nominal, can rank genetic disorders against each other or against a normal life. And certainly no scale is generally accepted that ranks abortions against birth on the needs or wants of the expectant mother. The decision models only formalize the personal values of individuals making abortion decisions.

Or try a formalization of decisions to use or forego contraception. Assume again a Bayesian calculation that assigns probabilities and expected value to alternatives. Probabilities, first, are subjective, changing with experiences. A reasonable risk may have to be balanced against expected costs, as when assessing the failure rates of the IUD against the health risks of the more reliable pill. Second, expected value may undergo dramatic shifts with changes in life patterns. What is a rational decision toward contraceptive use may turn out in retrospect to have been irrational when confronting the attitudes of one's partner/spouse toward the resulting pregnancy. But, mainly, since rational decisions depend in general on the values subjectively assigned to alternatives, a rational decision in any area of sex, procreation, abortion, birth will depend on the more basic values applied to these practices.

Bayesian decision-rules do make one contribution to abortion decisions. They elaborate the pro-life position by showing in modern form the truth of the medieval preponderance of a certainty over an uncertainty. Condition: human life has a value far in excess of the utility of abortions. Then, no matter how low the probability that a human being exists in an unborn state, it is always rational not to allow individual discretion on abortion when uncertain on the beginning point for human life. Example: a hunter does not fire at a figure in the forest if uncertain whether the figure is a human being or a bear. Uncertainty favors pro-life. Or, Bayesian decision-rules reaffirm the validity of Pascal's wager.

Consider. God is, or He is not. If He is, there is the possibility of an infinite gain ("an eternity of life and happiness"). If He is not, there is the possibility of a finite gain (temporal rationality). Suppose I wager that God is. If He exists, I gain infinite happiness. If He does not exist, I lose only reason or knowledge. Suppose I wager that God is not. If He exists, I lose infinite happiness. If he does not exist, I gain only reason or knowledge. The infinite distance in value between gain and loss in each case makes the wager on the existence of God the more rational choice. [Blaise Pascal, *Pensées*, sect. 233.] Or, in a more recent language, the extremely high expected value of one of two alternatives renders the alternative a rational choice no matter how low the probability of its occurrence. And so abortion is disallowed, for the value of a human life is so high that it must be protected against such an assault even if the probability that the fetus is human is infinitesimally low. But notice that the reaffirmation of Pascal's wager appeals only to those who accept some probability that unborn states can be human beings. The pro-choice advocate who denies this as possibility will be unmoved by Pascal's interesting intersection with Bayesian decision-rules.

Standard decision-rules fail in general to provide much help in abortion decisions. A moral decision must settle precisely those problems that decision theory takes for granted. Does a fetus or embryo count as a human being? What is the value of human life? Deciding between the movies and the theatre does not involve strong and rational dispute over what the movies and the theatre are, and neither alternative is assigned a value beyond measure by a set of partisans. Conceptual dispute and claims for overriding values (for human life, for privacy) do, however, characterize abortion issues. At an even more basic level, the individual trying to make a moral decision on abortion wants *reasons* for choosing one alternative or another. This, if introduced to decision theory, is a request for why outcomes have the expected values they do in Bayesian models. Once more, the request must be met before the decision-rules can be used.

The individual trying to reach a moral decision on abortion is wiser after exploring moral arguments, biological theories, and decision-rules. But the wisdom is gained from a sharper appreciation of how things fail, rather than how they succeed. Moral arguments need biological theories. Biology needs moral assignments. Rational decision-rules assume as settled what is at issue in abortion. The principals thinking through abortion issues might well turn back to the hard cases that typically begin their reflections. If they do, and if they remember the circle linking morality, biology, and decision-rules, then they may be inclined to retrieve and expose the features of abortion that seem to be the basis of our intuitive responses to the hard cases.

(1) The embryo or fetus is not exactly like a human child. This observation, so vehemently denied by pro-life supporters, seems so obvious that resistance to it is puzzling. The genetic structure of human existence is constant from conception forward. But at no other time in life is so intimate and dependent a relationship found than in gestation. The unborn child, if it can be called that, is within the body of another. To deny the importance of this seems to miss the truly awesome nature of human creation in its early stages. It is, one might suggest, precisely this special quality of gestational life that leads many intelligent and sensitive people to allow abortions when human suffering is demonstrable — i.e., cases of rape, incest, physical handicaps, genetic defects, and unmarried teenagers who are pregnant. Few, if any, would endorse infanticide in these or any other conditions.

(2) The embryo or fetus is not simply a collection of cells to be maintained or destroyed at will. This observation, hostile to the main impulses of pro-choice people, also seems obvious. The embryo is, immediately at conception, an organized form of life that develops according to well-known laws into a human being. To draw parallels between this splendid creation and other human cells is to strain even metaphor to the point of absurdity. It is perhaps this special status of unborn human life that occasions resistance to easy or unreasoned abortions — those based on convenience, the wishes of others, or occurring late in term for no good reason. One indication that embryonic life is special is that late abortions distress many people who are otherwise pro-choice. Some of the distress is brought on by the possibility that late abortions may be homicides (and counted as such by prosecutors — see the Edelin case in the fourth chapter). But conversations with counselors at abortion clinics suggest that the human form of the fetus is the source of the distress. Thinking of embryonic life as just a collection of cells

cannot be sustained when the fetus is experienced visually. (3) Embryonic life is the result of a sexual union between two human beings. This simple and self-evident fact suggests that abortion issues, by their logic, extend to networks of individuals (even though affecting the woman most directly). An intelligible and comprehensive abortion practice will likely have to express connections between human sexuality, reproduction, and abortion, as well as the interests of all concerned parties in abortion. No intuition on the hard cases is exposed with this fact, but many complex ideas wait to be developed once it is accepted.

These three thoughts are basic propositions in any attempt to understand abortion issues. It would be sensible for both pro-life and pro-choice to accept them at face value as simple truths about abortion, especially if the realities of abortion law and practices are to be perceived correctly and organized sanely.

## For Further Reading

Becker, Lawrence. "Human Being: The Boundaries of the Concept," *Philosophy and Public Affairs* 4 (1975): 334–59.

Bellairs, Ruth. *Developmental Processes in Higher Vertebrates* (Coral Gables, Fla.: University of Miami, 1971).

Bennett, Jonathan. "Whatever the Consequences," *Analysis* 26 (1966): 83–102.

Brady, James, and Humiston, Gerald. *General Chemistry: Principles and Structure* (New York: John Wiley, 1978).

Brody, Baruch. "Thomson on Abortion," *Philosophy and Public Affairs* 1 (1972): 335–40.

Carrier, L. S. "Abortion and the Right to Life," *Social Theory and Practice* 3 (1975): 381–402.

Dinello, Daniel. "On Killing and Letting Die," *Analysis* 31 (1971): 83–86.

East, Sen. John P. "Report: The Human Life Bill-S.158," *The Human Life Review* 8 (1982): 81–112.

Finnis, John. "The Rights and Wrongs of Abortion," *Philosophy and Public Affairs* 2 (1973): 117–45.

Levy, Steven R. "Abortion and Dissenting Parents: A Dialogue," *Ethics* (1980): 162–63.

Noonan, John. *The Morality of Abortion* (Cambridge, Mass.: Harvard University, 1970).

Thomson, Judith Jarvis. "A Defense of Abortion," *Philosophy and Public Affairs* 1 (1971): 47–66.

———. "Rights and Deaths," *Philosophy and Public Affairs* (1973): 146–59.

Tooley, Michael. "Abortion and Infanticide," *Philosophy and Public Affairs* 2 (1972): 37–65.

Werner, Richard. "Abortion: The Moral Status of the Unborn," *Social Theory and Practice* 3 (1974): 201–22.

Wertheimer, Roger. "Understanding the Abortion Argument," *Philosophy and Public Affairs* 1 (1971): 67–95.

Wicclair, Mark R. "The Abortion Controversy and the Claim that This Body is Mine," *Social Theory and Practice* 7 (1981): 337–46.

# 3
## ABORTION AND THE LAW

1

The main disputes over abortion in recent years have concentrated on the legalization of abortion established by *Roe v. Wade* in 1973. Pro-life people tend to see the *Roe* decision as a revolution in abortion law. They want a restoration of an earlier time when abortion was illegal. But the earlier time is recent time. Laws prohibiting abortion in the United States occupy a restricted historical zone. James C. Mohr, in *Abortion in America,* has traced the laws that proscribed abortion (before *Roe v. Wade*) to legislation passed in the period 1860 to 1880. In the early 19th century, abortion was regulated only by the British common law and virtually invisible as an issue.

Mohr documents the intriguing changes that have occurred in the practice of abortion in America.

(a) From 1800 to 1825 women were free to have abortions until quickening (the perception of fetal movement by — usually — placing a hand on the abdomen). The general belief at this time, expressed in the common law, was that no human life existed in the embryo or fetus until quickening. Abortion was perceived as a safe procedure to terminate pregnancy. Whatever constraints existed were pragmatic, not moral — fear, for example, of the social consequences of being in a situation requiring an abortion. (And, since abortion was not much used at this time as a means to limit families, the act was associated in the popular mind with "fallen women.")

(b) The first wave of abortion legislation occurred between 1821 and 1840. But the aim was to regulate medical practices that were beginning to be perceived as unsafe. In effect, Mohr points out, the legislation was poison control, measures designed to protect the woman against the malpractices of apothecaries and physicians. All of these new laws accepted quickening as the (practical) beginnings of pregnancy. The main force behind this first set of legislation was the nation's professional (or regular) doctors. Their goal was to upgrade standards and drive the irregulars out of the practice of medicine.

(c) The next several decades witnessed a change in the frequency and nature of abortions. More women, and different types of women, were getting abortions. White, married, Protestant, native-born, upper middle-class women were using abortion as a means to control the size of their families. Abortion became a visible medical specialty. But it was still seen as closer to contraception than homicide. Indeed, an increased frequency of abortion is typically associated with an increased use of contraception, since a social change toward smaller families often precedes knowledge of how to use contraception effectively. And, since the decision has already been made to limit family size, abortion is seized as an absolutely reliable form of birth control (it always works).

(d) The upsurge of abortions was met by a physicians' crusade for more forceful regulation of abortion. The regular doctors were intent upon using state sanctions against their competitors on the abortion issue, and, in general, recapturing authority in public policy issues. The crusade succeeded in getting the anti-abortion legislation if 1860-80 passed in the various states. These new laws rejected quickening (sometimes resulting in the mere change of "a woman quick with child" to "a woman with child" to define pregnancy), made abortion a felony (typically punishable by a $5,000 fine and five years in prison), prohibited advertisements for abortion, and—most important—for the first time made the woman as well as the abortionist liable under the law. By 1900, abortion was once more no longer an issue. This time, however, it had restabilized as a practice prohibited by law.

The reasoning expressed in these state statutes proceeded to govern abortion in America through the first two-thirds of the twentieth century—or until *Roe v. Wade* in 1973.

## 2

The *Roe v. Wade* decision, however, cannot be isolated from a number of other cases and issues. The *Roe* case made abortion a legal practice by forbidding state regulation of abortion (on a sliding scale along intervals of pregnancy). But the *Roe* decision was preceded and followed by other cases that both expanded and contracted abortion liberties.

One helpful (though hardly the only) way to view the *Roe* decision is as an expansion of individual liberties and rights, especially privacy, against the regulatory powers of the state. In some ways, the abortion cases resemble the *Lochner* doctrine set down and developed in the first third of this century. In the early 1900s, New York passed a law prohibiting bakery employees from working more than 10 hours a day or 60 hours a week. Lochner, a Utica, New York baker, was convicted of permitting one of his employees to work in excess of the 60-hour limit.

In *Lochner v. New York* (1905), the U.S. Supreme Court reversed the baker's conviction. The Court read the Fourteenth Amendment due process clause as protecting the liberty of persons and the right of contract against the state's police powers. The Court recognized that regulation of the safety, health, morals, and general welfare of the public is within the state's powers. But the Court kept the contractual relations of employer and employee out of that regulatory zone. In effect, the Court expanded liberty and property to include values unmentioned in the Constitution. Economic liberties were mainly represented in this expansion. But the subsequent Lochner era of the Court also included other personal rights (such as civil liberties and the rights of the accused). In all cases, however, substantive values were introduced to the procedural guarantees of the Fourteenth Amendment.

"Substantive due process" merges basic rights with due process even when these rights are not found in the Constitution. In *Myer v. Nebraska* (1923), the Court reversed the conviction of a teacher convicted for violating a state law prohibiting the teaching of foreign languages to young children (!). Here First Amendment guarantees and rights to contract were both used (in different ways) to support the ruling. This decision also endorses the powers of parents to control the education of their children. A similar expansion of liberty in education is found in *Pierce v. Society of Sisters* (1925), where the Court sustained a challenge by parochial and private schools to an Oregon law requiring children to attend public schools.

A stronger fusion of basic civil rights and due process is forged in *Skinner v. Oklahoma* (1942). The state of Oklahoma had a Habitual Criminal Sterilization Act that required sterilization of individuals convicted three times for any felony involving a moral turpitude (which mysterious phrase excluded such morally upright crimes as embezzlement). The Court invalidated the law on the assertion that marriage and procreation are basic rights protected by due process and, in this particular case, the equal protection clause of the Fourteenth Amendment.

The most important precursor of *Roe,* however, is the case of *Griswold v. Connecticut* (1965). A Connecticut birth control law specified that "Any person who uses any drug, medical article or instrument for the purpose of preventing conception shall be fined not less than $50 or imprisoned not less than 60 days nor more than one year, or both." The law also covered those who helped anyone committing the offense. The Court, in finding the law unconstitutional, established the zone of privacy that was to play such an important role in the *Roe* decision. Justice Douglas, writing for the majority, recognized in the preamble to the First Amendment a right to privacy "older than the bill of rights, older than our political parties, older than our school system." The zone of privacy was drawn from First Amendment rights of association, Third Amendment prohibitions against quartering soldiers in houses without the owner's consent, Fourth Amendment rights of security in person, especially against unreasonable searches and seizures, the Fifth Amendment right against self-incrimination, and the Ninth Amendment's assertion that the Constitution does not deny or disparage those rights not listed. The association of marriage was granted privileged status by the Court as the locus for many of these privacy rights. Privacy, by this time in the Court's history, is supplementing substantive due process.

A miscegenation case further strengthened the importance of marriage. A statutory law in Virginia prevented interracial marriages solely on the basis of racial classification. The Court invalidated the law in *Loving v. Virginia* (1967). Again, the right to marry was affirmed. Justice Warren argued that "restricting freedom to marry solely because of racial classification violates the central meaning of the Equal Protection Clause." Marriage was introduced once more as a substantive right in the Fourteenth Amendment.

The right to privacy was clarified in *Eisenstadt v. Baird* (1972). Baird had been convicted of distributing contraceptives to an unmarried person. The Court, in overturning Baird's conviction, said (Brennan, for the majority) "If the right of privacy means anything, it is the right of the *individual,* married or single, to be free from unwanted government intrusion into matters so fundamentally affecting a person as the decision to bear or beget a child." The hole left from *Griswold* was filled. Privacy attaches to individuals, not simply to the institution of marriage or to married couples.

Several themes are evident in those pre-Roe rulings. The first, going back to the early 20th century, is the development of substantive due process. The procedural guarantees of the Fourteenth Amendment were being used to protect certain substantive values. Second, privacy rights were increasingly used to shield individuals from the regulatory powers of the state. Third, the values used in substantive due process and as the locus for the development of privacy rights were those associated with human reproduction and sexuality, and those heterosexual and monogamous practices — marriage, the family — that represent these values in Western societies.

### 3

The *Roe v. Wade* (1973) opinion struck down a Texas statute that made it a crime to get an abortion except "by medical advice for the purpose of saving the life of the mother." The challengers to this state law were Jane Roe (a pregnant single woman), John and Mary Doe (a childless couple, with the wife not pregnant), and Dr. Hallford (a licensed physician). The suits were class actions. The District Court decided in favor of Roe and Dr. Hallford, declaring the Texas statute unconstitutional under the Ninth Amendment. The U.S. Supreme Court upheld the lower court ruling.

The opinion of the Court rested heavily on privacy rights. Justice Blackmun, delivering the Court's opinion, acknowledged that the Constitution does not mention privacy. However, the Court had, in earlier opinions, established a zone of privacy from various of the first nine amendments to the Constitution. The Court viewed this right as "broad enough to encompass a woman's decision whether or not to terminate her pregnancy." For Blackmun, at least, the issue was not a right to control one's body. It was rather a right of individuals to be shielded from state regulations, to have private discretionary authority on procreation.

The Court recognized the interests of states "in safeguarding health, in maintaining medical standards, and in protecting potential life." But Blackmun interpreted the criminal abortion laws as designed primarily to protect women. Now, with the advent of antiseptic surgery, abortions in the early months are relatively safe (physically safer by a small margin, according to most authorities, than carrying to term). The state can still regulate the standards of medical care. But the Court saw no need for the prohibition of abortion on the concern for the woman's health and safety given the reduction of risk in medical abortions today.

The appellant claims, of course, asserted a "compelling state interest" in the protection of prenatal life. If sustained, such interest would normally override privacy rights. But the Court did not accept these claims. Blackmun argued (1) that the Constitution is unclear on what constitutes a "person," but (2) the fact of widespread legal abortions in the early 19th century suggests that the use of the word "person" in the Fourteenth Amendment does not include the unborn. Further, the Court recognized a variety of theories on when life begins, with the life-begins-at-conception only one of these competing theories. Broad segments of popular and scholarly opinion could be found in each of the various theories. The most extreme theory from the point of view of the pro-life position is life-begins-at-birth. Yet even this theory, according to Blackmun, was endorsed by the Stoics, and is today supported by large segments of the Jewish and Protestant community. The Court reasoned that the law cannot override the rights of the pregnant woman by adopting one theory of life against all others. Rather, in the face of conflicting theories, the discretionary authority of the individual woman becomes paramount.

The point at which the state has a compelling interest in the protection of fetal life is, in the Court's judgment, "viability." The reasoning here is that a proof of independent life — outside the mother's womb — does call for state protection of life. The state may, after viability, proscribe abortions except those needed for the life or health of the mother. The Court thus at once (1) found the Texas statute unconstitutional (as too sweeping, without distinctions among stages of pregnancy), and (2) set up (by the logic of viability) a sliding scale along the continuum from conception to birth. Let Justice Blackmun summarize:

A state criminal abortion statute of the current Texas type, that excepts from criminality only a *life-saving* procedure on behalf of the mother, without regard to pregnancy stage and without recognition of the other interests involved, is violative of the Due Process Clause of the 14th Amendment. (a) For the stage prior to approximately the end of the first trimester, the abortion decision and its effectuation must be left to the medical judgment of the pregnant woman's attending physician. (b) For the stage subsequent to approximately the end of the first trimester, the State, in promoting its interest in the health of the mother, may, if it chooses, regulate the abortion procedure in ways that are reasonably related to maternal health. (c) For the stage subsequent to viability, the State in promoting its interest in the potentiality of human life may, if it chooses, regulate, and even proscribe, abortion except where it is necessary, in appropriate medical judgment, for the preservation of the life or health of the mother.

In *Doe v. Bolton,* the companion case decided at the same time, the Court declared a modern statute on abortion (enacted in 1968) unconstitutional. The Georgia abortion law at issue set out conditions under which a legal abortion could be performed. The portions of the law struck down included (1) the requirement that the patient be a Georgia resident, and — more important — (2) the procedural requirements specifying the "manner of performance" of an abortion and linking the performance to a state interest in the protection of the potential of independent human existence. The Court concluded that the attending physician's "best clinical judgment . . . should be sufficient." Since no other surgery requires more, the Georgia law's requirements that abortions be approved by a hospital committee and confirmed by two other physicians were deemed unconstitutional. Also, the law's restriction of abortions to licensed hospitals (instead of other licensed institutions — like abortion clinics) was rejected. This last provision, however, was qualified later by the Court in *Gary-Northwest Indiana Women v. Orr* (1981), when the Court upheld an Indiana law requiring that abortions for women more than three months pregnant must be performed in hospitals.

**4**

The *Roe v. Wade* decision obviously transformed abortion law in the United States. It also extended a particular concept of privacy that does not exhaust all understandings of private choices and actions.

Students of the law recognize two different senses of privacy. One is the right of selective disclosure. This is the ordinary sense of privacy recognized in many, if not all, social practices. To have privacy in this first sense requires a control over information, especially about oneself or one's associates. A second sense of privacy is discretionary authority, or autonomy of choice. In this sense, privacy is satisfied if the individual is shielded from social interference in making decisions.

The Court in *Roe v. Wade* endorsed the second sense of privacy. The area of privacy established in *Griswold* and earlier cases that marked off marriage and procreation from state interference was zoned to include abortion rights. The *Roe* decision was also like *Lochner* in selecting certain substantive values for unusual protection when these values are not mentioned in the Constitution. Privacy is the right drawn by the Court from the first nine amendments (though the Constitution is silent on privacy). But of more importance are the particular values accorded privacy rights. These values seem to be found in the heterosexual and monogamous family.

The distinction between such family values and other values is sharpened by several subsequent Court decisions on privacy. In *Doe v. Commonwealth Attorney for the City of Richmond* (1976), the Court affirmed, without hearing arguments, a federal court dismissal of a challenge by male homosexuals to a Virginia sodomy law. In *Kelley v. Johnson* (1976), the Court accepted local regulations of the length and style of a policeman's hair. The Court also, in *Hollenbaugh v. Carnegie Free Library* (1978), refused to review a federal court decision sustaining the discharge of two public library employees for "living together in a state of 'open adultery.' " In each of these three cases (and others), the Court could have extended privacy rights to the plaintiffs. That the Court demurred is one strong indication of the types of substantive values that the Court is shielding from state regulation—those of the traditional family.

The development of family law in the 1970s demonstrates further how family values attract the U.S. Supreme Court. In *Moore v. City of East Cleveland, OH* (1977), the Court invalidated zoning restrictions against the extended family (and granted the sanctity of the family substantive due process). The authority of parents over their children—a particular type of family value—was affirmed in *Parham v. J. R.* (1979). In this case, the Court ruled that parents can commit their children to mental hospitals without formal adversary proceedings. The right to marry was decreed fundamental in *Zalalocki v. Redhail* (1978), a case in which the Court rejected state regulation of a man's marriage rights in order to insure his child support payments. The Court, it is fair to say, loves family life; and the type of family it loves is traditional: male-female, with parental authority over children.

The first sense of privacy, selective disclosure, has found no such privileged substantive value. In *Whalen v. Roe* (1977), for example, the Court reversed a lower court ruling that a computerized data bank (acquired by New York State from pharmacists) on patients receiving dangerous drugs invaded zones of privacy. Justice Stevens, writing for the majority, saw no threat in such a data bank either on individual interests in disclosing private matters, or on individual autonomy in making important decisions. It is clear that the Court wants to protect the privacy rights of individuals to make decisions in certain areas and on certain values, but not others; and that abortion is an issue that the Court recognizes as falling within the general substantive values of sex, marriage, and reproduction that are to be protected from social interference.

5

The *Roe* decision has been controversial to both legal scholars and pro-life partisans. But it is not so clear that imagined legal alternatives to *Roe* would have been more desirable. Look first at what might have been.

(1) Suppose that the Court had not decided the abortion issue. (No *Roe* decision was made.) There is reason to believe that various state legislatures would have repealed the statutes prohibiting abortion. (New York had already—in 1971—legalized abortion.) A no-*Roe* society would likely have been pluralistic on abortion, with legal access in some states and prohibition in others. It is not clear that this outcome would have been more desirable than current practices, however. Women wanting abortions who, by the fact of geography, had no access to them would travel (if feasible) to states with liberal abortion laws. Uneven laws would thus have added the costs of travel to abortion, favoring (unfairly) the mobile and wealthy in society. Also, as indeed seemed to be happening in New York during 1971 and 1972, some states would have become abortion mills. Current resistance to *Roe* surely would have formed also against such state practices. Social divisions over abortion still would likely have occurred without *Roe,* though with different goals.

(2) Suppose that *Roe* had been decided in the same general way, but with a different determination for the point at which state protection of the fetus is required. Several criteria compete for the establishment of a right to life. The most general—life itself—is too inclusive. An insect does not have the same right to life (if it has any) as a higher vertebrate. The criterion of rationality is too exclusive. It fails to explain our natural reluctance to kill higher animals needlessly. It also cannot accommodate those hard cases of autistic children, mental defectives, the senile—those who have human equipment without the component of rationality. The Court used viability—the capacity to live successfully outside of the womb. Among the problems with this criterion are that it does not (as we have seen) clearly distinguish among types of dependency (artificial *vs.* bodily life support systems) and it cannot successfully address those later stages in term when the fetus is dependent on the mother's body, yet capable of independent life.

L. W. Sumner (1981) has argued persuasively that *sentience* is the most adequate criterion for a right to life. It admits of degrees, from lesser to greater, that accord with the progressively stronger rights to life we attach to more complex life forms. It also expresses that feature of life valued for centuries and which is most fearfully destroyed in death — a conscious mind. The issue in abortion then becomes — when does sentience occur in fetal development? Zygotes have no central nervous system. The spinal cord is formed in the third week of gestation. The forebrain, midbrain, and brainstem are distinct in the eighth week. The brain is anatomically complete by the end of the seventh month. Sentience depends on the presence of a brain and nervous system. First trimester fetuses feel nothing, are not conscious. The physical conditions necessary for sentience have not yet developed. If the developmental process is frozen, if potentiality is suspended, a first trimester fetus is identical to lower forms of life that are not sentient. Neither consciousness nor feelings occur. But a third-trimester fetus is sentient. It is a higher form of life, clearly unlike non-sentient organisms, and as such has a strong and pronounced right to life. Embryonic human forms, then, seem dichotomous on a sentience criterion in terms of their right to life.

If the Court had used sentience instead of viability to mark the point at which the fetus is to be protected by the state, several interesting consequences might have followed. The obvious practical consequence of a sentience criterion is that only very early abortions are permitted. The end of the first trimester is the very last point at which abortions are allowed, and perhaps even earlier thresholds would be established. One problem with early abortions is that pregnancy is not usually known until mid-way through the first trimester, and sometimes later. First trimester abortions are timed closely with the discovery and validation of pregnancy. Early abortions are safer than late abortions. But by legalizing only early abortions, a sentience criterion might have institutionalized in law a set of abortion rules that only the most organized and diligent women could have followed. The prospect of enforcing through the criminal law a set of rules requiring validation of early pregnancy for abortion and the prohibition of all abortions among women who slip through the validating net is a nightmare to contemplate.

(3) Suppose that a different set of concepts had been used by the Court to justify its decision to liberalize abortion law. *Roe*'s argument rests on a dubious attempt to find and extend various privacy values in the Constitution. A woman's decision to terminate her pregnancy is shielded from state regulation early in term. The Court, however, could have made a decision to override fetal rights to life with other principles. Equality, for example, can be ranked ahead of life in special circumstances. (Racial integration of public schools in America in the 1950s was sometimes marred by violence that took lives, but the fact that lives would be lost was not accepted by the Court as a reason to deny educational equality.) Suppose that *Roe* had been framed in terms of sexual equality, without any attempt to decide whether the fetus is either a human being or a person. The legal right to terminate pregnancies then could have been assigned on the argument that the fetus might have a right to life but no right (on Thomson's distinction) to the use of the woman's body, on the grounds that such use offends the equality that women are guaranteed under the Constitution. Abortion then would more clearly be articulated as expelling a form of life from the body of another, with fetal rights to life mandating cautious medical intervention and all warranted medical resuscitation and maintenance when separation occurs.

The arguments for such a restructuring of the *Roe* decision are impressive. First, the Court would not have had to decide the morality of abortion. The fact is that a substantial number of people in America believe that life begins at conception. The Court's adoption of "viability" in *Roe* denied the validity *in law* of this belief. Since the Court itself rejected the possibility of settling when life begins, the use of "viability" has no validity that might warrant opposing the sincere beliefs of anyone. Moreover, the denial of these beliefs has created volatile political problems that might have been avoided by leaving the moral issue of when life begins completely outside of the law.

Second, the issue of person-hood for the fetus could have been confined to specific social practices. The inertia of that body of law that does recognize fetal rights to life (inheritance, damages) could then have been duly recognized. The use of viability unnecessarily complicated a number of other areas of law. Third, the rights of third parties in abortion decision, in particular fathers and parents, could more easily have been negotiated. A freedom to continue or terminate pregnancy that is justified on sexual equality would not lead to the issue of family rights in abortion decisions. The woman would have been the uncontroversial authority over her pregnancy.

Fourth, the restructured *Roe* would have at once clarified the nature of abortion while obscuring the moral issue of life that is currently at the center of abortion disputes. Abortion-as-separation does not necessarily require killing the fetus. With continued developments in neonatology, it is conceivable that only first trimester abortions would result in the certain death of the fetus. The popular linkage of abortion with murder might have been broken; a woman's decision to terminate her pregnancy would have been limited strictly to termination and not to any authority to kill her offspring; and the medical procedures used to abort might have been forced to undergo change to recognize the fetus' right to life (though not right to the woman's body). At the same time, the avoidance of any tests for determining when life begins might have blunted the sharp claims of pro-life partisans, leaving to another day and perhaps another issue whether abortion is homicide.

The arguments against such a restructuring of *Roe* are also impressive, though their acceptance does not so much defend the actual *Roe* decision as question whether any legal decision is possible on abortion. First, though equality might have concentrated legal attention on issues other than fetal life, it is an open question whether any resolution by the Court would have defused the popular conflict on abortion. Legal protection of the fetus is a logical consequence of the moral argument developed by pro-life. Any legal decision not extending such protection is, for pro-life, morally deficient. Also, the use of equality as a principle overriding a right to life might not be as effective in abortion as it has been in other areas of life. We know, for example, that any program to build bridges is going to cost some workers their lives. Further, the number of workers to lose their lives may be calculable with some accuracy for particular projects. But no one can say who in particular is to be killed in the building project. The projects, representing social efficiency and perhaps progress, proceed on such needed ignorance. Abortion, however, causes particular fetuses, with unique genetic endowments and family heritage, to cease living. It is as unlikely that equality can dominate such cessations of particular lives as it is that efficiency in bridge-building, or even equality in education, could be secured if the names of workers and students who are to be killed in the name of these principles were posted ahead of time.

But, second, the flaw in the *Roe* case may be a larger fault in the structure of law as a device to resolve abortion disputes. Two sets of claimants have opposed beliefs about abortion. Each claimant wants to express in social practices some particular beliefs. It is not clear that these needs are best satisfied by fixing either of the opposed beliefs, or any other beliefs about abortion, in law. If no test for the beginning of human life has validity beyond simple measures of utility, and if competing principles like equality do not respect the beliefs of pro-life when these principles are encoded in law, then a political resolution might best resolve abortion disputes — a theme to be taken up in Chapter 5.

The *Roe* decision is a consideration of interests — of the state and of the woman. Justice Blackmun appears to be searching for a middle ground between the state's compelling interest in the protection of prenatal life, its more general interests in the preservation of the life or health of the woman, and the interests of the woman in being able to decide whether to continue or terminate her pregnancy. This middle ground, moreover, is to be presented in *Roe* without reference to morality. The less charitable critics of *Roe* might say that Justice Blackmun is looking for a majority in the American population where none exists. The search for a middle ground utterly fails, however, as soon as the legal argument on interests leads (as it must on abortion) to a moral test, in this case viability as the demarcation between the state's compelling interests and the woman's freedom to make a decision. One might have wished that interests would also have been assigned to the unborn, still without mentioning rights to life. Then the Court might have left to subsequent legal cases a determination of what fetal interests are in such areas as property and inheritance law. But negotiating fetal interests raises yet more interesting questions than the law can answer. At stake are the status and meaning of hypothetical and unborn persons, a subject that is probably best elaborated by models of rational choice before being addressed by standing courts.

6

The internal logic of *Roe v. Wade,* as actually decided, has generated several continuing issues, and another issue, funding, has arisen from political resistance to the decision. This resistance, in the years immediately after *Roe,* came primarily in the form of state efforts to restrict abortions within the constitutional limits set out in the *Roe* decision. Let us, in deference to the reality of *Roe,* survey the major issues that have continued to divide partisans in recent years, listening as we do so to the views of abortion activists.

The first "internal" issue is the status of family relations in abortion decisions. Abortion is viewed by the Court as a practice to be controlled by the individual woman, not the state (subject to the sliding scale of *Roe*). But minors, subject to parental authority, can get pregnant. And pregnancy itself is witness to the union of two people, male and female. What then are the rights of parents (and relatives in general) in their children's decisions on abortions? And what are the rights of fathers-to-be in abortion decisions?

The issue of family relations is legally more interesting given the fascination of the Court with family values. The Court has generally maintained the autonomy of the individual woman, however, in making an abortion decision, though with some internal dissension and with signs that parental interests are to be given some recognition. In *Planned Parenthood of Central Missouri v. Danforth* (1976), the Court, by a 5-4 vote, struck down a provision in a (post-*Roe*) Missouri statute requiring parental consent for an unmarried woman under 18 to obtain an abortion. The Court ruled that the state cannot delegate authority to any particular person, even a spouse, to prevent abortion. This ruling set abortion off as distinct from all other forms of surgery, which legally require parental consent before the physician can touch the child.

In a companion case, *Bellotti v. Baird* (1976), the Court allowed that a law might be able to give parents veto over an abortion if the judge could override the veto. But the parents need not be consulted. The local court could decide if the minor is mature and well-informed enough to decide on her own with parental authority or consultation. Recently, the Court upheld a Utah law, in *H. L. v. Matheson* (1981), requiring that a minor advise her parents of her decision to seek an abortion. Parental consent is still not required.

The father-to-be has fared less well. The Court has recognized (in *Planned Parenthood*) the husband's "deep and proper concern and interest in his wife's pregnancy." But since the woman "is the more directly and immediately affected by the pregnancy," then her interests prevail. The woman, and only the woman, is authoritative in abortion decisions during the first trimester of term.

Activists are perhaps as intense about the role of family members in abortion decisions as any other issue.

*O'Brien:* How about fathers-to-be? Do you think they should have a say?

*Baird:* No. I've always said that death rates for women are nine times more frequent if you go through child birth and I'd like to see any male listening to this tape or reading about it tell me what the death rate for us men waiting in the waiting room is. The ideals would be, so I'm not misread, ideally it would be fantastic if you could say, Mom, I'm pregnant and your mom says, let's discuss it, let's see what's best for you. Or your Daddy, or you go to your boyfriend, your husband, whatever the case may be, and say, I'm pregnant, what do you think we ought to do. That's fantastic but if you said, wait a minute, maybe this isn't my boyfriend's pregnancy, or my husband's pregnancy, or maybe my parents will react adversely. So ideally if the man could sit down and discuss with you and you felt at ease with that, sure. When I debate this from coast to coast, men will say, if it's my pregnancy, I have every right to say something. And I say, wait a minute, first of all, what makes you so egotistical? What makes you think for sure it's your pregnancy? We men can have intercourse. We men are told we can go out and sow our oats before marriage, even outside of marriage. Society won't admit it but it goes on. Okay, but if men can do that, we say to women, but you can't. You're not allowed to go out and do these things. I maintain, I'm not saying if it's right or wrong, but I deal with reality, a lot of women do have intercourse outside of marriage. I've had more than one women, but you can't. You're not allowed to have intercourse, you're not allowed to go out and do these things. I maintain, I'm not saying if it's right or wrong, but I deal with reality, a lot of women do have intercourse outside of marriage. I've had more than one woman say to me, please you've got to help me. Her boyfriend might have red hair and her husband has black hair, so that woman's got to make that judgment. The tragedy though is that many men think they own women and up until a few years ago, women needed permission of their husbands, not only to get a divorce, but if you were my wife, and if you wanted your tubes tied, you had to get my permission, but if I wanted my tubes tied, called a vasectomy, I don't need your permission. . . .

*Frohock:* Should the father-to-be have any say in whether a girl gets an abortion?

*Kisil:* I think they should have a lot to say. It's part of their genetic make-up and it took two to be procreative, so they certainly should be at least considered.

*Frohock:* How about the parents? When minors are pregnant?

*Kisil:* Oh, absolutely. That's another reason why I stay in the movement. They have taken that right from us and by what justification? . . . The point is if your kid was going to kill your grandchild, would you want the kid to have her reproductive organs ruined, so that when she came out of this tail-spin and maybe wanted to have a family, but she's having problems, because it was done like a production line. You wouldn't want your kid to have cancer. But if your kid had cancer, you'd like the best surgeon. You got to go down on a busy Saturday afternoon and sign for them to have their ears pierced. But the same [girl] could be aborted, a more serious surgical procedure, and I don't have any input? We have spent our whole lives and dollars on the best orthodontist, the best dentist, the best pediatrician, come on, Fred. Those fool women – they'd rather go play bridge, and play golf, and they'd rather belong to all those volunteer organizations in the world, but they won't wake up to the fact that if they took that right away from me, what next is coming down the pipes? . . . They talk about women's rights. I, as a woman, have a right over my child. At least, input, because you have to be careful. But if you say I have a right over my child, you don't. Your children come through you, they're loaned to you, but they're not yours. But, by damn it, we certainly have their interest at heart, don't we?

*Gordon:* No [the father should have no say], because from experience we know that the father will almost always abandon the child and mother. They have little or no responsibility. It would be all right to discuss it with them, but I think the final say should be with the mother. It's the mother who has to bear the child, and it's the mother who bears the life-long burden of the child, because almost all the men, under these circumstances, will abandon the family.

*Frohock:* What about the parents?

*Gordon:* The parents should have absolutely no voice.

*Frohock:* Should they be consulted?

*Gordon:* Consulted, yes, if it's possible. But what if the father of the 14-year-old says to the child, "Listen, if you ever get pregnant I'll kill you?"

What if the father is the father of the child? There have been so many cases of incest, hundreds of thousands of cases. What if the father is a child abuser? What if the father is seducing his own daughter? What if both parents have threatened to mutilate this child? It is reported that 400,000 girls run away from home every year. Are we going to consult those parents, where the parents are abusing the child? We have a million cases of child abuse every year, a million cases! One hundred thousand children are so abused by their parents that they are hospitalized, and 4,000 children are murdered by their parents every year. Are we going to consult those parents? So the point is this: if it's possible, and it seems like the parents are reasonable and can deal with it, and the girl can be convinced of it, fine, but I wouldn't require it.

*Frohock:* Do you think parents ought to have any say in abortions for pregnant minors?

*Hughes:* No, absolutely not.

*Frohock:* Why not?

*Hughes:* Because that girl who is pregnant is the parent of that child. Her parents don't have the right to force her to have an abortion (which many parents do try to do when they are involved), and they don't have the right to force her to have a baby. I think it's got to be her decision.

*Frohock:* What about the father-to-be? He's a parent.

*Hughes:* I think that reduces a woman, a girl, to a uterus. There's more to her and to her life than that, and that's not the most important part about her. I don't think a woman should have to reproduce for someone else, because someone else wants her to.

Curiously enough, however, two well-known respondents gave complex and even ambivalent answers to the question of family-member roles in abortion decisions. The Willkes were in favor of parental and spouse consent, but were also concerned with abuse of rules requiring such consent. Ms. DeCrow saw consent as an intriguing legal issue.

*Frohock:* Do you think then the father-to-be should have a say on whether a woman should get an abortion?

*Mrs. Willke:* If he's married, if it's the wife, the mate, yes, very definitely.

*Frohock:* What if he's not?

*Mrs. Willke:* If he's not, in that instance, again, I think that the girl should discuss it with him and see if there is some support there, and I think that this is where we've again failed in education. What have we taught our men? Are they really responsible for the children they bring into the world? Just as decent human beings, what do we owe a new life that we bring into the world? Are we ready to accept the responsibility, or aren't we?

*Dr. Willke:* That's a hard one to do. In the adoption thing now, we have a Supreme Court case out of Illinois which says that if the girl, unmarried, wants to give her child up for adoption, there must now be the consent of the putative father. Heavens, it could be a rape case, and very often, this is a very casual affair and the girls . . . come to me and they say, I hardly knew the guy, I got drunk, or something or other, and now he's holding it over me, and I don't think I can take care of my baby and in all great unselfishness, they have a life ahead of them. They want to place their baby in a good home. They want their baby to be loved and here through some kind of interpersonal spite, maybe these two fought or so forth. He wants the kid to get back at her or some other destructive interrelationship, and we run into these things. If a girl like that comes to me, I advise her, you don't know who it was. Tell them there were five or ten, you don't know who. But the girl must prostitute herself to get out from under that ruling. I don't think the father ought to have complete rights, of course not. There should, however, be a safeguarding of the parental/father/husband in the intact marriage situation. It's just as much his kid as hers. Of course, we have to honor that. Just as we should honor 'the parents' rights with the minor daughter.

*Frohock:* You think then the parents should not only be consulted, as the Supreme Court has said in the Utah Law, but also give approval?

*Dr. Willke:* Of course. An escape clause for a destructive relationship, yes, sure. Some kind of an appeal outlet, yes. But it should be pretty tightly honed. We give these parents absolute right to all kinds of things over kids, ear piercing, elective surgery. You name it, up and down the road we go with these children, and rightfully so. We've all kinds of teaching and opinions. Who really overall, forget the hard cases, in our culture, loves that child the best? A judge? Or the woman who's borne her or the father who's nurtured her? The answer is only too obvious. Do we have destructive relationships? Of course. But we safeguard against that. An analogy . . . husbands beat wives, sometimes brutally; therefore, we should not let women live with husbands.

*DeCrow:* There are two answers to that. One is what should be and the other is what the legal standard should be. I think ideally parents and children should be in communication; parents shouldn't be so uptight that they can't talk to their children about contraception and sex education in general. Ideally, if a young girl finds herself pregnant the first people she should go to are her parents, and she should tell them she's pregnant and together they should decide what she's going to do. (I personally think the best thing for her to do would be to get an abortion.) In other words, they should be her confidants in this situation. However, that happens not to be the case in many families, and if it is not the case, if the kid is afraid to talk to her parents (and in some ways a lot of parents don't want to hear about this either), then I think it's a terrible burden on the girl to require her to talk with her parents if she can't, and who can be a better judge of that than she. I think it's also an unfair burden on the parents although it sounds like parents' rights versus something else. But I would say if a girl is too upset to talk to her parents about an unwanted pregnancy then there is something in that communication situation that means it's going to be uncomfortable for both parties. And I think if a girl is old enough to get pregnant and she feels it's going to be calamitous to speak to her parents then she shouldn't be forced to do that. Also I don't think it should be required, although the Supreme Court upheld a Utah statute which said you had to get permission. . . .

*Frohock:* It said that you have to inform the parents but they don't have a veto over it. You do have to tell them about it. [Note: This is the *Matheson* ruling.]

*DeCrow:* And practically it's like the husband's consent thing. Even if that's in the law it can't be enforced because a person just goes to another county and does it.

*Frohock:* That's my next question. Do you think the fathers-to-be should have any say, legally? The Court has said no but do you think, if you were constructing your argument in the legal world, that the fathers-to-be should have any say in whether a woman gets an abortion?

*DeCrow:* That's a fascinating question. I'm currently the attorney for a guy in a paternity suit [author's note: this is the Frank Serpico case], and the legal argument that I've framed is he chose not to be a father. The woman chose to have the baby (they're not married), and I'm using an equal protection argument. He had no right to force her to end that pregnancy and therefore, since male persons do not have the right to choose, you can't have a unilateral decision in the hands of the woman and then say he's got to pay. In this case she told him that she was on the pill, but when he was informed she was pregnant he said, "I don't want to be a father. Have you thought about abortion?" She said that she wanted the child. So the answer to that is that it is very complicated. I don't know how I'd construct a law. Right now the law is definitely unequal; men have no stake in the say of what's going to happen. It comes to the whole right to choose parenthood, or to choose non-parenthood. After New York made abortion legal and before the Supreme Court decision I wrote a speculative piece on what this might mean, legal abortion, what it might mean in general, legally. One of the things I concluded was that if abortion is legal then men shouldn't have to pay child support for a child they chose not to have. Now men can't choose to have a child because of biology. (If you pay a mother-for-hire that's illegal, which I don't think should be. If it is a contractual arrangement between two people then you should be able to do it.) So men can't choose to be biological parents alone, but I think someday we'll have test tube babies, so then a man can choose to be a sperm donor, just like artificial insemination. But right now a man cannot choose to be a parent unilaterally, and I don't think he should be able to force the woman to have an abortion, although I think he should be able to opt out of support if she chooses to have a kid. If she is pregnant and wants to have an abortion (I'm a big expert on these cases because I've used them in my paternity case showing how the father has no right), the court has held uniformly that he has no right to force her to bring the child to term, and I guess since it's the female body I would go along with that, though with great ambivalence. I can't see myself as a judge or legislator saying that Mr. Smith should be empowered to force Miss Jones to carry a child for nine months, but I think it's a problem, that it's discrimination against men. I just don't see how at this stage in scientific knowledge we can correct it. I have a lot more problems with that than I do with parental consent. In one case a husband and wife had together planned to have a child and then she decided to have an abortion. I guess she was going to get a divorce and an abortion. This was really a contractual arrangement — they had decided to have a child. And he tried to get the court to stop it and the court wouldn't. Additionally one would have to say the court couldn't because if the guy got a court order in New Jersey (I think this was in New Jersey), she could have gotten on a bus, gone to New York and had one. So it would be very hard to enforce.

## 7

The second "internal" issue is what constitutes viability. Again, the issue arises from the Court's own logic in *Roe v. Wade*. If the measure to be used in determining state interest in protecting life is the capability of the fetus to live independent of the womb, then it is natural to ask about the criteria for independent life. In one of the more macabre lower court decisions, Circuit Judge Clement Haynsworth ruled in Federal Court in *Anders v. Floyd* (1978), that a fetus which lived 20 days on its own after an abortion was still non-viable.

In *Colautti v. Franklin* (1979), the Court invalidated a (post-*Roe*) Pennsylvania law that attempted to assert state interest in protecting fetuses potentially able to survive. The law prescribed a standard of care when the fetus "is viable" or when there is "sufficient reason to believe that the fetus may be viable." Physicians not following these statutory requirements were subject to criminal liability. The attending physicians in an abortion are to make the determination of fetal viability. The Court found the law deficient on several points. First, the standards to be employed in caring for the fetus were ambiguous. Second, differences between "is viable" and "may be viable" were not mentioned. Third, the introduction of criminal penalties was said to have a chilling effect on constitutional rights, especially since the penalties were attached to such vague criteria. Justice White dissented sharply. He pointed out that the *Roe* decision did mean by viability the point at which the fetus is potentially, not actually, able to survive outside of the womb — and that is largely what the Pennsylvania law sought to express. White viewed the majority decision as tacitly disowning the concept of viability described in *Roe*.

Pro-life activists reject viability as a test for state protection of human life, linking it with euthanasia, while pro-choice partisans accept viability as a reasonable test. In one case — Kathy Hughes — the respondent accepted euthanasia as a sensible proposal.

*Frohock:* The Supreme Court in the *Roe* decision used "viability" as the point at which human life warrants protection by the state. Could that view in any sense be compatible with your own views, that human life begins at conception? Do you have with the Court decision at least the possibility of a separation between the moral determination of when human life begins and the test for state protection of human life?

*Jackson:* I'd respond by saying that "viability," which is a human judgment on a particular biological artifact, is precisely flawed by the problem of deciding who is doing the judging and precisely on what grounds. As has been well pointed out, "viability" means the possibility of surviving, and this is being pushed back slowly, incrementally, as medical technology improves. So I see it as a very problematic sort of distinction. The other thing I was going to add was that I do see, and this has often been pointed out, that once you invoke viability as a criterion, you can by the same token say we may apply viability to born people of whatever age or condition and say that they are viable or non-viable, according to whether we think they are socially useful, whether we think that their lives are worth anything, even to them. You know the Philip Becker case, which incidently has recently had a happy resolution, I don't know if you've heard that. Becker was the 12-year-old boy, who's now 14, in California, who's mongoloid, and whose parents were denying him a surgery which would relieve him from pain. And he would have probably lived to about the age of 30, but they refused it on the grounds that his life was not viable. It was appealed, and recently the court allowed that the couple who had defended the boy, Philip Becker, and got to know him and love him, could adopt him, and they, therefore, as the adopted parents, now have the authority to mandate the surgery required to relieve him from his pain and guarantee a longer life.

---

*Frohock:* Do your views on abortion also accommodate euthanasia — I mean euthanasia of course to apply to both ends of the scale?

*Hughes:* Yes.

*Frohock:* Could you elaborate on that?

*Hughes:* There's a question of control, of having control over your destiny and yourself. For myself, I think I should be able to specify the circumstances under which I want my life to continue. And then on an ideological level I think again it comes to limited resources — for me it is immoral to spend millions of dollars to save one life or prolong one life one day. I just don't believe in it. It's immoral to me.

*Frohock:* Would that view depend on something like the claim that those who are here on earth now have a higher priority?

*Hughes:* Yes, I think it's a question of stewardship. When I bring someone into the world I want to provide the most I can, and for the generations that are coming I want to do as much as I can to make this a better world. And when I'm on my way out I don't think I should stand in the way of my family.

*Frohock:* Would you think, because of the limited resources we have on earth, that someone else should have the right to tell you the conditions under which you ought to die?

*Hughes:* I can't say. The will to live is pretty strong and I don't know. I would hope that I would take it on myself, that I would feel a responsibility to take it on myself and not have someone tell me. Now let's say that I changed my mind or that a law was passed saying that I didn't have any right to make that choice—I think that would be unfortunate. Right now I'm willing to let other people spend the money to freeze their bodies so they can come back, but it's costing me, through the insurance companies and through society in general in terms of medical care, to keep people alive who are probably never going to come back. It bothers me a little bit but I'm not out there saying turn off the life support system for them, yet.

*Frohock:* You understand that the problem, at least from the pro-life perspective, is that the infant child doesn't have the capacity for choice. The analogy at the other end would be the person who, because of physical debilities, wouldn't be able to say, shut off the oxygen and let me die, so that decisions are made by others.

*Hughes:* Right, it's a rough decision. I'm comfortable with power and making decisions. But it's not as though a fetus . . . to me, it's not an infant; it's inside somebody's body. I wouldn't want to make the decision to have my left leg cut off but I would, or to have a tumor removed. And that's the way I view it—to me it's a negative thing. An unwanted pregnancy is like a tumor; it's a living cell but it's got to come out.

*Frohock:* Wouldn't then the question of when it achieves the status of human being be relevant?

*Hughes:* Yes, it might. We make hard decisions, choices, all the time. I think little baby cows are adorable. I didn't go into the Peace Corps because when I was in college I heard this couple talking about their experiences—they had to kill chickens, butcher goats. God, I couldn't do that. I probably could if I had to, if I had to survive, but it wasn't a life style that I wanted. That's innocent life, that's killing. These choices are hard, and we have a responsibility as human beings to make these hard decisions. We make them all the time. I think a vegetarian could make the same argument the right-to-lifers are making. I'm not a vegetarian but I think they could make the same argument: "They're killing poor, innocent animals, innocent life." They have no choice, they don't have the capacity for choice, and neither does a fetus. It doesn't have the capacity to make a choice.

## 8

A third, "external," issue (one not deriving from the logic and language of *Roe*) is public funding for abortions. The Court has refused, first, to require states to fund non-therapeutic abortions for indigent women. In three companion cases in 1977 — *Beal v. Doe, Maher v. Roe,* and *Poelker v. Doe* — the Court saw no compulsion from either the Constitution or federal law to change local decisions on abortion funding from public money. The test, for the Court, was not one of strict judicial scrutiny. Justice Powell, for the majority in *Beal* and *Maher*: "An indigent woman desiring an abortion does not come within the limited category of disadvantaged classes so recognized by our cases. [T]his Court has never held that financial need alone identifies a suspect class for purposes of equal protection analysis. . . . [T]he right (in *Roe,* to abortion) protects the woman from unduly burdensome interference with her freedom to decide whether to terminate her pregnancy. It implies no limitation on the authority of the state to make a value judgment favoring childbirth over abortion, and to implement that judgment by the allocation of public funds."

The Court, second, refused also to invalidate a number of restrictions on public funding for many medically necessary abortions. Between 1976 and the present, the U.S. Congress has passed several versions of the Hyde Amendment. These amendments restrict Medicaid funding for abortions except under extraordinary circumstances. The most restrictive of these amendments was first in effect for fiscal year 1977, which permitted federal money for abortion only when the life of the mother was in danger (roughly the same bill ratified — again — by the U.S. House of Representatives and Senate in June 1981). A more generous version was passed in 1978 that also covered reimbursements for abortions for "victims of rape or incest when such rape or incest has been reported promptly" to an official agency. These amendments were attacked in *Harris v. McRae* (1980) on the grounds that they all violated substantive due process, equal protection, and the religion clauses of the First Amendment to the U.S. Constitution.

The Court rejected all of these attacks and, in effect, assimilated *Harris* to the *Maher* decision. The Court ruled that not even health reasons entitle a woman to financial resources for abortions. The *Roe* decision removed state impediments to abortion. Freedom of choice on abortion was granted constitutional protection. But the Court refused to see indigency as an impediment that violated constitutional rights. Whether to use public money for abortion was viewed as a decision measured only by its rational relationship to a state interest. It was, in short, up to legislative bodies, not the Court, to make funding decisions on abortion.

*Hyde:* Well, the issue first arose in my life in the Illinois General Assembly when I was a member back in 1968 and at that time the move was to liberalize the then existing abortion laws which provided criminal penalties for abortionists and I was asked if I would co-sponsor such a bill. I'd never thought much about abortion. I hadn't studied the situation. So I said let me delve into it a little bit and I'll get back to you. So I did, I read some material on abortion and rather than co-sponsor the bill I decided that I would oppose it because I felt that a human life was involved. However small and microscopic and vulnerable it still was the beginning of a person and so it ought to be protected. So that became my position. Now as the legislation moved forward, it became clear that it wasn't a sort of subject that a lot of people wanted to get involved in or would take the time to become expert in. There always was a vacuum on the side of opposing such legislation. So we were able to defeat that legislation in the state legislature. Then along came Roe-Wade in 1973, where the Supreme Court pre-empted it, said there was a constitutional right for a woman to have an abortion and it no longer was appropriate for state legislative action. In 1974 I ran for Congress, got elected, showed up here in 1975. At that time, again the issue (of abortion) wasn't uppermost in my mind. The action in Congress by most of the pro-life people was co-sponsoring amendments to the United States Constitution. But everyone realized there didn't exist a two-thirds majority to pass anything and so opposition to abortion took the passive form of co-sponsoring amendments and then letting it go at that. So, one day in 1976 the HEW appropriation, I was advised by another member, had $15,000,000 in it for 300,000 abortions, and a simple amendment knocking that out would be appropriate. So he didn't want to offer it and I said, you know, what the hell, I'll offer it. So . . . we scribbled it out and I offered it. I did not expect it to pass but we were looking for a recorded vote to see who was with us and who wasn't. We debated the thing, the vote was had and to my surprise it passed. Immediately, the people who strongly supported abortions energized, Bella Abzug and the girl from California, nice looking woman, I can't think of her name, Yvonne Braithwaite Burke, Pat Schroeder, etc., galvanized their forces. And at the end of the bill, it is permissible procedurally to demand a separate vote, so that was demanded on that amendment, and we picked up even more votes that time. So we were delighted, overjoyed, and it went over to the Senate. The

Senate finally decided to accept, secure in the knowledge that the federal courts would knock it out as denying equal protection, etc. And so they accepted it to avoid a long battle, not easily nor quickly but they finally did. And sure enough, they found a judge in Brooklyn, New York, who immediately enjoined the enforcement of the Hyde Amendment. So it wasn't operative but for a couple of days before it was enjoined. And over the ensuing period it was litigated extensively. The Supreme Court, as I recall, issued an order dissolving the injunction, but ordering the court to continue with the hearing, which they did. Meanwhile as the years went on the Hyde Amendment, so-called, was offered every year. The first version of it, which was (that) no funds appropriated herein may be used to pay for any abortion except where the life of the mother would be endangered if the fetus were carried to term, was amended in succeeding years by adding other qualifications—the health of the mother where certified by two physicians, serious physical health rather than mental health, and that sort of thing; and then rape and incest were cranked in and these were very vigorously debated. Then finally we got back to the original Hyde Amendment, with the sole exception for the life of the mother—where we are now. At this point, Congress is so weary of debating the issue on an annual basis for the appropriation that the amendment really is accepted, and isn't battled over in the continuing resolution.

These three additional issues—the rights of family members, viability, and funding—derive directly and indirectly from *Roe v. Wade.* The first two are not completely resolved. The rights of parents in the abortion decisions of their children are still unfolding in court decisions. These rights, unlike the (disputed or nonexistent) rights of the unborn, are expressed in law. A long tradition has recognized the authority of parents over their own children, especially in the area of medical therapy. The exact relationships between these rights and abortion rights are yet to be worked out. One item, among others in this area, is whether the sense of privacy established by the Court shields the individual from family as well as social interference. Since the Court has consistently championed the integrity of the family, the balance between these two rights will not be easy to set.

The issue of viability is also unsettled. There is first the acknowledged ambiguity in the concept itself. Who is to determine viability? By what criteria? Is viability to be settled by actual or potential life outside of the womb? Is the duration of independent life to be a test (remember the *Anders* case)? If so, the Court will have to forge a rule that distinguishes one length of time from another. A live birth currently counts under the law as a person even if the child dies immediately. Then there are the medical techniques that encourage human life. Viability is a function of medical technology. Neonatology (the subspeciality of newborn care) has pushed viability for the fetus to much earlier points since the *Roe* decision. Many infants today who weigh as little as a pound and a half at birth are able to survive and lead normal lives. Physicians predict that babies born as early as 24 weeks gestation will eventually survive. But, also, great uncertainty surrounds what independent life means. Since death itself has no unambiguous meaning in the law, it is not at all clear what life means. Can seriously damaged infants — with epilepsy, blindness, mental retardation, cerebral palsy — who are kept "alive" with elaborate life-support systems meet legal tests of independent life outside the womb?

The issues of *who* and *what* determine viability are particularly pressing in view of the gravity of homicide. The case of *Commonwealth v. Kenneth Edelin* (1976) is instructive. Dr. Kenneth Edelin, Chief Resident in obstetrics and gynecology at Boston City Hospital, performed an abortion by hysterotomy (medically equivalent to a Caesarian carried out without regard for the fetus) on a 17-year-old unmarried woman in late September of 1973 (approximately 8 months after *Roe v. Wade*). When the woman appeared for the abortion, the attending physician, Dr. H. R. Holltrop, diagnosed the pregnancy as 20 weeks in term. He advised and approved a saline abortion (the introduction of a 20 percent sodium chloride solution into the amniotic fluid). After the woman was admitted to the hospital, a medical student and junior resident set the term at 24 weeks. Dr. Holltrop reexamined and concluded 21-22 weeks. Dr. Edelin set gestation at 20-22 weeks.

The problems began when Dr. Edelin tried to insert the needle into the amniotic sac. The tap was bloody, indicating that the needle had not penetrated the sac. Dr. Edelin stopped the probes. He consulted with Dr. James F. Penza, his supervisor (and associate director of obstetrics and gynecology). Dr. Penza agreed to attempt the intra-amniotic instillation of the salt solution on the following day. These efforts failed also. Both agreed that the safety of the woman in the abortion procedure required a hysterotomy. Dr. Edelin went ahead with the surgery. He removed the fetus, and, according to later testimony, put his hand on its chest to check for a heartbeat. Finding none, he placed the fetus in a stainless steel basin for examination by the pathologist. A later autopsy found a partial expansion of the fetal lungs. Either the fetus had sucked in amniotic fluid inside the sac, had taken in room air through the uterine incision, or had taken in room air outside the uterus. The latter possibility suggested some type of postnatal life.

The state of Massachusetts indicted Dr. Edelin for manslaughter. The grand jury indictment judged that the baby boy (the fetus was a male) died when removed from the body of the mother. The manslaughter charge was that Dr. Edelin waited "3-5 minutes after he manually separated the placenta from the uterine wall and before he removed the person from the abdominal cavity of his mother," thus killing the person by a wanton and reckless act before its delivery. The grand jury assumed that the fetus became a person "upon the detachment of the placenta" (Gunther, 1980, p. 359). The defense contended that manslaughter could occur only where a fetus was born alive completely outside the mother's body.

Dr. Edelin was convicted in Superior Court of manslaughter. He appealed. The Supreme Judicial Court overturned the conviction, holding that there was insufficient evidence that there was a live birth. Dr. Edelin returned to his practice. But the case is ample demonstration that viability is an open and continuing issue. A closer look at the *Colautti* decision suggests why the issue has not been settled. The U.S. Supreme Court maintains (in *Colautti*) that there is viability when, in the judgment of the attending physician, "there is a reasonable likelihood of the fetus' sustained survival outside the womb, with or without artificial support." The Court has argued, reasonably enough, that since viability (defined in this way) may vary with each particular pregnancy, legislatures and courts cannot specify an objective single standard for viability, such as weeks of gestation, fetal weight, etc. Instead the attending physician must be given broad discretionary authority to judge viability. The problem (Wood, 1980) is that abortion techniques affect fetal viability. To give discretionary authority to the physician, then, is to allow the physician to determine, not judge, viability. (The woman also has power to affect or even terminate the fetus' life insofar as she can choose abortion techniques.) One objective of the Pennsylvania statute invalidated in *Colautti* was to separate the act of abortion from viability by requiring the physician to consider the life and health of the fetus in selecting abortion techniques. The Court pointed out that the parameters of these standards of care were poorly defined. The statute, for example, did not stipulate that the life and health of the woman are to prevail if in conflict with the life and health of the fetus. But critics maintain that the *Colautti* decision empties viability of effect when the judge of survival — the physician — also holds power to determine survival.

States continue to define viability in different ways (Wood, 1980). Idaho and Utah follow the definition set forth in the *Roe* decision. Iowa, Kentucky, Maine, Missouri, and Nebraska use the slightly amplified version in the *Danforth* decision: "that stage of fetal development when the life of the unborn child may be continued indefinitely outside the womb by natural or artificial life support systems." Other states — Indiana, Minnesota, Montana, North Dakota, Pennsylvania, Tennessee, and Wyoming — use a test that is constitutionally ambiguous, if not dubious — the actual ability to live. Two states, Oklahoma and Louisiana, employ even less constitutionally sound grounds: a test of potential ability as drawn from premature births, not from abortions. Twenty states have statutes protecting a fetus delivered alive. It is interesting to note that "born alive" is not equivalent to "viability," for a fetus who takes one breath is born alive though not necessarily viable. Aborted fetuses' rights to life are identical with those of post-natal infants. But state protection of fetuses aborted alive can have extensive implications for abortion conditions even when they do not constrain the selection of abortion techniques. Five states, for example, require that medical equipment to resuscitate, and in general care for, fetuses be nearby during abortions. If such equipment is not present in abortion clinics, the practical effect of such state requirements is to require hospitalization for middle and late term abortions, which then extends state regulation of abortions in additionally complicated (and controversial) ways.

Few abortions are performed late enough in term to raise the issue of viability. The continuing concerns over viability are thus marginal issues in numerical terms. But they capture the core differences over abortion in identifying the complex overlaps between abortion and birth late in term, and in addressing the conflict between the physician's discretionary power and the fetus' potential for life.

The third issue—public funding of abortions—is at least clearly determined by the Court. But it is an issue of extreme and growing controversy. Even the Court was sharply divided (5-4 in *Harris*). Justice Stevens, who had been with the majority in *Maher*, argued that the *Roe* decision rejected state interference that assigned greater value to potential life than to the mother's health. Further, government programs in general must distribute funds using neutral criteria. He concluded that the Hyde Amendment fails both the reasoning in *Roe* and impartial tests of distribution within a medical program (Medicaid) designed precisely "to alleviate some of the hardships of poverty by providing necessary medical care . . . "

The divisive nature of the funding issue may be partially explained by the fact that it cuts across substantial ideologies of the state. Imagine that

(a) $x$ is a right to do $a$

(b) $y$ is a necessary condition for doing $a$

(c) one can have $x$ without $y$.

Now the classical liberal version of the state (17th to 19th century—now the conservative view) maintains that having $x$ guaranteed by law does not entail having $y$ guaranteed by law. This is roughly the position of the Court on the funding issue—that the right to be free to choose abortions without state interference does not require social guarantees on the (financial) means to effectively exercise that right. But a more recent view of the interventionist state (the contemporary meaning of liberal) views the proposition in (c) above as a proof of the vacuity of (a). Unless the necessary conditions for an action can be guaranteed along with the right, then (on this view) having the right is meaningless.

The Court may be consistent in keeping government regulation totally out of abortion decisions (though Justice Brennan, in dissent on *Harris,* sees the issue as restricting the state from using its power to constrain the woman's freedom to choose on abortion, in effect through coercive financial incentives favoring childbirth). But whether proposition (c) above does or does not nullify proposition (a) above is a difference in conservative *vs.* liberal ideologies. And ideological issues are notorious sources of acrimony.

**9**

Abortion decisions, like all other decisions, depend on images, or metaphors, of the central figures involved in the practice. One unusual feature of abortion issues is that disputants cannot even agree on how many central figures are involved in abortion—whether just the woman, or the woman and child. But the pro-choice and pro-life perspectives in law do represent different images of the individual woman.

(1) The law leading up to *Roe v. Wade* and the cases following this decision develop privacy rights. The individual woman is conceived as a figure shielded from regulation. She may seek advice, counseling. But no values may be imposed on her by others. Indeed, the general philosophy of pro-choice is expressed as private choice by all individuals on matters of sex, reproduction, and marriage. The individual is to be a self-sufficient figure on these issues, though many of the values in privacy protected by law are dominant in American society (involving the monogamous, heterosexual family).

Where is the support for this image of the private individual?

(a) Both senses of privacy—as control over information and autonomy in choice—are justifiable on moral grounds. Control over information is an important way of ordering the relationships in one's life. The individual who denies information to his business associates that he provides easily to his wife is arranging patterns of intimacy. What and how much to reveal of oneself is always a device to structure one's social order. To lose control of information about oneself is to lose that capacity for self-definition and social ordering that information establishes. So it is that the second sense of privacy, autonomy in choice, easily complements the first. To be free from social regulations in making choices affecting one's interests is a natural companion of being able to control information about one's life.

To be in control over one's life is an important condition for moral action. Some (Hart, 1955) argue that if there are any natural rights, freedom must be one of them. Any right, after all, is a restriction on the freedom of others to stop the bearer of the right from exercising that right. The right to vote, for example, restrains the freedom of registrars (and others) from stopping qualified individuals from voting. Unless it is assumed that individuals are free to act, the restrictions that rights impose on freedom make no sense. There is an even larger point here. The starting premise for any theory of rights (natural or legal) is the thought that individuals are free and self-legislating creatures. The business of governing then becomes, in part, the development of rules to adjust those rights and insure social welfare. It is impossible even to conceive of what moral practices would be like without the premise of individual authority over private issues.

(b) But, second, there is a rational defense of privacy. This defense has been developed by Nozick (1974) on a paradox introduced by Sen (1970). Assume first the standard liberal view that if a value is preferred unanimously in a society, then that value ought to rank higher for society than those values not preferred unanimously. Then listen to the following story (adapted from Sen, 1970). One woman, Mary, is a pro-life supporter. Another, Jane, is pro-choice. Three alternatives confront the two individuals: x = Jane is allowed to have an abortion; y = Mary is allowed to have an abortion; z = no one is allowed to have an abortion.

The pro-life woman — Mary — orders the alternatives as z > x > y. The pro-choice woman — Jane — orders them as x > y > z. (There is some malice in the pro-choice ordering with the y > z ranking. But it is not inconsistent to feel so strongly about pro-choice on abortion that one assigns its benefits to others, especially to pro-lifers, ahead of banning pro-choice completely.) Now one of the rational conditions for an ordering of alternatives is transitivity — if y is preferred to z, and z is preferred to x, then y must be preferred to x. (If a man is taller than his wife, and his wife is taller than his son, then the man must be taller than his son.)

Let one more condition embellish the story. Each individual is to be authoritative for the other over two of the three alternatives. Mary (pro-life) is allowed to dictate rankings between z (no abortions) and x (whether the other individual is to be allowed to have an abortion). Naturally the ranking is $z > x$. Jane (pro-choice) is allowed to dictate rankings (for both individuals) between y (whether the other individual is to be allowed to have abortions) and z (no abortions). Here the ranking is the expected $y > z$. This respective dominance over pairs of alternatives produces a surprising outcome when the rankings are combined. If $y > z$ and $z > x$, then (on transitivity) $y > x$. Or, carving out niches of orderings (something the liberal mind respects) results in a collective preference for Mary (pro-life) rather than Jane (pro-choice) being allowed to have an abortion. This is very peculiar. It is even more peculiar when one notices that both individuals prefer the opposite, $x > y$.

What does this rational anomaly tell us? Mainly, that giving authority to individuals to fix alternatives for others (for society) can lead to contradictions. Neither individual in our story wants abortion rights for Mary. Yet this is the social outcome. Privacy rights can avoid this rational problem by granting each individual authority over their own lives, not the lives of others. Thus one important justification of privacy is that, by marking off space for individuals to make their own choices, the rational dilemmas often encountered in aggregating choices can be avoided by excluding certain alternatives from social choice.

(2) The pro-life perspective conceives of the individual woman as an extended figure. She is part of a set of mutually beneficial obligations that individuals have to each other. Or she is fulfilling the role of Good Samaritan. The joys and pains of childbirth are well documented. Viewing pregnancy as the fulfillment of beneficial obligations requires a stress on joy instead of pain. The Good Samaritan role—roughly, rendering assistance beyond that which duty requires—stresses the painful character of pregnancy. In both roles, however, the individual woman is an extended figure. She takes her values from a network of offspring, family, and friends. The private figure of pro-choice gives way to the individual who merges self-interest with the interests of others.

Where is the support for this image of the extended individual?

(a) Though the social sciences, especially economics, assume routinely the concept of a self-interested individual, social reality easily provides instances of individuals who identify strongly with others.

Family units, for example, are clusters of separate individuals with overlapping and common interests. It is hardly surprising to hear that parents often define themselves in terms of their children, that lovers and spouses sometimes merge parts of their identities with each other, that — in general — individuals are members of networks of associates strongly attached to one another. The first pillar of support for the extended individual, then, is that it is a realistic concept.

Morality provides additional support. Though autonomy of choice — the central idea in privacy — is a condition for moral action, the references of choice need not be simply the self. Indeed, a totally self-oriented system of values seems morally inferior to one that takes others' interests into account. (Saints are self-less figures, after all.) Abortion is also precisely the type of issue that introduces the interests of others. One of the continuing issues after *Roe v. Wade* is whether and how the interests of family (spouse, parents) are to bear on abortion rights. (The pro-life perspective would add the interests of the offspring to this network.) Certainly any moral point of view can accept extended senses of an individual even within a zone of privacy rights.

(b) The image of the extended individual can also avoid those rational contradictions found in the summation of preferences. But it does so by avoiding summation rules. The rational problem of combining preferences among individuals represents a failure of combination rules. The two individuals on abortion rights (example above) cannot put together their preferences rationally without violating a unanimity rule (y is preferred to x in the collective outcome, even though both individuals agree on x > y). One way to avoid this problem (as suggested) is to allow private decisions. Another is to impose decisions authoritatively, without summing preferences. The U.S. Supreme Court has decided in favor of privacy rights on abortion. The Court can as easily impose abortion restrictions without rational contradiction. The rational problems of preference-summing justify both privacy and authoritative decisions in collective choice. Voting, as the source of rational problems, is the one method made suspect by the rational contradictions.

Which image of the individual is more persuasive — private or extended? No general argument can subordinate one image to the other. It is important to see how they operate within the contrasting perspectives on abortion. But to adjudicate between the two images requires a reconstruction of society along each of the images. Then these questions arrange the inquiry—what would society look like if each of the contrasting images were society's microcosm? And, which version of society is more desirable as a human community? It remains to observe that the main conflicts between the two images of the woman—private *vs.* extended—are embedded in the law because of the moral endorsement found in the *Roe* decision. *Roe,* remember, modestly set aside the higher ambitions of philosophers and theologians to determine the point at which human life begins. But then the Court turned to "viability" as the practical demarcation between the authority of the woman to end her pregnancy and the rights of the fetus to state protection. "Viability," however, writes a membership criterion into the law that is morally repugnant to those who believe that life begins at conception and requires state protection at that point. The Court thus entered the moral dispute over abortion by endorsing one moral test—viability—and rejecting, as part of the law, all others. It follows from the moral test that privacy rights must be found in law and assigned to the woman to shield her from state regulation before viability occurs. An acceptance of conception as the beginning of life would have led to the endorsement of those mutual obligations that require public regulation of abortion at all stages of term.

The question that seems to require further treatment is: Does the law have to subscribe to one or another of the moral values on abortion? Is there a legal or political resolution of abortion problems that does not require the legal expression of moral values?

**For Further Reading**

Bryant, M. D., Jr. "State Legislation on Abortion After *Roe v. Wade:* Selected Constitutional Issues," *American Journal of Law and Medicine* 2 (1976): 101–32.

Decker, Raymond. "More Christian Than Its Critics," *Commonweal* 51 (1975): 384–92.

Gunther, Gerald. *Cases and Materials on Constitutional Law,* 10th edition (Mineola, New York: Foundation Press, 1980).

Hart, H.L.A. "Are There Any Natural Rights?" *Philosophical Review* 64 (1955): 175-91.

Mohr, James C. *Abortion in America* (New York: Oxford, 1978).

Nicholson, Jeanne Bell. "The Court, Abortion Policy and State Response: A Preliminary Analysis," *Publius* 8 (1978): 159-78.

Noonan, John. *A Private Choice: Abortion in America in the Seventies* (New York: Free Press, 1979).

Nozick, Robert. *Anarchy, State, and Utopia* (New York: Basic Books, 1974), pp. 164-66.

Ramsey, Paul. "Protecting the Unborn," *Commonweal* 50 (1974): 308-14.

Regan, Donald. "Rewriting *Roe v. Wade*," *Michigan Law Review* 77 (1979): 1569-1646.

Rubin, Eva. *Abortion, Politics, and the Courts* (Westport, Conn.: Greenwood Press, 1982).

Sen, Amartya. *Collective Choice and Social Welfare* (San Francisco: Holden-Day, 1970), chapters 6 and 6*.

Sumner, L. W. *Abortion and Moral Theory* (Princeton, N.J.: Princeton University, 1981).

Trinkaus, Walter. "Dred Scott Revisited," *Commonweal* 51 (1975): 384-92.

Wood, M. A., and Hawkins, L. B. "State Regulation of Late Abortion and the Physician's Duty to Care for the Viable Fetus," *Missouri Law Review* 45 (1980): 394-422.

# 4
## ABORTION REALITIES

### 1

Abortion disputes are over an act that is not widely understood. It is, as a physical act, a medical intervention. Four types of abortion are performed today. Menstrual extraction, and dilation and curettage (D&C), are the two most common types. They are administered mainly in the first trimester. In menstrual extraction, done usually in the first seven weeks of term, the embryo is sucked out by a vacuum pump without dilating the cervix. In a D&C, the cervix is dilated and the embryo is either scraped out by hand (with a sharp-edged curette) or sucked out with a vacuum pump. Approximately 95 percent of all abortions are either menstrual extraction or D&C. A variation on D&C is dilation and evacuation (D&E), in which the fetus is extracted later in term (12-17 weeks) by a stronger vacuum pump. (Some doctors avoid this procedure entirely because of the grisly effects of the suction on the more developed fetus.) D&E abortions are almost always performed in hospitals, since the woman must be at least sedated, and often anesthetized.

A third type of abortion procedure is intra-amniotic instillation (administered mainly in the second trimester). Water with a 20 percent salt solution is injected into the amniotic fluid by catheter. The sodium chloride is poisonous to the fetus, causing its death within two hours. A spontaneous abortion then follows. Sometimes prostaglandins are injected instead of the salt solution. These compounds, drawn from the human seminal vessels, do not have the same toxic effect on the fetus as the salt solution. Fetuses, as a consequence, are more likely to be aborted alive with prostaglandin than with saline instillations. Less than 4 percent of all abortions are intra-amniotic instillations.

A fourth type of abortion is the hysterotomy. This consists of a surgical incision in the abdomen and uterus, and the removal of "the products of conception" — the fetus. This type of abortion is performed usually before 20 weeks into pregnancy. If the pregnancy has reached five months, the procedure is surgically identical to a Caesarean delivery without continuing the life of the fetus afterwards. Sometimes the procedure is combined (for other health-related reasons) with a hysterectomy (the removal of part or all of the woman's reproductive organs). All forms of hysterotomies amount to one-tenth of 1 percent of all abortions.

The physical features of abortion tell us that it is a medical event needing trained technicians for success. No one who observes, or undergoes, an abortion can doubt the importance of antiseptic surgery in abortion. Nor can any participant deny the radical differences between D&C abortions and hysterotomies — especially where viability becomes an issue late in term. But, mainly, it is instructive, when exploring abstract arguments or inspecting aggregate data on abortion, to keep in mind what physical events occur when the term "abortion" describes the purposeful end of pregnancy. It is especially important to see that beneath the layers of social predicates assigned to abortion is a physical act of intervention that women experience as reality, not as theory.

## 2

Who gets abortions?

All categories of women along age or socioeconomic status are found in abortion figures in the United States. But pregnancies are terminated through abortion more frequently among the very young and the middle-aged. In the decade following *Roe v. Wade*, about 3 in every 10 abortions were obtained by teenagers. Annually 1.1 million teenagers get pregnant (11 percent of all teenagers).

Approximately 400,000 of this 1.1 million get abortions. The pregnancy rates go up as the socioeconomic status goes down. But it is not clear that abortion rates increase with lower socioeconomic status. In a study of Rhode Island, a state with a predominantly white and Catholic population, 56 percent of all pregnancies in teenagers at the highest socioeconomic status ended in abortion, while only 22 percent of pregnant teenagers living in poverty areas got abortions. Best estimates are that the greater number of poor women who get pregnant at least evens out these percentages, so that the number of abortions among poor teenagers equals, perhaps exceeds, those among more affluent teenagers. In New York State, the highest abortion rates among pregnant women occur in girls under 15 and women over 40. More abortions, however, are obtained by women in their twenties. Thirty-five percent of all abortions in the United States are performed on women in the 20 to 24 year old age group, another 20 percent on women in the 25 to 29 year old group.

Why women get abortions is not clear. The one universal observation, axiomatic to abortions, is that women get abortions because they do not want to have a child at that time in their lives. Informal surveys of counselors at abortion clinics and pro-life organizations reveal that the reasons women offer for not wanting a child vary enormously. They include financial considerations (too poor, too involved with a career), a desire to limit family size (from one other child to many others), that they are unmarried, that the lover-or-husband does not want a child, that a child would wreck a fragile relationship with the man or (conversely) make the relationship permanent, fear of birth defects, because of parental pressure, that they are too young or too old, and (strange though it may sound) even that they love children too much to bring one into the circumstances of their world. Among the very young, however, it may be safely speculated that age itself is an influential factor in abortion decisions.

Pro-life activists believe that most abortions are the result of "selling" techniques by organizations like Planned Parenthood, while pro-choice activists see the decision to have an abortion as a free and informed choice made by the woman.

*Kisil:* . . . people will have abortions according to whose hands they fall into, except for a few—a few women are really decisive by nature and they really know what they're doing and this is the decision for them. There are very few of them. Millions of people go into abortions according to whose hands they fall into.

*Frohock:* So then—I'll just ask the question, because you've partially answered it—why do women get abortions?

*Kisil:* Women get abortions because, first of all, society has managed to make it sound very simple, very non-threatening, very safe, and I think most of us equate legal with "it's O.K." And, I think legal isn't always the best thing for you.

*Frohock:* What about those who believe in free choice? How do they come to have their beliefs?

*Kisil:* O.K. The people, particularly the people who cry freedom of choice, they're either extremely dishonest to themselves—or they have bought such a story that they're not on to themselves, and let's say, they do believe in freedom of choice, they truly believe—they're not going to stand out on a street corner and drag you into an abortion clinic. They truly believe it's a nice comfortable situation, it's not for me, but at least the gal should have a choice. Well, there are two things wrong with that philosophy. First of all, it's not a true choice if you have failed to tell the girl all her options, all her possible complications, and if you haven't told her—explained to her—fetal development—a lot of—not just using teenagers, but a lot of young married women—go into it, not realizing what they are doing until after it's over. And the same people who cry freedom of choice, they really try to stop laws of informed consent. I can show you things in the files. Those kind of people—the pro-choice people, the pro-abortion people—they actively have letters out to all the people on their mailing list, in their clinics, in their meeting rooms, whatever organizations, they are the same organizations that opt for freedom of choice, are the same people who are encouraging other people to say "Don't allow informed consent." How can you be against informed consent and say you have freedom of choice?

*Frohock:* Do you think that if women were more informed, there would be—

*Kisil:* There would be less abortions. I know it, I don't think that, I can guarantee, and I can show you where the woman who has been informed has looked into what fetal development is, and—you see, it's a euphemism that has fooled the woman and during a period of crisis, too, it's easy to grab on to a euphemism and let yourself be fooled. But when it's over with and there is a bigger problem, then you say, "Why don't they make it a law that doctors have to tell you what it's really all about?" We've got women all over the country who have had abortions, who have formed organizations and tell about their experiences.

---

*Frohock:* When girls go to the various agencies in a community—do these agencies do an adequate job counseling?

*Gordon:* I don't think Birthright does, or that any of the Right to Life people do, because they invariably discourage girls from having abortions, whereas I think Planned Parenthood does because they provide an option. They say one option is keep the child, or . . . they don't pressure a child to have an abortion. That's a total lie. I never have heard of a Planned Parenthood that didn't do the following: They encourage the child to tell her parents, they always encourage the child to tell her parents, and they always give an option, abortion, keeping the child, adoption, and so on. They are very careful about providing options, whereas the other groups are not. At one time Birthright did provide options, but they're losing their grip on this thing right now. Of course, the pro-life groups never give options, and they provide very bad services, not professional services.

*Frohock:* Do you think the decisions on abortion, pro and con, made by women are made as a consequence of consulting with agencies, or are they made prior to coming to these agencies?

*Gordon:* They're often made prior, most of the time.

*Frohock:* Take it at the individual level. Let's imagine that you are a counselor for one or another agency. What would be the signs that you would look for that would make you suggest to a girl or to a woman that she really ought not have an abortion? Are there any?

*Gordon:* I think in discussing the matter, if you felt . . . I would still allow the final decisions to be the woman's. I've been in situations where the 14-year-old is pregnant, the mother and father are totally opposed, they want the child to have an abortion, and the child refuses. In those cases I support the child, even though the mother and father wanted the child to have an abortion, and in my judgment it would have been far better for the mother to have the abortion. I have no question about it in my mind. There may be situations where the child wants an abortion, and quite clearly she's going to be overwhelmingly guilty about it. I may say, "Listen, I want you to think about it. You may feel guilty, upset. Having the child may be less punishing than your guilt later on. Think about it, but whatever you decide

I'll go along with it." On the other hand there may be a girl who says, "Listen, I want to have this baby. I'm 12 years old, I can take care of it." I might say, "How are you going to take care of it? How much money do you earn? Are your parents going to help you? Where are you going to live? Do you know what it means to take care of a child?" I'm not just going to go along with whatever it is. I as an adult have a right to provide what would be a sense of circumstances, options, give a sense of reality. I've worked with many retarded children who get pregnant, and they say, "Oh, I'm going to have a baby, it's going to be great," and I say, "Hey, if it's all so great, why don't you work for this nursery school for little kids." Half of them change their minds when they have to take care of a kid for 24 hours, so one is obliged to introduce some reality. But in the final analysis the person has to let the individual decide.

---

*Frohock:* Tell me in a general way what happens in an organization like Planned Parenthood when women who are pregnant come in to see you. They're not looking for sex instruction but are actually pregnant and considering an abortion. What happens?

*Hughes:* I'll go over what I do. First I find out what leads her to think she's pregnant, what kinds of symptoms she has and what she has done to verify that that is actually the case. Once in awhile it turns out that she's wrong, that she's not pregnant. And then, what are her feelings about it, what does it involve for her at this point in her life, who has she told about it, discussed it with? Once in awhile in rare cases there is a woman who cannot discuss it with anybody but most of them have discussed it with someone. "Have you made a decision? If so, what went into the decision? If you haven't made a decision, how do you see the situation? How would you feel about abortion? What would be the pros for having a child right now? What are the cons?" And then giving information about what's involved in an abortion, how it's done, answering any questions about the procedure, if there are problems with financial resources, if she will continue the pregnancy. Adoption — very few women ever want to consider that.

*Frohock:* Why is that?

*Hughes:* Because if they went through nine months of pregnancy they're going to keep it, they're not going to give it away, they couldn't do it. That to them is more painful emotionally, for the rest of their lives, than abortion is.

## 3

The number of abortions in the United States has increased

yearly since legalization. In 1970, 193,000 abortions were performed. In 1971, the year that New York State legalized abortions, 486,000 women got abortions. By 1977, 1,270,000 abortions were being performed in the United States each year. The figures for 1981 show 1.5 million abortions annually. Almost one-third of all pregnancies currently end in legal abortions. Seventy-four percent of women getting abortions in 1978 were unmarried at the time of the procedure. Most abortions are performed in the first trimester. But teenagers are more likely to delay abortions until later in term. Among girls under 15, less than 33 percent of abortions are performed within the first eight weeks of gestation, while 41 percent of abortions among 15-19 year old category, and almost 60 percent of abortions obtained by women 30-39 years old, occur within eight weeks of term. Indeed, over 13 percent of abortions performed on the under-15 population occur at 16 weeks of term *or later,* compared to 5.7 percent, and 3.4 percent, and 4.6 percent late abortions in (respectively) the 15-19, 20-24, and 30-39 age categories.

One explanation for relatively late abortions among very young teenagers is ignorance about both pregnancy and the possibility of abortions. Another is hesitation in informing parents—and, since the *Matheson* ruling in 1981, telling parents is a requirement of law. Difficulty of access to abortion clinics has also been cited as a cause. Eight in 10 counties in America do not have abortion clinics. Abortion services are found primarily in metropolitan areas on the East and West coasts. Only 18 percent of public hospitals in 1975 performed any abortions. Since very few girls in the 15-and-under age groups pay for their abortions, costs must be borne by parents, guardians, partners, or public funds—another source of communication and consent delays. It is in principle possible, of course, that the very young are more troubled morally by abortions—and thus deliberate longer. But the more likely causes of delay are the increased difficulties in perception, understanding, and access facing the very young.

Is abortion safe?

Most studies show that it is. Major complications from abortion in the United States are in the range of 0.7 per 100 abortions. In one representative year, for example (1975), about 77,000 women had complications from abortions. This is a large number. But only 29 of these women died. The "only" here is not meant to convey callousness. It is an evaluation drawn from comparisons with other surgical prodecures currently performed. This safety record is important because abortion is one of the most frequently performed types of surgery. The comparison of abortion with its only alternative to those who are pregnant—childbirth—is also instructive. The death-to-case rate for pregnancy and childbirth in the years 1972-75 in the United States was 14 per 100,000 live births, compared to 1.6 deaths per 100,000 abortions performed at 12-weeks gestation or earlier. Abortion, as the supreme Court assumed in the *Roe* case, is safer for the life of the mother than carrying to term.

The two most important factors influencing complications are gestational age and abortion technique. The longer the woman waits during pregnancy, the more likely she is to have problems. The lowest rate of complications is during the 7-8 weeks period in term (which is very early, since knowledge of pregnancy is usually not sought or secured much before this time). The complication rate increases at a fairly even pace after this point, reaching a high of 2.26 per 100 abortions at 21-24 weeks. The second factor affecting complications, abortion technique, is in part determined by the first. The safest abortion procedure is suction curettage, with a complication rate of 0.4 per one hundred abortions. The next safest is sharp curettage (using scraping methods), which is 4.8 times more likely than suction curettage to have complications (though still with the low rate of 1.9 per one hundred abortions). The complication rate increases dramatically with abdominal operations. Hysterotomies and hysterectomies have complication rates 37.3 to 40.3 times higher than suction curettage. Since suction curettage can only be used in early abortions and abdominal surgery is required with late abortions, an abortion is much safer when performed very early in term. Even a delay of suction curettage from 8 to 10 weeks gestation increases the risk of a major complication by 60 percent (though still at the relatively low rates of 0.27 to 0.45 per hundred abortions).

It is reasonable to assume that legal abortions are safer than illegal abortions, though there is some controversy over whether this has always been true. It is true that, since 1970, abortion-related deaths have been declining at a more rapid rate than other causes of death in pregnancy and childbirth. Abortion mortality has declined even more rapidly since 1973, the year that abortion was legalized in the United States. The same accelerated decline in abortion deaths is found in England and Hungary after legalization of abortion. Legal abortions in the United States currently have a lower mortality rate than any other surgical procedure. Infection is the main cause of death from legal abortions in the United States. From these facts—the correlation of lower mortality rates with legalization and the role of infection in abortion mortality—it seems to follow that illegal abortions (which one would assume are less hygienic) carry a greater risk of death and complication in general. But data on illegal abortions before *Roe* in 1973 are not easy to assemble. Certainly the "kitchen abortions" inspiring the drive toward legalization were hazardous experiences. But no one knows how many hospital abortions were disguised as routine dilation and curettage treatments. And the number of "kitchen abortions" is impossible to determine with accuracy. But there is no doubt that abortions performed under the guarantees of antiseptic conditions are safer than those that are not, and that legalization has made antiseptic conditions a routine expectation in abortion procedures.

Long-term complications are not known with any reasonable certainty. Studies of physical complications have used unsound methods of control; and psychological complications are still in the area of guesswork. There are some indications that abortion can be a traumatic experience even when the procedure avoids physical complications. A *New York Times* article presents one version of abortion experiences. Parkmed, a private outpatient clinic in New York City, performs around 300 abortions a week. Linda Maddocks, a counselor, reports that "most of them [the women] have the attitude, 'I don't like it—I wish I didn't have to make this choice, but I do have to make this choice.' " Sometimes the experience is one of overwhelming relief. "I'm having trouble raising a puppy," one woman observed afterwards. "I know I'm not capable of raising children." She was pleased to have had the abortion. But a disturbing number of women have bad experiences. One 29-year-old businesswoman who had just had her second abortion admitted that after her first abortion "I had terrible nightmares of being a child murderer and having to chloroform babies" (*New York*

*Times,* February 27, 1981). Though reliable studies of the post-abortion psychological states of women have not been made, informal reports like this one suggest that abortion can be a difficult experience.

Pro-life activists emphasize the harmful effects of abortion, while pro-choice people dismiss complications as nonsensical or so negligible as not to be seriously considered given the alternative complications of carrying to term.

*Frohock:* So that if I ask you to say almost in a single sentence, what is the most important thing that leads you to oppose abortion, it would be —

*Kisil:* It would be the deception of the female. . . . I think if they really understood that they were carrying a new life . . . They'd heard nothing but that abortion is O.K. All your prime time television went to abortion. I won't go into it in detail but it's been going around that it's like a dentist's appointment, like it's an easy thing to do. There are very, very few women who go through an abortion without being hurt, psychologically and physiologically.

*Frohock:* Do they come here to see you?

*Kisil:* Sometimes we get them through the phone. Sometimes Birthright gets them. But — they end up in Hutchings [Psychiatric Center] with psychologists and psychiatrists. Some of them just cope with it and they're all right. Some of them have a bad time on the anniversary of what would have been the birthday of the child. Others maybe can cope with it pretty well until they start thinking — maybe they are fortunate to have another child. No one can say that if I have one abortion, I may not have another child, but then when they do have that other child, as that child starts developing, they realize what they did at the beginning — well, then, they have that coping to do, too.

*Frohock:* So, what would you say that feeling is?

*Kisil:* I think it's a feeling of being cheated — you weren't told the truth. It must be awful when you feel you've been cheated.

---

*Frohock:* Right-to-lifers have said that if women of all ages were informed about abortions, very few would have abortions, because they just are not told the dangers, the physical risks, and the emotional problems associated with abortions. How do you respond to that?

*Gordon:* First of all, the emotional problems they have made up. All of our studies that we have developed over the years reveal that the greatest trauma is when a mother gives up the child for adoption, and the next traumatic is when the mother keeps the child. The least traumatic, the least emotional implication, is abortion. People handle abortion, generally speaking. There are a few, there's always a headline of one or two who regret the decision, but the number of people who are emotionally scarred by abortion is infinitesimal compared to those scarred by actually having the child and giving it up for adoption, or keeping it. Sometimes the person who is scarred is the baby who is kept, because of abuse and lack of care, and so on, and we have to keep that in mind, too. So the myth, the Right to Life people have carried out this myth based on no research whatsoever that I have ever been able to examine, that it's all this emotional trauma . . . of course you can always get a few case histories. And so that's number one. There's no question in terms of the current research that the risk of abortion is far less than that of actually having the baby if it's medically done in the first trimester. The risk, the medical risk, leaving aside some problems of multiple abortion, but the medical risk of the first abortion — and most people have not had more than one abortion . . . a certain percentage, 10-15 percent, have more than one. But it's a small percentage. So they're lying.

---

*Frohock:* Do women ever feel that abortion is immoral? Does that come up at all?

*Hughes:* Yes, for some people.

*Frohock:* How do they phrase it? What are their concerns?

*Hughes:* About killing. For some women who have children they think it means that they're bad mothers; if they don't have children they think some of them, it means that somehow they don't love children. Some of them will say, "I love children. I love babies," meaning to tell me that they've always thought of people who had abortions as doing it because they hate babies, because I think that's a prevalent image. Many of the women who come in considering abortion have always been opposed to abortion themselves, until they find themselves in that situation.

*Frohock:* After you talk with them what do they do?

*Hughes:* First we need to verify that they are pregnant and some sort of estimate how far in the pregnancy they are. And then the decision is up to the woman. If she wants to be scheduled for an abortion we make the appointment, explain exactly what's going to happen. For someone who is undecided we say, "You can make an appointment and you can call us up and cancel it," or "You can not make an appointment and call us later if you want to make an appointment," or "We can make an appointment for you to come back and discuss it further." Or if she's made a decision not to have an abortion, she will not have to do anything.

*Frohock:* Roughly what percentage of women who consult with you in Planned Parenthood go on to have abortions?

*Hughes:* Most of them. I think many women, most women, have already made up their minds by the time they come here. They may have reservations, they may be scared, but they've really made up their minds. A small percentage are ambivalent to the point where they leave without making a decision.

*Frohock:* Then having made up their minds they come in to have the abortion. Do women have problems emotionally or physically with abortions?

*Hughes:* I think it's really different for each person. I think many women feel a tremendous relief because most of the agonizing is done beforehand. That's the worst time for people—making the decision and anticipating it. It's really awful. And so once it's over I think most would say they just feel really relieved: "It's over, it's done. I got through it, I'm okay. Now my life can get back to normal." For some women, and I think for all women but in varying degrees, there's a feeling of loss mixed in with it, as there is even with women who have miscarriages. There's a hormonal reversal that their bodies go through, our bodies go through, during pregnancy and after pregnancy. It's a loss and as with any other loss they have feelings of anger and so forth, but most people have dealt with these kinds of problems before. Some have not, like young teenagers. But I feel that most women are strong, most people can deal with their problems, and life goes on.

---

*Baird:* . . . Obviously, thousands of people were either killed or seriously maimed (before legalization of abortion). One of the things that was an unrecordable factor, many of the women considered suicide. I remember I had a patient who drove to me all the way from Detroit, Michigan, and I asked her why she made it a point to tell me that not only did she drive, but she rented a Volkswagen, and she told me very clearly that if I couldn't help her, she didn't want to hurt her family's car, she was going to take the Volkswagen, the rented car, and drive it off the bridge, and take her life. So we had 55,000 people approximately who were dead every year of automobile accidents, and you sometimes wonder how many of those could have been people who deliberately did this. The greatest crime I saw was what women had to go through. I had many a woman come to me, and the next thing I knew, they would start to undress, and I'd say, what in the world are you doing? Well, I had to pay $50 for your phone number from a man in a bar, and he said, you go to Bill Baird, he'll help you but just to make sure, why don't you undress and be nice to him. Quote, unquote. And I said, please get dressed quickly because I never know who's in the waiting room. Suppose there are police there. You don't have to do that. But many women are programmed that they had to give their body and tragically many of the people they had gone to previously, the quack abortionists, made them do that. They'd say, okay strip first and they'd give them some sort of . . . or some drug. Many times, as I mentioned yesterday, they'd go to motel rooms, give them drugs to relax them, and they'd come to find two or three men abusing them sexually at the same time. So the abortionist would collect a fee from the women for their so-called abortion and also collect a fee from these guys who wanted to have sex with a semi-conscious young woman, and the woman was in a box, she couldn't go to the police because if she did, they'd say well, what were you doing here in the first place. And it was a felony to aid and abet an abortion.

The possible trauma of abortion and the ready availability of contraception raises the question of why women get pregnant when they do not want children. The question is deceptively simple, however. Many women do not know about either the risks of abortion or the full range of contraceptive techniques (and their varying effectiveness). Risk calculation on pregnancy may itself vary with the same woman as her life changes. One study (Luker, 1975) suggests that women calculate the risk of pregnancy as remote before they are pregnant. "Taking chances" just does not seem like taking a chance. Then, after they are pregnant, they calculate these risks, in retrospect, as considerable indeed. Though the skeptic who doesn't believe in unwanted pregnancies can chortle at these revelations, the point is that women may not be able to perceive the exact nature of the risk they are running without adequate contraception until after they are pregnant (or until their own personal fail-safe system has failed). This is one (among others) explanation for unwanted pregnancies.

Special types of caution and ignorance are two other explanations. The pill and the IUD are the two most effective methods of birth control. The use of these two devices among teenagers almost doubled between 1971 and 1976, but declined by 8 percent in the years following. Surveys show that teenagers, like others, are sensitive to the publicized dangers about the pill and the IUD. The least effective method of birth control is withdrawal. This method seems to be an increasingly used substitute for the pill and IUD. Surveys show a 45 percent increase between 1976 and 1979 in the use of withdrawal as a method of birth control. Other less effective methods—the condom, diaphram, and foam—also increased in use during this period. A rational caution over hazardous methods of birth control may have caused young women to turn to less reliable alternatives on birth control. Since premarital sex is now general, if not universal—7 in 10 women are sexually active by age 19, and only 4 percent of teenagers are married—the causes of unwanted pregnancies among teenagers are self-evident. More recent studies, however, show that the birth control pill reduces the risk of ovarian and endometrial (uterus lining) cancer in young women by one-half. If avoidance of the pill is due to rational caution, then an increased reliance on the pill should now follow.

### 4

The attitudes of the public on abortion are not easy to determine. The main polling organizations indicate support for the pro-choice side. The ABC-Harris polls show a 60 percent approval of the *Roe v. Wade* decision legalizing abortion. A strong majority—80 percent—endorses abortion in cases of rape, incest, or where the mother's life is in danger (the qualifications found in the Hyde Amendment). But only 40 percent accept abortions for other reasons. A Gallup poll taken in May, 1981, however, reveals a sharper division over the *Roe* decision—45 percent in favor and 46 percent opposed. The Gallup survey indicates that views toward *Roe* depend on beliefs about when human life begins. Among those believing that life begins at conception, only 27 percent favor *Roe,* with 66 percent opposed. Among those who believe that life begins at birth, 73 percent favor *Roe,* 20 percent oppose. A substantially higher percentage of women than men (50 to 49 percent) reported that they believe life begins at conception. Another Gallup poll taken in the summer of 1981 indicated that the percentages of people who take extreme positions on abortion are about equal – 23 percent feel abortion should be legal under all circumstances, 21 percent feel it should be illegal under all circumstances. An ABC-*Washington Post* poll reported in August 1981 that the vast majority of the public feels abortion should be legal when the woman's life is endangered (87 percent), when pregnancy is a result of rape or incest (81 percent), or when the mother might suffer severe physical health damage (83 percent). Where there is a chance that the baby might be deformed, 69 percent approved abortion. In cases where the woman's mental health is endangered, 72 percent approved of abortions. Disapproval is greatest when abortion is viewed as a form of family planning.

Let it also be recorded, however, that pro-life people have maintained that pollsters ask the wrong questions, and that mistakes in phrasing questions distort the public's views on abortion. For example, pro-lifers point out that many members of their organizations would not say that abortion should be illegal under all circumstances (reserving legal abortions for, say, pregnancies threatening the life of the mother). Thus, say pro-lifers, the 21 percent recorded in the "extreme positions" category in the Gallup poll of summer 1981 understates the pro-life support. A more accurate count, according to this argument, would require different questions.

The complex dialectics between public opinion and legal decisions on the abortion issue can be expressed by two questions. Did the Supreme Court reflect public opinion in the *Roe v. Wade* decision? Did the *Roe v. Wade* decision influence, and even legitimate, the pro-choice view? In a study of national polls and legislative policies on abortion, Uslaner and Weber (1979) give a mixed *yes* to the first question, and a more straightforward *no* to the second.

Support for the legalization of abortion was increasing before the *Roe v. Wade* decision in January of 1973. The Harris polls in June 1972 show 48 percent of the public in favor of legalized abortions up to four months of pregnancy. Two Gallup surveys, taken in November 1969 and December 1972, indicate a sharp increase in support of the pro-choice view. In 1969, 40 percent favored legal abortion. In the 1972 poll (taken one month before *Roe*), 46 percent favored legal abortion. The Gallup poll reported the largest increase in support (9 percent) from men. College-educated persons and those under thirty increased their support by 5 percent for pro-choice. Protestant support of legalized abortion increased 5 percent. The Supreme Court, then, did reflect a trend in public opinion in favor of legalized abortion. But the trend was by no means decisive. At no time prior to the *Roe* decision did a majority of Americans favor legalized abortion. Substantial groups maintained their opposition, or increased support for pro-choice only incrementally. Catholic approval of legalized abortion remained low (increasing from 31 to only 36 percent). Women's support increased only 4 percent. The *Roe* decision did not represent a majority view of the public, nor did it represent a view widely distributed among all important groups in America. The decision did, however, reflect a growing support (slight though it was in some cases) across most of the major demographic categories in American life.

The *Roe* decision did not, however, legitimize the pro-choice view. Students of politics are familiar with the spectacle of increased support for a government position after an authoritative decision has been taken. The most dramatic example of this (cited in Uslaner and Weber) is the Cambodian invasion of 1970. Before the invasion, only 7 percent of the American people supported an invasion. After President Nixon ordered the invasion, 50 percent supported the move. Military policy is not always the best case study for generalizing the effects of policy decisions on public attitudes. The "rally round the flag" syndrome is especially strong when the country is at war. But even on more relaxed standards, the Supreme Court decision in *Roe* did not create strong or widespread support for the pro-choice view. Though abortions were legalized by *Roe,* they were not by any means legitimized — accepted as right — by the public at large as a consequence of the Court decision.

The trend of support for abortion did continue through the *Roe* decision. The Harris polls show 48 percent in favor of legalized abortion in June 1972, 52 percent in April 1973 (after *Roe*), 54 percent in April 1976, and 60 percent in 1979. The National Opinion Research Center surveys, on different questions, support the Harris polls' indication of growing support before and after *Roe*. But the

Gallup polls suggest a slowdown in the increase of approval after *Roe.* The national figures show a 40 percent approval of legalized abortion in November 1969, 46 percent in December 1972, and 47 percent in April 1974 (fourteen months after *Roe*). College graduates continued apace with their support for pro-choice (5 percent increase from 1969-1972, 4 percent from 1972-1974). The categories of men and Protestants slowed their increase of support (for men, from 9 percent in 1969-1972 to 2 percent in 1972-1974; for Protestants, 5 percent to 3 percent in these respective time periods). Catholics reversed their support trends after *Roe,* from a 5 percent increase in support during 1969-1972, to a 4 percent decrease in 1972-1974. A favorable response from women increased from 40 to 44 percent in 1969-1972, then declined to 43 percent in 1972-1974. By any measure, the *Roe* decision failed as a catalyst for public support of the pro-choice view. Indeed, recent events suggest a polarization of views on abortion, not a reconciliation.

## 5

Since *Roe v. Wade* legalized abortions, pro-life organizations have focused on the political system. The pattern is familiar. After *Brown v. the Board of Education* in 1954, blacks turned to politics to amplify the victories they had won in the courts. In the case of the pro-life movement, the opposite inspiration has occurred. They have lost in the courts. Their efforts are now directed toward recovering these losses in legislative bodies.

All popular movements can adopt one or both of two strategies in influencing legislative decisions. One is lobbying — influencing the votes of legislative members. The other is electoral activity — changing the composition of legislative bodies. Pro-life organizations, like others before them, have used both strategies. Lobbying efforts have four goals: (1) denying public funding (at both federal and state levels) for abortions; (2) passing, in the U.S. Congress, a Human Life Statute; (3) passing, in the U.S. Congress and then among the several states, a Human Life Amendment to the U.S. Constitution; and, more recently, (4) passing a constitutional amendment that would enable Congress and individual states to adopt laws banning abortion.

The first version of the Hyde Amendment passed the U.S. House of Representatives in 1976. On June 24 of that year, Representative Henry J. Hyde from Illinois stood up on the floor and proposed an amendment to the Labor-HEW appropriations bill for fiscal year 1977. The amendment was simplicity itself in its wording: "None of the funds appropriated under this Act shall be used to pay for abortions or to promote or encourage abortions."

To the surprise of many, including especially the pro-choice people, the House passed the Hyde Amendment, after an unusually brief debate, by a vote of 207-167. A second vote later that day upheld the Amendment, 199-165. The U.S. Senate, however, voted later that month, 57-28, to strike the Hyde Amendment from the bill. The House-Senate conference committee could not reconcile their differences. The amendment went back to both chambers. Again, the House accepted, the Senate rejected, the proposal. The deadlock was broken by a compromise clause allowing federal funds for abortions when the life of the mother is endangered. This version of the amendment passed in both the House (256-114) and Senate (47-21). The 1980 version of the Hyde Amendment also allows federal funding for abortions in cases of rape and incest. Otherwise, abortions are no longer financed by federal money.

The Human Life Statute, co-sponsored by Hyde and Senator Jesse Helms, attempts to define human life. The U.S. Supreme Court, in *Roe v. Wade,* declared that no consensus exists among experts on the point at which human life begins. Blackmun, for the majority, said that the Court cannot arbitrate this disagreement. Discretionary authority to abort or not was granted to the woman in substantial part because there is no dominant theory on the starting point for human life. The Human Life Statute offers a definition of life aimed at filling this gap: "For the purpose of enforcing the obligation of the States under the 14th Amendment not to deprive persons of life without due process of law, human life shall be deemed to exist from conception."

The purpose of the statute is to provide a legal definition of life in order to bring the fetus or embryo under the due process protection of the Fourteenth Amendment. States could, under the statute, pass laws defining abortion, at any stage in term, as murder. In a frequently quoted remark, Representative Hyde observed that "If the fetus is human life, as of course it is, it ought to be accorded equal dignity with the snail darter and the sperm whale." The legal strategy derives from Congressional extension of voting rights to Fourteenth Amendment guarantees. The U.S. Supreme Court ruled in 1959 that literacy tests do not discriminate. Congress decided that they did, and in effect added to the rights protected by the due process and equal protection clauses of the Fourteenth Amendment. The Court, in *Katzenbach v. Morgan* (1966) and *Oregon v. Mitchell* (1970), accepted the Congressional extension of rights. The thought behind the Helms-Hyde bill is that the right to life can also be extended through legislative action to the Fourteenth Amendment.

The Human Life Amendment to the Constitution would actually reverse *Roe v. Wade.* No Congressional action has been taken on any Human Life Amendment. The only hearings held in the House and Senate took place in the 95th Congress without any recommendation being made. Pro-life supporters are themselves divided over whether to accept abortions performed to save the life of the mother. But one popular version of the Amendment is the following (supported by a majority of the National Right to Life Committee):

Section 1. The right to life is the paramount and most fundamental right of a person.

Section 2. With respect to the right to life guaranteed to persons by the fifth and fourteenth articles of amendment to the Constitution, the word "person" applies to all human beings, irrespective of age, health, function, or condition of dependency, including their unborn offspring at every stage of their biological development including fertilization.

Section 3. No unborn person shall be deprived of life by any person: Provided, however, that nothing in this article shall prohibit a law permitting those medical procedures required to prevent the death of a pregnant woman; but this law must require every reasonable effort be made to preserve the life and health of the unborn child.

Section 4. Congress and the several States shall have power to enforce this article by appropriate legislation.

In 1982, new efforts were made to pass a proposal introduced by Senator Orrin G. Hatch, Republican of Utah, that would give Congress and the states "concurrent power to restrict and prohibit abortion." State laws that are more restrictive than national laws would prevail. Hatch's amendment, in wording designed to overturn the 1973 *Roe* decision, says "A right to abortion is not secured by this Constitution." The Hatch amendment has general support in the pro-life movement and was the first anti-abortion amendment supported by a Congressional committee when the Senate Judiciary Committee voted 10 to 7 in favor of the proposal on March 10, 1982.

The problem for the pro-life movement with a constitutional amendment, however, is the same problem facing any who would change the Constitution. Massive support is required in numerous legislative bodies (two-thirds vote in both the U.S. House and Senate, passage by three-fourths of the state legislatures within seven years). As a consequence, constitutional change is typically a drawn-out process, even when successful. The short-range strategy of the first two legislative measures—cutoffs of federal funding for abortion and efforts to introduce rights to life to the Fourteenth Amendment (represented by the Human Life Statute)—will likely dominate pro-life lobbying activities for the foreseeable future.

The effect of lobbying activities on legislators is uncertain on abortion issues, however. Several studies of legislative voting patterns doubt any clean causal patterns between group lobbying and pro-life votes. Studies of state legislators [summarized in Uslaner and Weber, 1979] indicate that the religious affiliations of legislators are the most important determinants of abortion votes (and this affiliation is obviously not created by lobbying efforts). One study suggests that even representatives in Congress from heavily Catholic constituencies are not more likely to vote a pro-life view on abortion funding. A study of the passage of the 1976 version of the Hyde Amendment presents a complex set of cause-and-effect relationships (Vinovskis, 1979). The personal values of legislators on abortion are important in voting decisions. These values are personal and resistant (on the whole) to lobbying tactics. But legislators are also uncertain about constituency reaction, and so prone to avoid abortion issues when possible. Lobbying acts as a catalyst on these values, forcing them to the voting stage. The conclusion is that pro-life lobbying may not change anyone's mind so much as it forces legislators to transform (reluctantly) their personal convictions into explicit voting records.

Pro-life groups have had several spectacular successes with the second of the tactics—electoral activity. In 1978, they could reasonably claim victories over three heavily favored candidates: Senator Dick Clark (D., Ohio), Representative Donald Fraser in the Democratic primary for Senator in Minnesota, and State Senator Minnette Doderer for the Democratic nomination of Lieutenant Governor of Iowa. The Right-to-Life Party also surprised many by its fourth-place finish in the 1978 New York election, bumping the Liberal party to fifth in the first electoral effort in New York by pro-life forces. In 1980, pro-life groups claimed additional victories. These included Senators George McGovern (South Dakota), Birch Bayh (Indiana)—both of whom were defeated by candidates having a Right-to-Life label—and John Culver (Iowa). Even the election of Ronald Reagan as president was counted by some as an affirmation of the basic pro-life view.

Claims for electoral power must be carefully examined before acceptance, however. First, many candidates are elected and re-elected in the face of pro-life opposition. Governor Hugh Carey was easily reelected in New York in 1978 even though he supports state funding for abortions. Senators Alan Cranston, Gary Hart, Patrick J. Leahy, and Bob Packard were reelected in 1980 in spite of being targeted for defeat by anti-abortion groups. Second, it is not always easy to say that a candidate loses because opposed by special interest groups. Elections can (obviously) turn on many issues. Third, the history of special interest groups suggests that demonstrations of electoral power are often met by renewed opposition that begins limiting this power. Opposition to the Vietnam War, to school busing—many movements of the 1960s and early 1970s quickly generated electoral opposition from other groups, some leaders in the major political parties, and, sometimes, the government itself. Though substantial differences separate the pro-life movement from opposition to the Vietnam War and busing, the very success of pro-life efforts in highly visible electoral strategies may herald a diminishing rather than a heightening of power. Hit lists have a tendency to mobilize one's opponents, and even one's supporters. Three United States Representatives—Henry Hyde, Robert Young, and Martin Russo—and one United States Senator—Jake Garn—resigned in June 1981 from an advisory panel of the National Pro-Life Political Action Committee after the organization targeted nine members of Congress for defeat in 1982. The resignees did not like the idea of hit lists.

The opposition to pro-life is the coalition of organizations under the pro-choice label. In many ways, the pro-life forces stole the thunder, and even great amounts of the lightning, from pro-choice groups in the 1970s. Even effective language was appropriated—pro-*life* and pro-*family* (an appellation now commonly assigned to anti-abortion views). Wes McCune, president of Group Research, an organization that monitors the political right, told an annual meeting of the Abortion Rights League that the anti-abortion groups "had pre-empted the right to use the term 'family.' They stole it right away from you. They got it, and I don't know how you'll ever get it back" (*New York Times,* February 16, 1981). The pro-choice groups lagged behind in lobbying and electoral activity in the years following *Roe v. Wade.* Most of the influence on abortion issues was brought to bear by the pro-life side.

A simple chronology of resistance to legalized abortion demonstrates the pro-life influence in the years following *Roe v. Wade.* Shortly after the *Roe* decision in 1973, Congress passes a "conscience clause" proposed by Senator Frank Church. The bill frees individuals and hospitals from compulsion to perform abortions just because they receive federal funds. An amendment to the Legal Services Corporation Act in 1974 prohibits attorneys paid by the Corporation from representing clients seeking non-therapeutic abortions. The first Hyde Amendment passes in 1976. The U.S. Supreme Court upholds the Hyde Amendment in 1977. An amendment in 1978 prohibits the National Institute of Child Health and Human Development from using family planning funds for abortion and abortion-related research. In 1980, the Bauman Amendment passes Congress. It absolves states of any responsibility for funding abortions, even to preserve a woman's life. The Bauman Amendment gives states the right to set their own minimum standards in funding abortions, freeing them from federal guidelines.

(The Court, in accepting the Hyde Amendment, had only freed states from funding abortions Congress refused to fund.) Both birth control and amniocentesis services come under fire in the decisions to renew Title X of the Public Health Services Act and the National Genetics Diseases Act. And of course the Human Rights Statute and the Human Life Amendment are on the legislative agenda.

Abortion is still legal. But the greater influence of pro-life organizations from 1973 to early 1981 is obvious. Several reasons help explain what happened. First, and least disputed, the pro-choice position was affirmed in law with the *Roe v. Wade* decision. What had been vigorous opposition to abortion laws was transformed into celebration of the status quo after 1973. Relaxation of political effort is a rational response to political victory. Karen Mulhauser, executive director of the National Abortion Rights Action League, observed that "It's been hard to convince them [members] that in order to take the politics out of abortion, we have to get political" (*New York Times,* November 8, 1980). Second, the logic of the pro-choice view naturally avoids a careful inspection and communication of arguments pro and con on abortion. The point is subtle. A pro-life perspective sees abortion as *the* moral problem of contemporary society. The view that abortion is immoral must be transmitted to all, and, ideally, endorsed by all—uniformly. Pro-choice, by contrast, turns the issue of abortion over to the woman for a decision. There can be as many reasons for and against abortion as there are women—as far as the pro-choice view goes. Put bluntly, proponents of a pro-choice point of view do not have to think through the morality of abortion. The woman does. The pro-choice view simply wants to guarantee that she has this opportunity. It follows that pro-choice spokespersons will not be as concerned to argue the morality of abortion in public forums. The rule of individual decision on abortion is the pro-choice goal. And this has been enshrined in law since 1973.

The strong efforts of pro-life organizations to change or bypass *Roe v. Wade* mobilized pro-choice groups in the late 1970s and 1980s. More than one-half million people contributed a total of $5 million in 1980 to pro-choice causes. The National Abortion Rights

Action League increased its members by 10,000—to 100,000—in the months following the 1980 presidential election. In general, pro-choice groups organized grass roots volunteer organizations and telephone networks after the November 1980 election. Planned Parenthood, the Religious Coalition for Abortion Rights, and the National Organization of Women are the principal lobbying organizations for pro-choice. Other groups, like the National Abortion Rights Action League, ·organize political action committees and chart legislative votes. The renewed efforts seemed to swing the power balance on abortion back toward pro-choice by late 1982. When the U.S. Senate defeated in September 1982 a proposal by Senator Jesse Helms that would have restricted freedom of choice on abortion, the director of the Washington office of Planned Parenthood, William W. Hamilton, Jr., was inspired to observe of Senator Helms: "For all his huffing and puffing, we now see that the emperor has no clothes." (*New York Times,* September 20, 1982.) The hyperbole in that statement should not distract us from the fact that pro-choice was more comfortable politically in 1982 than in earlier years. Substantial monetary contributions to political candidates by the National Abortion Rights League made pro-choice reasonably good politics, though all observers would agree that candidates in general wish that the issue would disappear entirely.

It is an axiom of interest group theory that whenever an interest group is threatened by opposing groups or the larger social system, the group whose interest is threatened will organize to protect that interest. This simple notion of response-to-threat seems to be clearly at work in pro-choice activities in the 1980s.

## 6

Several issues are clustered around the political activities of abortion groups. Some, like techniques, are either contemptible (fire bombing of abortion clinics) or simple expressions of emotion (the use of graphic photographs by pro-life groups, disruptions of Congressional hearings by both groups). Other issues are deeper, touching on the logic of interest groups, the nature of political ideology, and a possible conflict between morality and justice.

One issue that has generated a fair amount of discussion is the role of single-issue interest groups in American politics. Though both pro-life and pro-choice organizations endorse a cluster of values (the consistency of which will be explored in a moment), it is safe to observe that each type of group is dominated by the abortion issue. Indeed, pro-life groups have urged voters to support or oppose candidates solely on the basis of their stands on abortion. Pro-choice groups can be expected to follow suit as the abortion issue becomes more salient in political life. Is one-issue voting rational?

Many of the standard interest groups in American politics are, and have been, pluralistic associations. The economic groups representing farm, labor, business, and professional sectors have pressed their interests along several fronts, rarely gambling everything on a single issue. The received wisdom on the American voter complements this pluralism. He is typically portrayed as a member of multiple, and often overlapping, interest groups. Variable ranking of issues, trade-offs among issues, are more nearly the norm than straight single-issue voting. To support a candidate solely on the basis of a single issue means that all other issues, all of the pluralism of American politics, is subordinate absolutely (without trade-offs or compromises) to the single issue.

Yet there is nothing inherently irrational about single-issue voting so long as the voter invests the issue with sufficient importance. Any time a moral issue is introduced to the political system, the prospect of single-issue voting is raised. Abolitionist movements judged authorities in terms of one issue—how they stood on slavery. The history of the black movement, especially in the early periods before the *Brown* decision in 1954, consistently supported politicians friendly to the black cause, opposed those who were not sympathetic. Opponents of the Vietnam War in the 1960s frequently subordinated all other issues to that of peace. Many feminists judge politicians solely on their attitudes toward the Equal Rights Amendment. Some Zionists are prepared to give or withhold political support entirely on a candidate's responses to Israel's national interest.

Moral commitment to a single cause can transform the costs of even participation itself. One of the least attractive paradoxes of political life is the demonstration that it hardly ever pays to vote in large electorates. The costs of going to the polls outweigh the minuscule chance that any single voter will affect the outcome of an election involving millions of people. Moral commitments, however, attach benefits to participation itself. The individual donating money or time to either pro-life or pro-choice organizations may get benefits from the donation itself independent of the effects of individual effort on the collective outcome. Those internal rewards — feeling good about acting on one's moral principles — may make even the most ineffective participation rational for the individual.

Yes, one-issue voting is rational if the stakes are high enough. A German Jew who voted against the Nazis in the early 1930s because he perceived correctly the coming holocaust would have been eminently rational on the single issue of survival. Even less intense issues can make participation rational on the basis of internal rewards. The irony is that moral commitments may be exactly what is needed to correct the negative incentives of pragmatic politics. If no issue is really important, then it pays to be a "free rider" — consume the benefits of collective action without incurring the production costs (especially if one's contribution does not matter more or less in the social outcome). But moral issues require a more personal payment. Those committed one way or the other on abortion may have a stronger, not weaker, rational incentive to participate in politics precisely because the issue is important enough to override all others.

The objection to this line of argument is that a single cluster of values will always transmit itself into a variety of related political issues. Suppose the obvious — that some moral endorsements can be traced back to a small set of core values. Pro-life relies on the integrity of human life (a premise shared by pro-choice, though few pro-lifers will admit this). From this core, the pro-life arguments spread a web of legal protection for the fertilized ovum, on the extension of rights to life to the zygote. Critics maintain that there are less-traveled but equally sound roads from the core values to political issues. For example, racism and tobacco are both hazardous to health, indeed affront the integrity of human life. Yet Senator Jesse Helms, linked in the popular mind to at least the latter, consistently receives pro-life support because of his prudent (or, who can be sure, moral) backing of pro-life measures in Congress. Or consider support services for unmarried pregnant teenagers. Suppose a candidate for political office opposes abortion, but is either indifferent to the tragedy (and this is what it is) of pregnancies among unmarried teenagers or subscribes to unrealistic solutions (chastity, say). Does the core value of "integrity-of-human life" require unqualified support for this candidate simply because she opposes abortion?

There is a problem of logic and a problem of value in single-issue politics. The logical problem is that moral principles seem always to lead to a cluster of political values. Both Aquinas and Machiavelli worried over the application of moral generalities to political contexts (and came away with different theories to assuage their worries). But no moral or political philosopher, past or present, has ever argued for a linear, one-to-one relationship between one's deeper values and the complex world of politics. The problem of value is that the only way to dismiss the attendant issues illuminated by core values is to assign such a premium value to the most representative issue—abortion, for pro-life—that all else is subordinated to it on tactical and strategic grounds.

Such subordination is of course what pro-life has done. When pro-life representatives draw parallels between abortion struggles today and the abolitionist opposition to slavery in the last century, or compare liberalized abortion practices to Hitler's genocidal politics, the statements are not mere hyperbole. They are necessary blinders to those political issues any "pro-life" organization would naturally support in the absence of absolute value attached to the one issue of abortion.

## 7

Another issue is the consistency of the values clustered under abortion banners. At the surface level, some particularly bad fits occur. Though no unambiguous relationship has been established between sex education and the use of contraceptives, some evidence suggests that increased knowledge about sexual functions and methods of birth control does result in a lower rate of unwanted pregnancies among unmarried women. Studies also show, however, that sex education does not change a person's sexual habits — making them neither more nor less responsible sexually. Also, the main evidence suggests that awareness of contraception and access to birth control methods do not guarantee that contraception will be practiced (reviewed in Gordon, 1979).

Both sides in the abortion debate react to these studies in incomplete ways. Since unwanted pregnancy is a result of attitudes toward risk and (as a complex package) cultural attitudes toward sex, a simplistic reliance on sex education and birth control clinics obviously is not going to solve the problem of unwanted pregnancies. A change in the values of the young is required. Yet the literature of pro-choice chronically stresses the mechanics of sex over the deeper values that individuals bring to their sexual lives. Conversely, pro-life organizations ignore the thin, but promising, connections between types of sex education and the use of contraceptives. Worse, the religious element in pro-life is also strongly opposed to birth control as such. Individuals and organizations are entitled to their own values. But since abortion would not be such a grave social problem in the absence of unwanted pregnancies, one would think that the intensity of views over abortion would translate into consistent reforms to avoid the problem. It has not, on either side.

*Frohock:* One of the things that impresses me as I look through all of the data on abortion is that so many young girls are getting pregnant. If I had to design my perfect universe, women wouldn't be able to get pregnant until they were emotionally mature. But we live in a world where, for whatever reason, divine or otherwise, accidental or planned, physical maturity comes long before emotional maturity. So then you have 11 and 12-year-olds getting pregnant —

*Kisil:* Which, may I bring out a point, this is another sad thing. They are always dropping these little gems that the younger the child, the worse it is for her to get pregnant. Let me tell you — it is worse for her to get pregnant the younger she is as far as her psychological maturity is concerned, but did you know the younger the child is who goes through an abortion, the more vulnerable she is to have complications later. Far better that she should get all kinds of loving support and go through with the pregnancy, as young as she is, than rip that baby out via a suction machine or D&C and then she is more vulnerable to complications the younger her body is. But *they* present it the other way. Because who isn't going to say, "Oh, my God, 11, 12, 13, 14-year-old kids having a baby." Nobody's going to, anybody will feel bad about that, whether you were the parents of the child, the social worker, the hospital worker, the people in the church who might be helping—you've got to identify with that. That's why they always use those little things. Why do we have so many abortions? Why do we have so many girls being pregnant?

*Frohock:* Why?

*Kisil:* Do you have any ideas on it?

*Frohock:* Well, I do but I'm not being interviewed. I'd rather have your ideas.

*Kisil:* . . . the very people who promote abortion, the very clinics, they all think it's tied up with—if you get the kids in the sixth grade and we teach them sex education and we teach them all the kinds of contraceptives and encourage them to find the best ones for them, and so on, then we're going to stop pregnancies. They had 10 years, they had the government money. They started teaching it, and they have been getting into public schools, and they get into the church groups and they get into the Girl Scouts, they *have* been at our kids. And what do you have as a result? More pregnancies, more abortions, and more VD.

---

*Frohock:* Do you link your own views on abortion to any type of program on sex education, sexual instruction, with the view toward the possibility of eliminating unwanted pregnancies, at least in the very young? Do you see any relationship?

*Gordon:* Of course I do. I feel that abortion is a medical procedure, just like any other medical procedure. It has some risks in it, and it should be avoided whenever possible. The ideal situation would be when there's no need for abortion, but we don't have 100 percent safe contraception for people who use contraception. I strongly believe, and this is why I think it's so political, that massive sex education can have a big impact. It won't eliminate abortion. We're not going to eliminate the need for abortion until we eliminate poverty, until we eliminate racism, until we eliminate any chance factor in sexual intercourse, but we can reduce by 10, 15, 20 percent by sex education. The reason why it strikes me that the pro-life movement is so totally irrational is that their argument is, "Look at all the sex education we have in this country, and therefore we have this increase in promiscuity and unwanted pregnancy," the view that sex education causes unwanted pregnancy. When as a matter of fact less than 10 percent of American schools have anything approaching sex education. It's not sex education, but the lack of it. I can't say causally, because I can't use the argument the other way around. But we have enough evidence that young people who are well informed have a tendency to delay their first sexual experience, and when they have sex they use contraception. Their irrational argument of causality: I'm reminded of the fact that the period of time in this country when prayer in the school was the most prevalent was the time of the Great Depression. Suppose I argued that prayer in the school caused the Depression. The thing is laughable. Also they say it's the pill that's causing promiscuity. How can it be the pill if less than 20 percent of sexually active children, teenage girls, use any form of contraception? It's the lack of the use of the pill, not the pill, that's causing the problem. So the arguments that the pro-life people use have a tendency to be enormously irrational, because it's not just that they're pro-life, they're against everything else. And therefore their arguments don't carry for me any element of rationality or respect.

*Frohock:* . . . in the studies I've looked at, many girls, at least many young girls, will not employ birth control methods because that would be an endorsement of sex, that would be to plan for it. Would one of the changes here be in the way that you morally look at sex in the long run, so that you think of it as something rational that you can plan for, and thus avoid unwanted pregnancies in that way?

*Gordon:* I don't think there's any doubt about it. I personally, for example, don't think teenagers should have sex. I think it's a health hazard. There's no question in my mind that they're too young and too vulnerable and too readily available for exploitation. I think that society in a lot of ways is responsible for the idea that if you plan for sex, that means you are promiscuous, or in some way endorsing it. We have to turn this concept around and say that we're all sexual, and that if you're not planning, if you're going to have sex without planning you're not being romantic or spontaneous, you're just being stupid. So there's a double bind. Teenagers are encouraged by the so-called moralists not to even think about sex, not to have it because if they don't educate themselves about it, then they won't be thinking about it. And so what happens is that it's spontaneous combustion, it's the immaculate conception, which is ridiculous. Millions of children, half of all high school students, half of all teenagers in America today will have had sexual intercourse before they finish high school. So we're talking about millions and millions of young people, and we had better get across the message as part of our education that we're all sexual and we all have sexual desires and impulses, but that it's better to control it if you can, and we as adults know from experience that self-control is a good idea. I myself propound the idea that the best oral contraceptive is "no," and I've developed many publications and ideas and materials to encourage girls to say no, not to fall for the lines that boys use to seduce girls, to come up with answers. I'm saying that sex is never spontaneous, that sex is never a test of love, but I've been in this field more than 25 years, and in that 25 years no teenager has ever asked me my consent for sex. They don't ask me, and they don't ask their parents, and they're not asking their churches, and they're not asking the pro-life people either, and so we had better have more than one message. We can't just say, "No, don't, stop," because we've been saying that for centuries without any success whatsoever. So we had better say, "If you're not going to listen to us, if you're not going to pay attention to the wisest minds in the world today, at least use contraception so that you don't bring unwanted children into this world." Don't tell me that unwanted children become wanted, because no child of a 12 or 13 or 14-year-old, almost none of them, becomes wanted. I know from experience that almost every boy who makes a girl pregnant will abandon that girl, that almost all marriages that are the result of pregnancy are broken within three or four years. Almost every index of psychopathology goes along with being born to a teenage mother: child abuse, criminal addiction, it doesn't matter what pathology we're talking about, it will correlate positively with being born to a teenage mother.

---

*Mrs. Willke:* You have to back up a little bit and say, what do you hope to accomplish by sex education? What's your point for doing it? Your point for doing sex education is to hopefully make this young person more intact, healthier, better able in the years ahead to make a loving, lifetime commitment in marriage, if that's their choice. You don't want to point them toward failure. You're not consciously trying to say divorce is a good way to go, regardless of who's guilty. That's flunking marriage, divorce. So what you're trying to do is to help them be a more intact, loving person to make this lifetime commitment of love. Therefore, what must you teach and incorporate into sex education so their example is the best for the goal you're trying to get to? It's very obvious. First of all, you're going to teach certain society, life-preserving values. Then teach monogamy, as the best gamble, the best way to go for a happy, good life ahead. You're going to teach divorce for the failure it is. You're going to teach other . . .

*Dr. Willke:* . . . we're not talking about religion. We're talking about preserving a stable society. If you take the average Planned Parenthood approach, which at best makes the assumption that these children will be sexually active and at worst cynically laughs at anyone who would suggest anything except sleeping around because they all do it. . . . it's not a negative any more. And if the lady from Planned Parenthood, the Public Health Nurse, whoever, stands in front of this class and in effect says we know you're all going to be doing it or a lot of you children are, without condemning, just don't commit the mortal sin, don't get pregnant, and here's the rubbers and here's the pills and so forth and so on. You know, don't speed, but if you do, we'll get your ticket fixed. So there's an out. These kids, many of whom are obviously under pressure by our culture to conform to that peer, they really don't *know* that most of the kids are sleeping around. All they've heard about is the ones who are and of course the media and everything, the movies, the bare breasts and everything today just pushes them into this sort of thing. And here is an authority figure, my parents didn't talk to me much about this, in fact, at worst, I know my dad's got a lady on the side, or maybe we're divorced or separated at home, and here's an authority figure telling me that really everybody's doing it and isn't condemning doing it. In other words, there is an implied or actual endorsement of this activity and that's all I need to jump into the water.

*Kisil:* The answer is that you cannot teach sex education without morals. . . . What about the kids in the 6th and 7th grades, struggling with their hormones, struggling with the boy-girl bit, but nobody with any kind of authority says to them, "It is better to wait." Why can't we say it to the kids? Not one of them will say it. IT IS BETTER! There are less emotional scars, more chance of growth. Why can't people in today's age say, "We have cheated you, because we haven't had the guts to say it is better to wait." Now I don't mean, according to somebody's church it's better to wait. It's common sense that it's better to wait. Where are the people holding these kids' hands when they get into these relationships and the horrible feelings they have about themselves because that girl made a monkey of him or he took advantage of her? Nobody said, "Hey, it's less hassle if you can wait." Why can't the kids hear that?

---

*Hyde:* It's a very mixed record. We have had drug education courses in the schools. We've had sex education courses in the schools and I really haven't seen that they have done a lot of good. The matter of sex education depends, it seems to me, on the quality of the teacher and the ability of the teacher to elevate the subject out of mechanics and plumbing and the sensate level and to infuse into it the value system that depends on, really, a spiritual recognition. And this is very difficult in the public school, where one cannot talk about any higher laws or any notion of sin or of a sacrament and it really reduces itself to plumbing. And that may well do more harm than good. Again, with the sensitive teacher, very capable, some good could be done. I mean, my God, the mistakes that are made through ignorance are prodigious. They ought to be obviated, but I just have no conviction that sex education has done a hell of a lot of good. A lot of parents have felt relieved that they can abandon what is primarily their responsibility to the schools, and the schools take this on and can't do always under all circumstances an adequate job. So I'm unconvinced yet that basically that it has proven useful. I sure wish it would.

*Frohock:* So you would think that the change in values that the young attach to sex and procreation . . .

*Hyde:* I'd like to see the churches once more have a more active role to play, if the parents are going to abandon their responsibilities. And it seems like they have. The churches. Or the ACLU ought to look the other way, which they never do in terms of trying to teach kids that sex is not recreation. That it has responsibilities and there are some moral, spiritual responsibilities that are above and beyond pleasure-pain and economic. It's damned hard to do. You know in the old days we were supposed to be ignorant and really retrograde, but the abortion rate, the promiscuity that's going on, the failures of families at home, don't indicate that under the great permissive society that we've been reveling in that there have been much improvements. So I just think it's up to those who advocate these things to prove they do some good. I don't think that proof is available yet.

The interviews suggest that pro-life activists support a program of chastity for the young as a way of avoiding unwanted pregnancies, while pro-choice people urge a comprehensive dissemination of birth control techniques in the hope that sexual activity will not lead to pregnancy. Each side has deeply held justifications for their positions. Pro-life partisans have a comprehensive view of the moral individual developed on ideals of pre-marriage continence and marital fidelity. Pro-choice activists tend to separate sex from both procreation and marriage as such, seeing sexual commitment as an expression of love rather than a part of a legal contract like marriage. Neither side develops a program of sex education that both distributes information on birth control *and* teaches premarital continence as a desirable practice. Indeed, pro-lifers see such a program as contradictory and pro-choicers view as unrealistic any serious effort to convince the young that sexual activity should wait for the marriage contract.

Uneven, and even inconsistent, clusters of values in pro-choice and pro-life organizations are also found in the more fundamental areas of ideology. One short-hand definition of an ideology is any set of values that are not falsifiable and structure reality in general ways. Conventional designations today still recognize a *left* (socialist, liberal, etc.) and a *right* (conservative) in political practice. It is uncertain, however, where the various pro-choice and pro-life organizations are located on any ideological spectrum. Pro-choice is a feminist value, firmly lodged in the women's movement. It is also a liberal value in general, held by those who endorse an activist social state and a strong civil rights policy. Yet acrimonious disputes over abortion mar many of the National Organization of Women meetings. And the use of social utility arguments by pro-choice leaders — especially the claim that supporting abortions is less costly to the taxpayer than supporting welfare mothers and their children — has alienated influential minority leaders like Jesse Jackson.

The inconsistency is deeper than tactics. Leftist ideology grants a strong role to the state in setting social values and distributing resources. Yet the main pillar of strength for the pro-choice movement is the right of the individual to be shielded from state regulation — a conservative point of view. Obviously the values to be shielded differ from liberal to conservative. The liberal (pro-choice) preserve of privacy is sex and procreation. For the conservative, it is economic gain. But the acceptance of an activist state by liberals is the spectre now haunting liberalism in the guise of the Human Life Statute. Conservatives love to remind liberals of this acceptance when arguing for the legislative definition of life. Also, public funding of abortion denies to those morally opposed to abortions the right to refuse financial support — in short, their rights to choose on the issue of public financing.

The pro-life movement is no less vulnerable to charges of inconsistency. One of the main institutional supports for pro-life is the Catholic Church. It is the continuing interest of the Church to establish a buffer between religious and secular activities (a buffer permitting tax-free properties, religious freedom, autonomy of Catholic schools, and support for a voucher plan permitting individuals pro-choice—ironically—on public *vs.* parochial schools). The pro-life movement requires government regulation of the most intimate of moral items and the control of individual choice (on abortion) by statute law. Conservatives generally dislike government regulation. Yet making abortion illegal would probably require considerable policing of hospitals, clinics, some alarmists would say even homes. Public funds would have to be provided to support additional children and mothers unable to meet new financial problems. An anti-abortion society would contain more, not less, state regulation of individual liberty.

The odd assortment of values under the pro-choice and pro-life labels indicates that no systematic theory of state regulation has been thought out by either movement. Certainly no integrated system of thought, no available ideology, comes readily to view in the pro-choice and pro-life perspectives.

Pro-life activists, however, disagree with the thought that undesirable government regulations will follow the legal prohibition of abortion.

*Frohock:* I'd like to read you something and then I want you to comment on it: "Making abortion illegal will require a state interference in the lives of citizens so great, so extensive, that liberty itself will be the victim."

*Jackson:* If society has sanctioned a certain procedure, in this case, abortion, for a number of years, so that it has become more and more thinkable to do it, then naturally you would think that the taking away of that right would be a tremendous loss of liberty to you, if you are committed to that as a part of the liberties of a human being. If, however, you think that it is a tremendous aberration for that liberty ever to have been granted in the first place, and that people have become, or some people have become, somewhat used to that so that they regard it as a part of liberty, if you see this as in fact diluting the whole meaning of human life, then you're going to say that even though initially some people may feel that there was a great loss of liberty involved, eventually they're going to be reeducated back to understanding that to have abortions in this fashion is a terrible wrong, a willfully wrong thing, and there's no more loss of liberty involved than the loss of liberty anyone would experience by having certain actions proscribed, such as, obviously, taking the lives of those who are already born, or any other category of conduct that the government might legislate upon.

---

*Frohock:* How do you respond to the pro-choice person who says that the police powers in the state would increase in undesirable ways if abortion were made illegal under these measures?

*Mrs. Willke:* All we say to them is go back to 200 years before 1973 and were there police powers going on then? No. So why would there be now? That's again just total falsehood. There would be no way that would come about. You have to legislate that through your state legislature. The state legislatures are not going to put it through. No way.

*Frohock:* Would the woman be prosecuted under this . . .

*Mrs. Willke:* For 200 years she never was. Why would she be now?

*Dr. Willke:* None of us want it. In fact, we would fight it.

*Mrs. Willke:* Who would put it through?

*Dr. Willke:* Do you know a majority of any state general assembly that would put through a bill putting women in jail? Of course not, it's not going to happen.

*Mrs. Willke:* They've just dreamed up some lovely little things to get everybody worried and they're absolute lies and incredible that intelligent people do that.

---

*Frohock:* Wouldn't the state, though, have to explore distinctions that are very difficult to explore, for example, the difference between a miscarriage and an abortion, in order to determine criminal liability?

*Jackson:* They certainly would, in some cases. The law would not work perfectly. But it does not work perfectly. We know that's the case. Again, that doesn't mean you can't have a law. You know from the beginning that the law is not going to work properly, and yet because of the principle involved you enact a law. In some cases you would have to make a determination. Incidentally, with regard to the numbers involved, you're making the assumption at the beginning that essentially the numbers before 1973 will obtain after [but] there's a deliberate attempt made to falsify and inflate figures for women having abortions by those people who are crusaders for abortion, and the figures often cited for the United States and for England has been shown, upon more sober investigation, to be wildly inflated. There's a question as to how many are really involved. I also think that the law cannot only be a disincentive but an incentive. If the government can, for example, spend money, I think properly so, with regard to warning people of the effects of cigarette smoking or advertising the needs of the handicapped, I don't see why the government cannot enter, put a bit of money into, adoption agencies, and encourage people to adopt, and indicate how much a possible thing that is, because as far as we can tell, there's a rising incidence of abandonment, which is a terrible affliction. I think the government can certainly do that, in tandem with the same law.

**8**

One of the most difficult conflicts in each movement is between morality and justice. Both sides see abortion as a moral issue, though the perspectives differ on where moral predicates are to be located. Pro-life, we have seen, defines abortion as homicide. Pro-choice assigns moral value to freedom of choice on abortion. Justice, however, is different from morality. Justice is concerned with the production and distribution of (in John Rawls's phrase) "the burdens and benefits" of society. Equal opportunity, compensatory measures, full employment, inflation, in general who gets what, when, how — these are the problems that a theory of justice addresses. Scarcity is an assumption of justice. Imagine a society of perfect abundance, where every person is satiated with desirable goods. No productive or distributive issues can arise in such a society. Justice is not a problem. But morality still can be. Even in material utopia it is still possible to ask — what ought to be the moral practices of the society?

Abortion is first a moral issue. But because the issue arises in human societies — where scarce resources rather than abundance is the general rule — the issues of distribution normally covered by justice are also relevant considerations in abortion. The Hyde Amendment is the case study. Should society fund a practice that a substantial number of its members finds immoral? What is the relationship between the morality of abortion and the distributive issue of access to the practice of abortion?

*Frohock:* Now there is a standard approach to these arguments that depends on a distinction between morality and justice. Put in very simple terms, it would be that even if abortion is wrong morally, it is still unfair to deny access to it to poor people so long as it is legal. What is your response to that?

*Hyde:* Well, there is always a gap I suppose between what is legal and what is moral. There needn't be but there often is. I view the purpose of law, the role of law, is to protect the weak from the strong, and one of the basic reasons for government to exist is to protect innocent human life. If that is not a major, if not the major consideration, then government just becomes an exercise, a Darwinistic struggle between special interests and that sort of thing. The basic civil right is the right to life, and government exists to protect the defenseless weak people whose right to life is endangered by other people putting other values ahead of it. So it seems to me the duty, the entirely proper duty of government, is to protect innocent life. Now the fact that rich women are able, or women of means are able to kill their unborn children because the Supreme Court legislated a decision permitting it, setting a public policy contravening that of the legislature of the entire country, doesn't make it right. It is still wrong, although it may be legal. What I seek to do is to change the legality of that—to make it illegal. At least, the increment we have achieved thus far prevents the Federal government from subsidizing the killing of the unborn child—the preborn infant. Now it is the unborn of the rich that are in jeopardy under such an arrangement, I will concede that. But access to the procedure of killing your unborn is the sort of boon that I would deny to everybody if I could.

One of the main requirements in justice is that distributions of goods be *fair.* Strict equality is overridden by fairness. If two claimants for a slice of the social pie have unequal needs, a fair (though unequal) distribution would allocate more of the pie to the needier of the two. Theories of justice are richly endowed with multiple (and, unfortunately, conflicting) principles of distribution. Among these are need, desert, merit. But all (or almost all) theories of justice assume that the social pie is desirable—that those sitting at the table prefer more rather than less of the goods to be distributed *and* that all agree that the pie is a good, not a bad. Abortion is a case where those sitting around the table are divided over the quality of the pie (*really* divided). Some see the pie as a primary good (all should have access to it). Others see it as a primary bad, to be denied even to those at the table who want it.

For those who see abortion therapy as a good, the problems of justice are fairly straightforward. Standard discussions can proceed over the role of the state as provider of social services. Conservatives oppose, liberals support, the social provision of welfare needs. But for those who view abortion as an evil, the connections between morality and justice are more complicated. Suppose that a liberal who stoutly affirms the welfare role of the state also believes that abortion is immoral. One can consistently take either of two positions on state funding of abortions: (a) though abortion is immoral, if the rich under the law have access to abortion therapy, then fairness requires that all have access as long as abortions are legal—yes, on funding; (b) since abortion is immoral, better that few rather than many have access to abortion therapy—no, on funding.

Suppose that poisoned pie is the resource to be distributed to the eager diners. Only a lunatic would claim that, because a few upper class gourmets can eat the pie (and dutifully die), fairness requires that the pie also be available to those eating with the hired help. But perhaps the analogy is wrong, since there is no proof that abortion is like poison—some say it is more like effective medicine. Try fast cars. Or guns. If gun control effectively kept the poor from buying guns but still left weapons in the hands of the few rich, would this be a reason to make guns legally available to all? Or would social needs override fairness with this conclusion—better that few rather than many have access to guns?

But the analogies break down in yet another way. Abortion is a case where the consumers of the social pie disagree over whether the diners are benefiting or dying from the eating, and even how many people (mother—embryo) are affected by access to the social practice. Drugs may be a better (though milder) analogy. Imagine a table around which are seated users and non-users of drugs. (Some of the drug-users are pregnant.) Cocaine is on the table instead of pie. Cocaine is linked to some psychological and physical problems. Its effects on fetuses are unknown. Some at the table see the drug as beneficial (on a hedonistic calculus). Others see it as harmful. If some who view the drug as a benefit have access, should all who view the drug as beneficial also have access? Does it make a difference if the drug is alcohol? Aspirin? Tobacco?

Here again the analogy breaks down. We do in the cases of alcohol, aspirin, and tobacco legalize the drugs with appropriate social warnings. But society does not fund the consumption of alcohol and tobacco. (The opposite is true—taxes are imposed.) Aspirin is funded in health care programs. But the benefits and harms of aspirin are generally acknowledged (and use of it is a discretionary balancing of benefits and harms). Abortion therapy is once more unique in the deep disagreements that occur over whether it is a benefit or a harm. Funding an unpopular war might be the only apt analogy. But even here the connections between public funds and war efforts are not tight. Medicaid moneys for abortion, unlike taxes for the defense budget, are targeted for the specific practice at issue—abortion therapy.

The issue of public funding for abortion—in effect, whether individuals who feel that a practice is morally wrong ought to be taxed to support that practice—is complex and open. No analogies quite fit the issue. Competing positions seem equally authoritative. One additional reason that the issue is so difficult is that there is really no intuitively overriding rule of fairness that might govern distributive issues. Tax the rich to help the needy. Reward those of ability. Which is fair? If social distribution is zero-sum (as Thurow claims, 1981)—where gains to one sector of the economy equal proportionate losses to another—no intuitive sense of what is fair justifies losers and winners.

*Fairness* may be a wild-card term like *sameness.* The value of a wild card depends on the suit to which it is assigned. What it is for two items to be the same depends on the social practice in which the items appear. Two homicides may be legally identical, but medically quite different. Fairness may be similar, an empty term until assigned to a rule or principle. But the selection of a rule or principle of distribution then must be made prior to the settlement of what is fair.

Since one of the important determinants of social rules is morality, the pro-life rejection of abortion funding finds some support. The pro-life argument would be this—that the emptiness of *fairness* pushes the issue of funding back to morality; and morality demands as few abortions as possible. Thus funding is denied on moral grounds. Of course this argument simply moves distributive issues on abortion back to morality, where the opposed positions occupy even less common ground than typically found in arguments over fairness.

## 9

The realities of abortion divide and subdivide in many ways, and through what seems like inertia enter and partition normative concepts like equality, fairness, justice. The chronic decomposition of complex ideas may be what gives abortion practices the Rashomon effect. Three fragmented themes influence both our intuitive and systematic ideas on abortion. (1) One is the difficult connections between what is moral and what is just. Many goods that are distributed in society permit consistent, though uneasy, judgments on the moral and the just. But abortion does not. And the reason it does not is that the conceptual dispute is unsettled. If agreement is not possible on the population to be affected by distribution, and even whether the item to be distributed is a good or a bad, then it is hard to see how morality and justice can be made compatible. As replacement for compatibility, the morality of abortion dominates justice, determining for partisans the proper social arrangements on abortion. But morality is precisely the conceptual area where abortion disputes occur.

(2) The American public is divided over the morality of abortion. Though the opinion polls (there is little doubt about this) ask dichotomized questions that elicit, if not fortify, divisions on abortions, the evidence still suggests that by now almost half of the American people are polarized on the morality of abortion. Whether this polarization would have occurred in the absence of *Roe* is an intriguing question. But the current division does make a moral resolution on consensual grounds near to impossible. It seems to follow that a resolution of abortion issues must be framed in terms that do not require an either-or, for-or-against, social state. In current realities, some non-moral resolution is the only practical hope.

(3) The data on abortion introduce another victim — the unmarried and pregnant teenager. In a world where over one million teenagers get pregnant every year, and where 400,000 of these teenagers secure abortions — amounting to one-third of all abortions obtained in the United States — it is impossible to spin out arguments on abortion as if the fetus were the only concern. No moral or political resolution of abortion can ignore the social reality that children, in effect, are among the main recipients of abortions in America today.

## For Further Reading

Callahan, Daniel. *Abortion: Law, Choice, and Morality* (New York: Macmillan, 1970).

Gordon, Sol; Scales, Peter; and Everly, Kathleen. *The Sexual Adolescent* (North Scituate, Mass.: Duxbury Press, 1979).

Luker, Kristin. *Taking Chances* (Berkeley: University of California, 1975).

Osofsky, Howard and Joy. *The Abortion Experience: Psychological and Medical* (New York: Harper & Row, 1973).

Rubin, Eva. *Abortion, Politics, and the Courts* (Westport, Conn.: Greenwood Press, 1982).

Thurow, Lester. *The Zero-Sum Society* (New York: Penguin Books, 1981).

Uslaner, Eric, and Weber, Ron. "Public Support for Pro-Choice Abortion Policies in the Nation and States," *Michigan Law Review* 77 (1979): 1772-89.

Vinovskis, M. A. "The Politics of Abortion in the House of Representatives in 1976," *Michigan Law Review* 77 (1979): 1790-1827.

The data on abortions cited here and in other chapters were drawn mainly from two Guttmacher Institute Studies:

(1) *Safe and Legal: Ten Years' Experience with Legal Abortion in New York State* (1980).

(2) *Teenage Pregnancy: The Problem That Hasn't Gone Away* (1980).

the collection of pieces in:

Furstenberg, Frank, Jr.; Lincoln, Richard; and Menden, Jane, eds., *Teenage Sexuality, Pregnancy, and Childbearing* (Philadelphia: University of Pennsylvania, 1981).

and two publications summarizing studies by the Centers for Disease Control in Atlanta, Ga.:

(1) *Abortion Surveillance 1978* (November 1980).

(2) Grimes, David A., and Cates, Willard, Jr., "Complications from Legally-Induced Abortion: A Review," *Obstetrical and Gynecological Survey* (1979): 177-91.

# 5
# LEGAL AND POLITICAL RESOLUTIONS

## 1

The divisiveness of abortion is clearest when those on opposing sides come together for a debate. Witness the following exchange between Mildred Jefferson and Sol Gordon:

*Gordon:* You take the people who want a Right-to-Life Amendment. . . . The majority are the same people who are anti-black, the same people who are anti-Jewish, the same people who were the racists in Congress some years ago — are the people who are the great moral leaders of our time [on abortion]. . . . We're not bombing your offices. Why is that? That's the difference between our side and your side. . . .

*Jefferson:* . . . This great humanitarian trend [liberalized abortion law] has resulted in the deaths of more of those who are dark than ever died in the years of lynchings and slavery, stabbings on street corners and drugs in some tenements in the cities. This great human benefit that has the helpless and the vulnerable as the targets of the social planners inside and outside of the government who are acting out in collusion, using the funds intended to help the poor directed against the poor, acting out a fascist model of social improvement that they dare call liberal. Because indeed by getting rid of the people who are likely to run up the costs . . . one is acting out the old fascist model practiced and very carefully carried out in National Socialist Germany. . . . [Recorded March 17, 1981, on the Syracuse University campus.]

It is critically important in such an emotional atmosphere to acknowledge those small parcels of truth that might be recognizable to partisans on all sides of the abortion problem. The following list is proposed.

(1) Abortion is both a moral and a political problem. It is not clearly an issue to be governed by individual discretion. It is not an item easily regulated by social rules. It occupies that difficult space where morality and politics intersect. Resolutions of abortion issues will have to draw upon both moral and political considerations if all dimensions of abortion problems are to be addressed.

(2) "Origin-of-life" theories—bottom lines for both pro-life and pro-choice—are much more complex and limited than either side realizes. At least two different types of explanation on the origin of life compete with each other—(a) membership, and (b) metamorphosis. Neither triumphs. And since (a) prohibits many abortions and (b) tolerates early abortions—each on the assignment of a right to life to human beings—then origin-of-life arguments do not resolve as much as restate basic differences. Also, the social assignment of human status to individuals is itself a moral undertaking, not a biological exercise that breaks a moral deadlock.

(3) Rational choice theory does not help in solving abortion problems. Decision-rules simply formalize already formed values. They do not resolve disputes over values. There is one exception. Calculations of expected value against probabilities favor pro-life arguments if absolute value is assigned to human life. No matter how low the probability that the fetus is human, a high enough regard for human life will tip the balance against abortions. On the other hand, pro-choice advocates do not see the right to life as absolute, but as conditional on other things. Also, pro-choice does not regard the question of when human life begins as an issue of probability. Pro-choice advocates see the question as one of definition, and their definition of human life does not extend to early embryonic development. So the victory of pro-life in the logic of decision theory, like the use of origin-of-life models, is not recognized by the other side.

(4) The data on abortion (who gets abortions and under what circumstances) bring another player into the abortion dialogue—the pregnant minor. Pregnancy in the under-15-year-old group is (there is no moderate word for it) tragic. But whether abortion is salvation, or tragedy added to tragedy, is itself disputed. Also, the fact

of teenage pregnancies, no matter how devastating to those in that condition, cannot in itself justify abortion if the fetus has a right to life. But any resolution of abortion problems must give thought to the needs of pregnant minors if it is to succeed politically.

(5) Finally, each of the several sides in the abortion controversy is inconsistent. No coherent ideology justifies either pro-choice or pro-life. The role of the state in regulating the lives of its citizens, the zones of economic and moral privacy shielding the individual from the state — these are underdeveloped ideas. But the main inconsistency is between birth control and abortion. Abortion would still be a social problem even if all pregnancies were planned. Genetic defects discovered in pregnancy, a change in the relationship originating the pregnancy (husband or lover dies, leaves, etc.) — many events can make even the most desirable of pregnancies suddenly unwanted. But since the highest frequencies of abortion occur among girls under 15 and women over 40, and since three-fourths of all abortions are performed on unmarried women, it takes no great imagination to conclude that the majority of abortions are occasioned by pregnancies that are unplanned and unwanted in the first place. Even so, neither side — pro-life or pro-choice — has a coherent and effective program for eliminating unwanted pregnancies. This, in spite of the fact that the absence of unwanted pregnancies would collapse many abortion problems — including the issue of funding abortions — to much smaller and more manageable dimensions.

## 2

These observations, however, are tepid compared to the ways in which each side views the other side's beliefs.

*Frohock:* Why do you think the other side has the beliefs they do on abortion?

*Jackson:* In no particular order, I would say that what is not seen is not heard. I think that is fairly important, maybe a lot more important than I realize, that what we don't see doesn't exist. It's true in general terms in our society. For madness, you put people away in a hospital and you don't know what's going on. We're very, very remote from prisons, we don't really know what's going on. Many things we're remote from. One is remote from senility because again one puts people away in homes. And at certain extreme stages it may be better for an old person to be in a home, but only very extreme. Otherwise I think it's tremendously humanizing, both for them and for those looking after them, for them to be with you in your own family. But the degree to which these sorts of things are put away so you don't see them is the degree to which you don't hear them. I really do see that as one factor in the abortion matter. However, the question still remains, why should that have an effect on some people but not on others? For that I'd be inclined to say, okay, if that's true, then if your training would lead you to have a peculiar respect for the invisible, then you're more likely to take seriously what cannot be seen and what is not immediately tangible. It's interesting to me, for example, to discover that it's not only Orthodox Jews and Christians who have strong feelings about abortion, to look at it from the religious point of view. You also find that quite a number of people who come from the Eastern religious background, at least in the West, even though in India there's no such compunction about these things. But in the West you find that people who are "into" various sorts of Eastern religious things are frequently standing against abortion. It may be because it's just the principle of life is life is life and we must not touch it, but I think also there's a sort of conditioning toward respecting what you can't see, taking seriously what you cannot see. So I think of that as one factor. I don't know exactly how to play it, but that's the way I'm playing it right now. I think it is a factor. I also think that—the problem is that the statistics do not exist. I don't know whether Gallup has ever broken down his findings in this way, or who has, but I suspect that—well, it's more than a suspicion—on the whole, the more highly educated a person is, the more likely they're going to be for abortion, partly because if the movement towards abortion is in fact associated with many other opinions about society and life which tend to be moving away from the traditional things accepted by society in the past, then those people who are exposed to those opinions are naturally going to be influenced strongly. These people tend to congregate on campuses; you're going to find probably a disproportionate number of people in university faculties who actually without really examining the issue at all would tend to be pro-abortion just because they've been taught to think of it as a rights issue, and it's "my country, right or wrong" when it comes to a rights issue, you don't even think of that. For example, I discovered when I was on campus myself the tendency to uncritically accept certain positions because it appears right. For example, should we have a boycott of South Africa in . . . goods? "Well, of course, because . . . " But then you say, "Wait a minute. Do you really think you should sign your name to that when we're spending many more billions of dollars in trading with the Soviet Union and the satellite countries which have systems of oppression which make South Africa look like a kindergarten?" And then there's a sort of silence, you see, but why don't people think that? I think because things are initially presented in a certain way which satisfies particular presuppositions. I think insofar as people live on campuses, go through campuses, and read, let's say, *Time* magazine or *Newsweek* (which I think are very, very important in this regard), you're talking about a minority of people, not the majority. You tend to find a strong constituency there for pro-abortion views, even though there may be many nuances there, a fairly strong natural constituency. And the more we move away from that, you move towards the other sort of constituency, which in a way is more pragmatic, I think. I have a sense in talking to people who are not from a university background (I spent quite a bit of time with such) that they're fairly pragmatic, they're not looking at it in terms of rights, particularly. They're saying they're stumbling towards an opinion. They have a sort of gut reaction which is often something like pro-life, although they're afraid of being thought of as extreme, and they recognize the difficulties and they don't know how to handle these difficulties, and yet they're uneasy about it. I think that's where most people probably are.

*Gordon:* I can't imagine it to be a rational process. I feel comfortable with people and colleagues of mine who believe that abortion is not sound, that it is not a good thing, but I don't have a single friend who has then moved to make abortion illegal. Many of my colleagues and friends are strong Catholics, Orthodox Jews, but none of them have followed the sequence, "If I'm opposed to abortion, therefore I will oppose it for everybody. It must be illegal." I don't think it's a rational question at all because what I have noted in my own observation over the years is that 95 to 98 percent of all these fierce pro-lifers, all these people who are fierce, compulsory pregnancy . . . , they're not people I respect. They don't believe in social values. They're opposed to sex education, they're opposed to contraception, they're opposed to all the laws that improve society, they don't give a damn about mass starvation. . . . To compare [abortion] with the Holocaust, which angers me more than anything else. I've never known any of them, not a single one of them, to ever be a strong anti-fascist, a strong anti-Nazi, or any one of them who has ever taken an extreme position when it came to the mass murder of people. There are a few exceptions, there are a few liberals, and I know who they are, and you can just count them on the fingers of your hand, practically, there's so few of them. But mainly they are people who are reactionary. It's as though they are so preoccupied with the fetus, that when the fetus becomes a person they lose all interest. So their preoccupation now is with the fetal life, they don't care about people at all. This may seem like a grossly exaggerated generalization, but I strongly believe it, I have studied it, I have watched it. Especially the Congressmen who are in the pro-life movement, only one or two of them are interested in social legislation or care about people at all.

*Frohock:* So it's a kind of reactionary political package?

*Gordon:* Absolutely. It's no accident that most reactionary people in Congress, exemplified best by [Sen. Jesse] Helms . . . who is rotten to the core, a politician par excellence, who has accumulated a tremendous amount of power . . . who, along with his colleagues [Sen. Jeremiah] Denton and others, *they* represent, *they* are, *they* are giving us Sermons from the Mount? *They're* the ones who have any sense of morality? *They're* teaching us about what's moral and what's not?

---

*Hyde:* Sure, there has been, I hesitate to say, a deliberate confusion. When life begins is understood by those of us on the pro-life side to mean when an individual's life begins, not when life generically begins—the big bang theory or creationism—but there has been an enormous confusion by people who should know better. Biologists, doctors, a lot of the people who testify say, I know of no evidence to show when life begins. Well, we're not talking about that. We're talking about when an individual's life begins and that has always been clear. Then they confuse human and the value to be given to that life. That's not a scientific question. That's a value question which tradition, history, the law, philosophy—all of those forces animate or energize the decision to be made, not by scientists or doctors, but by the policy making body of society, which is Congress actually. These are very important distinctions . . .

*Frohock:* Then the remaining puzzle is how it is that so many people fail to be convinced by so conclusive a proof that human life begins at conception.

*Hyde:* Because it's inconvenient. It's terribly inconvenient. It's a reversal of the roles of Galileo and the misguided ecclesiastics. When Galileo came up with his theory of a unified cosmos, it shocked and was incompatible with the clergy than regnant. They refused to accept what was really scientific truth. Now today it is so inconvenient to recognize that human life is begun in some woman's womb by some microscopic little blastocyst that is making its way to her uterus to implant itself. Now it's always convenient to dehumanize the enemy. That's why they call it a fetus and the products of conception, and that's why we want to call it a pre-born child. We want to humanize it. When you're fighting the Germans, they were HUNS, the

Japanese, they were called the JAPS. You dehumanize the enemy and it's easier to kill them. And if you do anything but humanize the pre-born then it's easier to treat them as a statistic. So a teacher named Jean Garton, a Lutheran, has referred to the humanity of the unborn as the great 13th floor of society. Everyone knows it's there, but it's much more convenient to pretend it isn't.

*Frohock:* So let's see if I understand it. It would be that people who generally believe in pro-choice aren't able to appreciate the right of something unseen —

*Kisil:* Right.

*Frohock:* Or very small. They don't believe it's life. Is that why your side uses pictures?

*Kisil:* One thing I just learned. Birthright in their counseling do not use — I thought they did, but they do not use pictures. They use some pictures.

*Frohock:* They use replicas of the embryo or fetus.

*Kisil:* Right. Down at Planned Parenthood they have a profile of the uterus with a little microscopic baby there. And I heard a teacher ask them when they took us on a "Cook's Tour" — and one girl who selects the kind of movie films they would use in the different departments of the schools — and so she asked this girl, "Where do the babies go that they abort?" And she believes what she said, I suppose, or was trained to say, "There are no babies." And yet up here in their library room is the woman's uterus with the baby attached to the uterus at a very early gestation stage, but there's the baby. And in Allan Guttmacher's book in 1963, you know what he said — abortion kills the baby and threatens the health of the mother.

Pro-choice activists also recognize the impact of visually experiencing the fetus, especially at stages when it has human form.

*Frohock:* What is it about gestation that inclines you to draw a distinction between first trimester and second trimester abortions?

*Hughes:* Well, it's aesthetic. A woman in a second trimester abortion is the only one who participates. The doctor starts the process and leaves, and the woman is the one who is totally involved in the process. She has no choice but to participate.

*Frohock:* What does the participation consist of?

*Hughes:* Going into labor and delivering a fetus, seeing it. If my big toe had to be amputated I don't think I'd want to be awake to watch it. I think it's a hard emotional experience. But there's no doubt in my mind that I could do it.

*Frohock:* Is it the fact that the fetus has, as you said, quasi-human form that is upsetting to the woman?

*Hughes:* I think it's different for each person. For some people it's the pain; for some it's the gore; for some it's that the fetus is developed. I think I would be afraid I wouldn't be able to forget, that forgetting it would be hard, that you have to participate in it and watch it happen, that it would just be really untidy.

*Frohock:* In the first trimester the woman doesn't see . . . ?

*Hughes:* No, there is nothing to see. For many abortions, the woman can be asleep under general anesthesia, and people who can afford that and who have that option take it. I think most people would take it. Some people wouldn't, some people have a real fear of anesthesia. But it's a D&C and there's just blood.

## 3

One reason that abortion is so intractable a social problem is that the unborn are special types of future persons. Separate for a moment the concept of "unborn" from the pro-life point of view. Imagine, from a neutral perspective, the prospect of future generations. The demands on the imagination are modest. Every society is composed of past, present, future. Think of any society sliced open with time held constant. At any given moment, the recently born and the very old exist together, representing the future and the past. One small additional step takes us to the unborn. Re-start time. It is then an easy matter to see that birth and death are temporal events in any society. Since no generation in time seems to have morally privileged membership, and since societies typically exist beyond the life-span of their individual members, one need not turn to Edmund Burke to introduce the yet-to-be-born as members of society.

But future generations fare badly in theories of justice. Political philosophy offers many devices to establish justice. One, advanced by Plato, is intuition — seeing, without proof, the fundamental principles of social organization. Another is utilitarianism — which justifies those social arrangements that have maximum total or average utility. But the most powerful device to establish justice is the social contract. Social rules are just if those roughly equal in power and in conditions of moderately scarce resources agree, hypothetically, to have such rules govern their relations with each other. The social contract has been used for centuries — from Hume to Rawls — as a device to establish a just social order.

The unborn, however, are two steps removed from even hypothetical agreement. Among those currently existing in society, no actual social contract has been consummated. But the fiction survives, and even flourishes. Social rules and laws can be accepted on the Hobbesian thought of the alternative — disorder and conflict. We act as if a social contract had been struck because without a contract each person is his own authority; and, if there is parity of power, no one wins. (If Hobbes is right, everyone loses.) So it is in the interests of all who are equal in power to accept rules that govern society. The unborn, however, are hypothetical figures in this hypothetical agreement. Not yet existing, they have no power. Having no power, there is no reason for those who do exist to contract with them in that hypothetical agreement establishing social rules.

Aristotle saw politics as occurring only among equals. Interest groups in American politics understand the importance of power in social justice. Indeed, with the recent organization of women, blacks, the poor, those social costs traditionally passed on to these groups are resisted effectively. But future generations cannot oppose exploitation. Justice-across-generations — obligations to future generations — is hard to establish precisely because of the asymmetry of power from present to future. We can destroy the future. The future cannot affect us except in benign psychological ways (guilt over damage to the ecological systems). Abortion problems occur as issues in asymmetrical relations. The unborn are future generations; and as future generations, they suffer a considerable disadvantage in the social contract. Like Aesop's rabbits, they have neither teeth nor claws, nor even voices. The social contract does not easily extend to such beings.

Yet, unlike future persons, fetuses exist physically. Abortion terminates the gestation of actual creatures who look human sometime during the second trimester. The differences in effect here are striking. Social practices that indirectly kill, like the absence of safe mining procedures, can be tolerated in many societies. But a direct threat to life is often intolerable, a point made dramatically when massive efforts are made to rescue trapped miners. Some (Calabresi and Bobbitt, 1978) have argued that practices offensive to basic values must be obscure if they are to be successful. Abortions cannot be obscure. The fetus is real (whatever its moral status). It is understandable, then, that a substantial lobby has organized on behalf of unborn fetuses, but not for future persons not yet conceived. Present threats to the ecological system may kill substantial numbers of future persons. But we cannot see these persons. We can see aborted fetuses.

Abortion issues are thus lopsided in peculiar ways. Partisans speak on behalf of fetuses. But fetuses cannot express or represent their own interests. Opponents doubt that such interests exist, or that the unborn are persons in any sense at all. Inequality is coupled with disagreement over the existence of the alleged victim. Moral concerns over homicide further complicate the issues. The point, put in simple fashion, is that traditional political settlements adjusting the interests of equals is impossible given the asymmetry of power between born and unborn. But then the expected dominance (and even exploitation) of the strong over the weak is resisted by widespread perceptions of direct and explicit violation of a basic social value — the sanctity of life. And the violation of this value is itself disputed by substantial numbers of people. It is not surprising that neither legal nor political resolutions can work in standard ways on abortion issues.

4

Yet precisely in the paralysis of standard methods of resolution can be found the approaches that will provide rational solutions to abortion problems. These approaches address the problems of resolving moral claims by social decision-rules.

Theories that dwell on the connections between moral principles and social institutions have a long and uneven history. Classical political thought represents the most straightforward connections.

Plato maintained that institutions, ideally conceived, express the most fundamental principles of justice and morality. Social contract theory is less direct, assuming (most of the time) that social institutions are necessary conditions for the realization of natural law. Hobbes justified the state in part because it makes the moral life rational. Some political theorists see a basic hostility between the rational requirements of authority in society and the needs of at least ordinary morality. Machiavelli argues for the amorality of the prince on such considerations. More recent views, such as those of Max Weber, view political society and morality as separate social practices, never having to impinge on each other.

Various entry theories, stipulating more precisely how moral considerations bear on social institutions, have lately been developed. John Rawls (1971) uses (among other devices) hypothetical choice in an original position to generate principles of justice. These principles govern social institutions by specifying the fair distribution of burdens and benefits for individuals. Robert Nozick (1974) argues that certain natural rights operate as side constraints on the state, which in turn originates as a collective effort to establish security for individuals against physical attack. These grand and abstract efforts at theorizing are both well-known and of limited assistance in resolving abortion disputes. Each theory is primarily concerned with just or moral economic arrangements, not with methods for resolving moral disputes. (Except, as we will see shortly, Rawls's construction of collective choice is helpful in exposing some problems in abortion resolutions.)

More helpful entry theories can be found in the concepts of law developed by positivists and, more recently, by Ronald Dworkin (1978). Put briefly, positivists limit the term "law" to the rules of legal institutions, which institutions are specifiable by empirical conditions and need not intersect with morality to be completely described. If morality enters legal decisions, it does so with the discretionary authority of judges to decide hard cases. Positivists thus reject the major traditions of natural law, which all hold that legal decisions are moral actions that take into account the rules of legal institutions. Dworkin, by contrast, rejects mechanical (e.g., Hart's "rule of recognition") and empirical tests for saying what the law is. Law, on Dworkin's account, is a system of entitlements within which morality and law are inextricably linked. Individuals in legal systems make claims for rights, and these claims are adjudicated by judges deciding on principles. Hard cases are decided not on discretionary authority, but by identifying the deeper principles which govern legal decisions. Morality enters law in the form of background considerations that guide legal decisions when standard materials (institutional rights) provide uncertain guidance on the rights of individuals.

Abortion is a hard case, in many senses of that phrase, for both positivism and Dworkin's theory of law. Let's imagine an ideal legal forum where claimants for pro-life and pro-choice meet in the hope and expectation of a legal resolution of their dispute. The ideal judge will notice several things immediately about the dispute. First, claimants for pro-life and pro-choice not only disagree, but they cannot even agree on a test for resolving their dispute (each preferring a derivative decision-rule — the judiciary for pro-choice, a plebescite for pro-life — that is desirable because contingently instrumental to realizing their own views). Second, each side views the other side as wrong, so any judgment that one claim is right, or that both claims are wrong, or that both claims have equal weight, must be formed from outside the dispute. (This is a standard feature of moral disputes, but stating it here emphasizes the non-arbitrary character of any resolution of abortion — a settlement for either side, or neither side, will have to be justified with reasons.) Third, both sides accept a concept of human life as valuable and a principle forbidding killing human beings needlessly. But (a) each side extends (interprets and applies) the concept and principle in different ways to abortion, and (b) neither side's particular values on abortion are entailed by the starting concept or principle, or any of the additional considerations (e.g., biological data) introduced by the partisans. In this sense, both sides seem to be making non-cognitive moral arguments, though each side feels strongly that what they are saying is true and not merely the expression of emotion or sentiment.

The positivist ideal judge (if one could exist) would have an impossible task in trying to resolve the abortion dispute. He would first discover quickly that the law is not decisive on abortion. The common law permitted early abortions. Statute law (from the late

19th century in America) proscribed abortions. He might, as the Court did in *Roe,* look to some of the supporting reasons for abortion and explore their continuing validity. For example, a concern for the health of the woman has the opposite effect now on abortion practices, favoring instead of prohibiting abortion. But the morality of the dispute dominates such considerations. If fetal rights to life override risk to the woman, as pro-life believes, then the development of antiseptic surgery will not justify abortion. The positivist judge then seems to have discretionary authority to make a decision. But this will not do either. If he turns to morality he will find the same principle of respect for the integrity of life that yielded the two opposed conceptions of proper abortion practices. The positivist judge may yield to the temptation to put a decision into effect that is explicitly based on a noncognitive theory of value. But a resolution defended on emotive impulses is no rational resolution at all, least of all for a moral dispute.

So we turn to Hercules, Dworkin's ideal judge. She faces a more formidable task, though admirably equipped in will and temperament to fulfill it. She must decide which concept of abortion practices is the best elaboration of the principle respecting human life without resorting simply to her own emotive responses to abortion. This elaboration, moreover, will unavoidably require interpreting a cluster of other concepts like dignity, respect, perhaps equality and liberty (though not, one hopes, property). To succeed in this elaboration, she must construct a theory of constitutional government that explains the institutions of her society. This construction will be formed from institutional facts and political philosophy. The law governing abortion will be generated from the understanding of constitutional government and the coordinates of (a) legal fit with the common law and statutes, and (b) moral acceptability. The best theory of law on abortion, as on all other issues, will be that theory that is at the highest point on the moral acceptability axis among those theories beyond a threshold on the "fit-with-legal-materials" axis (Dworkin, 1978, Appendix; Alexander and Bayles, 1980). The rights of the claimants on abortion will be adjudicated on the basis of such Herculean constructions.

But it is not at all clear that Hercules will succeed in her efforts. The concepts found in abortion claims are what have been called "essentially contested" concepts (Gallie, 1956). They are (a) appraisive as well as descriptive; (b) the practice they describe is internally complex; (c) the rules of application are multiple; and, as a consequence (Gray, 1977) (d) there are intractable definitional disputes; (e) the conflict among interpreters is based not on isolated concepts, but on patterns of thought associated with rival forms of social life, and (f) the competing patterns of thought incorporate rival philosophical theses and reasonings within which resolution patterns occur. Now Hercules is as well endowed as any judge can ever be to discover the rights of claimants when essentially contested concepts are in the backgrounds of the dispute. But to do so successfully in moral disputes requires a homogeneity of background principles, rights, and understandings of the political society that may not exist among abortion partisans.

Suppose that Hercules begins by observing that the Fourteenth Amendment must be an inclusive rather than an exclusive rule, given that past mistakes, e.g., on race, were caused by limiting rather than expanding the Amendment's coverage. Then, as Aristotle would have urged, she turns her attention initially to the law on abortion. One plausible reading of *Roe* is that the due process clause and previous Court decisions did not dictate a decision on abortion. The Court then turned to the concept of fairness to decide the constitutionality of state laws prohibiting abortion (Dworkin, 1978, p. 125). Hercules will also turn to more basic concepts in deciding the abortion dispute, since an inclusive interpretation of the Fourteenth Amendment, attractive as a start, still cannot fix the rights or interests of the parties in the abortion dispute. Even, for example, with the proposition that an interest in life is weightier than an interest in the woman's freedom to choose, Hercules still will not know whether fetal life is an individual human life without exploring areas beyond the law.

It is certain that, since the legal fit axis in abortion is generous indeed given the conflict between the common law and state statutes, the requirements of morality — including the morality of the American community — will be unusually influential. But what will Hercules find when she begins her construction and elaboration of basic concepts? She will not be surprised at the trivial fact that the abortion decision, and the elaborate framework which finally states and justifies it, will be controversial (this can be expected even with sound answers to hard cases). But she may be more than astonished at the conflicting dimensions of background abortion beliefs. A right answer to claimants may not completely require a cognitive theory of value, but it surely needs some convergence of value. The chess referee constructs a single game's character to discover rights. Hercules on abortion may uncover any number of games, visions, and (in Wittgenstein's phrase) forms of life in American society. Think again of the constellation of beliefs in pro-life and pro-choice. Pro-life is committed not only to the view that abortion is murder, but also to a view of the human community that is organic in its extension of membership to all stages of genetic growth and in its acceptance of public regulation of that most intimate of decisions, whether to continue or terminate pregnancy. Indeed, such a decision does not exist on the pro-life view of society, for the fetus, from conception forward, is a member of the community with a standing equal to any other member. Pro-choice grants the woman the authority to end her pregnancy. The view of society embedded in pro-choice is of a human community where membership is restricted to independent and perhaps more developed life; and where the social practices of sex, procreation, and birth are carried out by discrete and autonomous individuals who choose and act in privacy and even in isolation from the norms of their society.

Hercules will dig deeper in her construction and elaboration. But what she will likely find is that neither American history nor political society can provide those deeper principles (of unification, of weight) that can arrange the rights of the abortion claimants in a way that satisfies morality. The long history of political philosophy is truncated along two distinct models of the political society. One, found in Aristotle, sees individuals as constituent members of an organic whole, with privacy displaced by the needs of the *polis* and individuals derived from a holistic sense of community. Another, originating roughly with contract theory in the 17th century, begins with discrete individuals fully formed and then attempts to derive society from these individualistic premises. Both organic and individuating political forms can be found in American theory and practice, from Madison and Jefferson to more recent conflicts between Friedman-like economics and various theories of collective economic responsibility. If the opposition between pro-life and pro-choice is delineated along two axes marking competing social ideals in political thought and reality, which ideal best constructs American social practices? And where can the right answer on abortion be located?

The problem for Hercules arises with the recognition that even the basic concepts in political and legal thought are developed on more primary models of a political society. Aristotle fused three items maintained as distinct in recent liberal thought: the individual, the state, and the society. One consequence of this fusion is that several issues important in liberal thought — civil disobedience, individual rights against the state, and anarchism — are simply unintelligible on Aristotle's concept of the *polis*. They mean nothing. Other concepts, like liberty, take on meanings radically different than they do in liberal political philosophies. Hobbes, by contrast, separated the individual, the state, and the society. In Hobbes's philosophy, in spite of his union of individual and sovereign interests, it is possible to construct an adversary relationship between the individual and the state. On this liberal model are built the shields of rights protecting the individual from state interference. The differences between organic and liberal political forms obviously order the primary goods of politics — community coming first in organic models, liberty usually prior in liberal models. But the more important effect is that the basic concepts of political theory are captives of these more fundamental forms. It seems unlikely that pro-life and pro-choice values can be ordered except in terms of these models of the political society; and nothing seems available to order the models themselves.

The problem for Hercules is that abortion disputes may finally be traceable not just to essentially contested concepts, but to two different and irreconcilable visions of society each of which is supported by history and political philosophy. There is no reason to believe that these competing visions are derived from some more fundamental set of concepts, and much evidence to doubt it; and so there is little reason to hope that the deep concepts of law (like, even, fairness) can be given a persuasive elaboration that any objective spectator will count as the right answer to the hard case of abortion. Even Hercules may find that her legal decision, like the concepts and traditions she explores, is essentially contestable (not just controversial); and thus, on the expectations of the parties, not right at all as a legal answer to abortion disputes.

## 5

Two problems diminish the effectiveness of any attempt to resolve abortion disputes through legal decision. (a) The disputants reasonably expect a right answer when none in this case can be provided; and (b) the even divisions in popular opinion on the issue make any right answer, even a sound one, difficult to implement. Difficulty in enforcing the law cannot (except at high thresholds) count as a reason for rejecting the legitimate rights of individuals. But when the law cannot, as in abortion (or so it is argued here), produce a right answer, then the responses of the public to a resolution are rational considerations.

Political resolutions, not burdened by the need to provide a right answer, may be more adapted to the needs of abortion problems. By "political resolutions" one can mean almost anything. But extreme political approaches to issues – anarchic, authoritarian – can be dismissed immediately. Anarchy, the dominance of individual authority, is not, in general, a satisfactory solution to homicide. Pro-choice supporters will instantly deny that abortion is homicide. But since one side, pro-life, does see the issue in these terms and nothing conclusive can be offered to rule the belief out of court, anarchy is disqualified as a consensual solution. Authoritarian methods can also be ruled out. Since neither pro-choice nor pro-life will accept the other's values, imposing one set of values or another is not an agreeable solution, rationally or morally. An imposed solution on this issue, given the general absence of consent, also carries with it all of the repugnant features of authoritarianism as such.

The most appropriate approach politically is to seek a consensus. Not consensus in fact, as things currently stand. This is impossible, given the divisiveness of the issue. A consensus may be constructed, however, as a proposed resolution of abortion issues. Such a construction can be developed at both idealistic and practical levels. At the idealistic level one might ask, what are the abortion practices that anyone would consent to if general rather than particular interests were expressed in rational choice? At the practical level one asks, what compromises can stitch together features of each position in a package acceptable to both groups?

One of the more powerful devices to identify a deep consensus on general interests is the method of hypothetical choice elaborated by Rawls (1971). Rawls asks us to construct conditions for a hypothetical choice of governing principles without knowledge of our assets and talents, location in the structure of rewards and benefits, or what (except in general terms) we value. The principles chosen on such exquisite ignorance, as modified by our moral intuitions, represent the interests of everyone. The basic device—hypothetical choice—can be extended to identify those rules that represent the general interests of all participants in a dispute. In abortion disputes we might ask: What would be a rational abortion practice if those choosing such a practice did not know which of the alternatives met their own particular interests? There are several ways to conceal the knowledge that allows individuals to realize their own interests. But one effective method in choosing abortion practices might be to introduce the unborn to the conditions where agreement is secured.

Three types of persons seem relevant to abortion issues. One is hypothetical. A hypothetical person is one who would exist if certain conditions occur. Think of all possible genetic endowments. These endowments would be a combination of all possible sperm with all possible ovums, past, present, and future. Only some of these endowments occur as the result of conception. The rest do not. The genetic endowments not realized through conception are hypothetical persons. A second type of person is embryonic. An embryonic person is one who is conceived, but not yet born. An actual person provides a third type—one who is born. All three types of persons can be regarded as homo sapiens. But each has a different status.

Suppose we imagine an idealized choice of abortion practices among rational individuals who do not know whether they are hypothetical, embryonic, or actual persons. This exercise is not a straw man, but a way of illustrating the special problems abortion introduces to political resolutions and perhaps a more general flaw in any attempt to resolve conflicts over ideals by means of idealized choice. Let a variant of Mill's harm thesis also be a premise of rational choice, in the sense that rational persons, knowing something about pain and injury, will choose to avoid being harmed by the social rules governing their abortion practices. What rules will be selected to represent the interests of all three types of persons?

If *harm* is interpreted as an experience rather than a deprivation, early abortions seem likely to be allowed and late abortions prohibited. The reason for this is that embryonic persons change radically during gestation in terms of their capacity to be harmed. They start with a full genetic endowment in the form of a blastula, with little physical or mental resemblance to actual persons. They conclude development in a form little different from newborn actual persons. Sumner's (1981) sentience criterion reappears as guide. Abortions in the first trimester do not harm sentient creatures, for no nervous system or brain is in place to experience harm. Early abortions do deprive the organism of life, and of the chance to develop into a rational, sentient creature. But so too does birth control. Limiting *harm* to experience suggests that a rational avoidance of harm will assimulate early abortions to birth control and middle-to-late abortions to homicide.

The alternatives to a moderate abortion policy are not as rationally appealing. Rules prohibiting all abortions overlook the possibility that the rational chooser may be one of the other victims in abortion practices — unmarried pregnant teenagers who might be (from their own point of view) best served by abortion, women threatened by ectopic pregnancies, etc. Liberal abortion practices risk the possibility that one might be an embryonic person developed sufficiently to suffer harm. The question raised and answered by a joining of hypothetical choice and a *harm* principle is not, when does human life begin, but: What are the conditions necessary for an organism to be harmed? A recognition that a brain and nervous system are requisites follows closely a rational definition of death based on the absence of brain waves on an electroencephalogram. Abortion rules become a rational avoidance of harm based on physical distinctions in gestation.

Leave aside the practical problems in enforcing an abortion practice permitting only first-trimester abortions (mentioned in Chapter 3). Does the construction satisfy an idealized political decision representing general interests? It does not seem so, for two reasons. First, *harm* is simply not limited to experience; and when it is not, several bizarre conclusions follow from idealized choice. Hypothetical persons have interests. On the reasonable assumption that existence is, on the whole, preferable to nonexistence, it is in the interest of a hypothetical person to be conceived (and then, as an embryonic person, to be born). This interest is not peremptory. Many conditions in which life is lived can make nonexistence preferable. Excessive and unrelenting pain, the failure of basic ideals—any brief reflection can produce conditions that can make living intolerable. A recent (and controversial) area of law allows suit for wrongful life. Shanna Curlender was born with Tay-Sachs disease. A laboratory had earlier tested her parents' blood and assured them that they were not carriers of the disease. A California district court allowed the parents to sue the laboratory for wrongful life. They settled out of court for $1.5 million (*New York Times,* April 12, 1982). Wrongful life suits are brought on behalf of handicapped children on the grounds that the child would have been better off not being born. But the legal acceptance that some lives are not worth living accompanies the more protean thought that some lives are better than no life at all.

The problem that life-value has for a rational choice of abortion practices is that several logical nightmares promptly follow the value assignment. If harm is extended to deprivation and thus can occur in the absence of the neurological conditions for sentience, then neither early abortions nor birth control (even the rhythm method) are rational practices. Not knowing whether one will be a hypothetical, embryonic, or actual person urges rational agents to select rules discouraging abortion and encouraging procreation. The possibility of victims will still qualify abortion restriction (severely handicapped fetuses, desperate women). But the general position of pro-choice gives way along with birth control. Here is the problem: abortion practices that are justified on the same grounds as those used to encourage as high a level of procreation as the world's resources will permit are simply bizarre.

The second reason that idealized political choice fails is that the method itself is unavoidably biased according to how the alternatives of choice are set up. Many reasonable people in both pro-life and pro-choice movements may have difficulty believing in hypothetical people (though "wrongful life" suits are unintelligible in the absence of some hypothetical construction of interests among those not yet conceived). But pro-choice denies reality also to embryonic people. Now notice that if hypothetical and embryonic people are not among the members of the population making idealized choices, liberal abortion practices are rational choices (for no person is harmed in abortion and many problems facing actual people are avoided). If, however, hypothetical and embryonic people are possible realities, then a restricted abortion practice is rational. The dispute between pro-life and pro-choice, in short, reappears at the most abstract level of idealized rational choice.

The fissure in an idealized choice of abortion practices is similar to the breakdown in applying law to abortion disputes. The conflict in ideals that is basic to abortion disputes carries over to the methods generally employed to resolve disputes. No single reconstruction of law can give right answers to claimants who draw on competing models of society (both of which are found in Western history). No hypothetical choice is independent of the values that are themselves disputed by abortion partisans. In the former, the conflicting ideals extend to the discovery of preexisting rights. In the latter, the conflicting ideals admit of no resolution because they reappear as conflicts over membership in the class of rational individuals selecting abortion practices (whether hypothetical and embryonic persons are to be included as realities). If the reality of, especially, embryonic persons is a core issue in abortion disputes, it is hard to see how any version of idealized rational choice can resolve abortion problems — even if bizarre outcomes could somehow be avoided.


6

Political compromise is a practical method for reaching consensus. "Compromise" is a word that fits badly with moral discourse. We speak of "compromising situations," where one's reputation or character are endangered, and compromising (as in giving up) one's principles or integrity — neither use particularly endearing to the ordinary demands of morality. The core meaning of compromise — mutual concessions to settle differences — is more easily applied to interests than moral principle. Since the abortion dispute is clearly over principles, not interests, it is not surprising that abortion activists maintain most of their values as nonnegotiable items. Traces of a possible compromise solution can be identified, however.

*Frohock:* Suppose you were locked in a room with someone who had total authority to represent the pro-choice point of view, and you had total authority for the pro-life movement, and you couldn't come out of the room until you reached some compromise defining social practices on abortion. What's the least you would settle for? What are the things that you would simply never give up, that you would have to have in that package, almost a nonnegotiable set of items?

*Jackson:* First in my package would be that my conscience remain intact in terms of whatever package I agreed to, what I think I went into the room with. That's what I think, and I don't regard the battle as finished until I get that. But if I've got to negotiate, then I will argue for abortion being permitted as close to following conception as I can get it. If that's three months, so be it, I'll accept it. I'll be glad. That's what I'll do, if that's the best I can get, I will fight for that.

---

*Gordon:* I think the bottom line is the Supreme Court decision. I wouldn't be happy or satisfied with anything else. It would have to be the mother's choice the first trimester.

*Frohock:* This is the *Roe-Wade* decision?

*Gordon:* Yes.

---

*Kisil:* I would insist on no taxation for abortions and a true informed consent because I believe that if there were informed consent — until we could pass the HLA, and who knows how long that would take — if we had true informed consent, I know we would cut back on abortions. And if we cut back the abortions, it wouldn't be just the babies we would be saving, because we're talking about a principle, not just 2, 3, 4, 500 babies, it is the principle of life — that we can't always defy the principle of life. The women, no matter what age they are, would not be getting so assaulted.

*Frohock:* So these two measures would be your bottom line. You wouldn't give up those? You don't have informed consent. The other measure you do have.

*Kisil:* In some states you do have informed consent.

*Frohock:* What does informed consent look like in the states that have it?

*Kisil:* The doctor that is about to do the abortion must notify the parents — it varies a little bit, but the parents would have 48-72 hours input into it. They must have knowledge of it. It's so dirty of them to fight it. Because we don't even say you have to have consent — just knowledge. And that the woman would be educated to fetal development. She would be educated as to the possible complications — the long-term, the on-going and the immediate. You would cut down.

_____

*Hughes:* That's hard. I wouldn't give away abortion. It's hard to think of what kinds of compromises I'd be forced to make. I wouldn't want to make any. I guess if I had to, if that became a compromise, I would say second trimester. I wouldn't give up first trimester abortion but I might give up second. It would be a lesser of evils kind of thing.

*Frohock:* How about funding?

*Hughes:* That's hard because I think about health care in general — I think it's a right and not a privilege. And I put abortion as a health concern. I think it is a health concern more than a moral concern for me, and I don't think anybody should be denied health care on this. I mean, talking about compromise, if the tables were turned I would want each woman who is pregnant to get full information about the risks and dangers of pregnancy, the fact that 300-400 women die each year because of complications of pregnancy and childbirth, whereas maybe ten die of complications of abortion. I think that we on the pro-choice side have done a lousy job informing people about abortions. I don't think most people understand it, what it's about at all, that it can be a healthy thing to do, both from a psychological and physical point of view.

*Frohock:* What if your pro-life authority said, "I want to have effective and informed consent for all abortions — no abortions until our side can get at the woman for 24 hours and show her all the hazards of abortion." Would that be fair?

*Hughes:* If I had the right to approve the information. I'd want to make sure they have their facts straight. No, I don't think it's fair. It's another burden. Abortion is safer than a tonsillectomy, and you know what can happen to you in the dentist's chair. Yet you do not have to sit down with the dentist and have him explain to you that giving you this shot of novocaine could kill you or that your jaw could be deformed the rest of your life or that you may never get feeling in your mouth again. I don't think that's fair emotionally to do to somebody. I think it's cruel. I could really conduct an education program so that no woman would ever want to have a baby. Pregnancy could be described in such terms that it would be a really negative, horrible thing for a woman to do to herself. I don't think it's fair. I think it's the same as asking me every time I go to the store to buy hamburger to watch them kill the calf, skin it, and grind it up.

---

*DeCrow:* . . . I believe in the First Amendment, and I believe that if there is a group in this country, whether 10 people or 80 percent of the population, which thinks a fertilized egg should be brought to term, then they have a perfect right to try to get that point of view across, by appearing on television shows, by marching in the streets. They should have a complete right to put their point of view across. If they believe that the use of condoms will send you straight to hell they should have a right to tell you this. So I have no problems with that. As far as making it a law, where are you going to stop? If a person had to watch a slideshow on brain surgery, that person might refuse to get an aneurysm treated. A lot of literature comes to me, and whether it's for abortion or not, I don't have any problem with that. They have a perfect right, except once (when I was speaking) there was a threat of a pie coming up on the stage! If someone is making a speech then people who think that person is wrong have a right to picket the auditorium, but not to prevent others from going in. Abortion is very bloody, and I think the same kind of horror would be created with operations in general. A lot of people don't react favorably to blood and gore. However, do I think they have a right to use whatever kind of appeal they want, emotional or otherwise? Sure. Planned Parenthood was picketed here several weeks ago. I think they have a perfect right to picket.

*Frohock:* But should they have access to the pregnant woman in the hospital for a period of time? In one state, and hypothetically in others, the law would require it.

*DeCrow:* I think not. If I choose to go into a hospital to have an abortion that's really my right. And as I'm wrapped up in the cloth and about to go in for the D&C I don't want someone running up to me with literature. I think there's a parallel with Jehovah's Witnesses. An adult person should have the right to say, "Don't do it." I think that's his right. But that would be like saying as I'm about to get a blood transfusion I would have to have a bunch of Jehovah's Witnesses around my bedside telling me that it says in the Bible that it's wrong.

*Hyde:* Well, first of all it's awfully hard to compromise when it's somebody else's human life you're compromising. It's human life and the other side would never concede to that and it's somebody else's human life. And before I really answer your question I think part and parcel of this whole discussion has to focus on the Bloomington baby, where this little Down's syndrome child was born with an esophagus difficulty; and the parents, rather than deal with it, wanted it to starve. And that was the treatment that was given, starvation. How Aesopian, referring to that as treatment. And the Supreme Court upheld their decision even though there were 10 families that wanted to adopt the child. And so the child starved to death, and this is a triumph of the quality of life ethic which is urged by the pro-choice people. Quality of life is important, if not certainly more important than the sanctity of life ethics. And here is a helpless little Down's syndrome — they wouldn't even name it because that would be too much dignity. So they call it baby boy Doe, and it starved to death in the Bloomington Hospital. Not in a ghetto or in an Appalachian mountain side, but in a modern hospital. You wouldn't do that to a dog. You wouldn't starve the dog to death. . . . So that is the logical extension, the slippery slope, as the phrase goes, of the quality of life ethic. Here's a little Down's syndrome. It's an emotional, financial drain — so starve it to death. If that isn't some hellish threshold that we've crossed, I don't know. With the sanction of the courts. What a lie to say that no man is above the law and no man is beneath the law. This little baby was born. So there's no question about when life begins and all that semantic gymnastics. It was human, it wasn't a puppy, it wasn't a guppy, it wasn't a wart, it was a little baby. By God, it might have had Down's syndrome and therefore it wasn't perfect and so it starved to death. Even the *New York Times* editorialized against that. That's where we are going with this quality of life ethic, as against protecting the most vulnerable whether they're handicapped, or little, or Down's syndrome, or what. It's an outrage. If we tolerate it, then we are slipping. Then we are regressing back to the jungle, in my judgment. Now what compromise? I would save as many unborn children as I could under any terms that I could. And that includes limiting it to surgical abortions. That would include abortions that save the life of the mother. Those exceptions, except abortions that would save the life of the mother. Beyond that, we'd have a struggle to see who could endure the most. Who could last the longest.

# 7

But the absence of any clear line of compromise in the current views of activists does not mean permanent conflict. It does mean that a compromise resolution will have to be constructed and proposed, rather than extracted from the publicly expressed thoughts of activists. The possibilities of compromise as a way of settling abortion disputes are drawn up from a rational ordering of social states.

(1) Hobbes developed his justifications of authority by means of a test that can be restated in simple terms. Ask whether conditions of authority (for Hobbes, guaranteed reciprocity in agreements) are better or worse than conditions of no-authority. If authority is rationally preferable, then rational individuals will contract to establish the civil society. If anarchy (the authority of individuals or groups) is preferable, then no contract is made. The test justifies authority for Hobbes on two failures of anarchy. One failure is caused by conflicting values. When autonomous individuals disagree — either they all want the same thing when only some fraction of the population can have it, or they want different things when the society can provide only some of these things — they may find that an authoritative resolution of their conflict is preferable to continuing the conflict. A second failure is caused by the absence of rational incentives to cooperate when all agree that it is best to cooperate. This latter failure is elaborated in game theory as the "free rider" problem. Authority is justified for Hobbes in this second case as the effective guarantee that no individual will find it rational to defect from collective efforts that are in the interests of everyone to pursue.

Abortion is obviously a case of conflicting values. It is also disputed within a civil society that has a political resolution in effect. But, though anarchy *vs.* authority is not the issue, current abortion practices enclose substantial conflict and do not entirely satisfy any of the opposed groups. Pro-life does not accept the *Roe* decision, pro-choice does not accept the Hyde Amendments. So it is reasonable to pose the Hobbesian test as a request to rank alternatives. Let $a$ = a continuing conflict over abortion practices, $b$ = a pro-life resolution of abortion issues, $c$ = a pro-choice resolution of abortion issues, and $d$ = a political resolution representing agreeable parcels of both pro-life and pro-choice. Each of the opposed factions on abortion will prefer a resolution in accordance with their own values. But each faction may also prefer a moderate political resolution to a continuation of conflict. Thus, for pro-life a ranking of b > d > a > c may be rational, for pro-choice a ranking of c > d > a > b. Given the impossibility of either *b* or *c* securing general support, both groups might settle for a political resolution that does not fulfill their own moral values and may even be coercive for many individuals. But the acceptance would have to be measured as a calculation of the best that can be achieved in actual social conditions.

The actual world of abortion practices is not encouraging for either pro-life or pro-choice. It is probably true, given what we know about pre-*Roe* abortions, that women will continue to get abortions no matter what the law says. An ideal world would not contain unwanted or defective pregnancies, or families fragmented by death or desertion, or the failure of love. But the real world does contain death and failure. And this real world suggests that the criminalization of abortion will result simply in riskier abortions, with increased mortality rates for women. Conversely, the prochoice movement must know by now that liberal abortion practices disturb great numbers of sincere people. These people will not disappear. Total authority for women to end pregnancies whenever desired, for reasons essentially unregulated by the state, will encounter increasing social resistance. This resistance, moreover, threatens a host of allied liberal values. More, not less, repression may follow the continuation of unregulated abortions.

The impulses favoring some compromise solution break from the Hobbesian test in one important respect. Given that abortion is a conflict over principles, not interests, none of the competing groups will favor just any authoritative settlement over the continuation of the conflict. Hobbes's state of nature is so deplorable that authority as such is preferable to anarchy. But no partisan on abortion can be expected to give up his principles just to avoid conflict. Compromise can apply to both (a) the procedures for reaching a settlement, and (b) the outcomes representing a settlement. The one consistent theme found in the expressed views of activists on abortion is that outcomes are more important than procedures. So even an imposed compromise may be acceptable so long as the right package of values is constructed.

(2) The endorsement of principles is not necessarily hostile to compromise solutions. Here let us follow the leads introduced by Wollheim's paradox. Richard Wollheim (1962) asks us to imagine an individual who morally endorses an alternative, *a,* and simultaneously endorses majority rule, *b,* as a moral decision-rule to settle disputes. An election is held and a rival alternative, *c,* wins majority support. The individual now faces the paradox of simultaneously endorsing two conflicting moral alternatives. He can continue to support *a,* but only by giving up his support of *b.* He can support *b,* but only by accepting the outcome of the election *c* and thus giving up *a.* Something like this paradox faces both pro-life and pro-choice. On the assumption that both groups accept the general framework for settling conflicts in American society, each group must decide whether to accept the procedures leading to undesirable outcomes (the Court in *Roe* for pro-life; the Congress on the Hyde Amendments for pro-choice), or reject the procedures in the name of the principles each side endorses.

At the moment, each side has chosen to maintain principles instead of procedures. Such maintenance, as noted, is consistent with principled dispute. Pro-life is clearest in its rejection of judicial authority, though there is little doubt that electoral procedures would also be abandoned by many in the pro-life movement if popular opinion were strongly pro-choice. Pro-choice activists have been more pragmatic, choosing to work tactically within legislative bodies to reverse policies denying federal funds for legal abortions. But each side still confronts a mild version of Wollheim's paradox in the spectacle of morally legitimate institutions producing outcomes antagonistic to at least some of their moral values.

One solution (or management strategy) to Wollheim's paradox illuminates an area where principles and compromise are compatible. The key is in a distinction between moral principles and the values and political programs the principles generate. Any important moral principle can be at least partially realized by a number of specific programs; and any moral evaluation will grant the principle more importance than a specific program. For Wollheim's individual, the paradox can be avoided by identifying the moral principle that leads to the endorsement of alternative *a* and then to a calculation of what practical choices will best realize that principle. The choice may well be to support *a* no matter what. But, as supporters of democracy have found out, a more successful realization of the moral principle may require maintaining the democratic decision-rule so that one's moral principles can be secured in the long run.

The introduction of *time* to moral reasoning orders social states longitudinally (Weiss, 1973). Imagine these alternatives: (1) everyone do *a;* (2) one-third of the people do *a,* two-thirds do *c;* (3) everyone do *c.* One might prefer (1) over (3) while still preferring (3) over (2); and if a decision-rule producing *c* means (3) over (2), but not (1), then one's moral principles might be more successfully fulfilled over time in the governed harmony of (3) than in the divisive implications of (2). The problem and solution are both familiar. The fulfillment of any moral principle in social conditions introduces considerations of what others will do. Once these considerations are introduced, however, actions to realize the moral principle may require the acceptance of compromise solutions immediately contrary to some of the values and programs generated by the principle.

John Rawls (1971) describes "partial compliance" theory — justice when reality causes ideals to fall short of complete success. One rational approach to non-ideal social conditions is to see to it that more rather than less of any moral principle is realized over time. This type of compromise is more reasonable when the compatibility between principles and programs across positions on abortion are understood. The respect for life informing pro-life mandates a concern for the life and welfare of pregnant women, especially those in their early teens who are unmarried. The respect for individual values guiding pro-choice requires a serious effort to accommodate the choices of pro-life supporters. Since both sides also share the basic principle of respect for life, a compromise position will at least start from some common premises.

Mutual respect is not always possible between conflicting moral positions. But in the case of abortion, it is at least conceivable that some resolution will represent a compromise respecting the moral integrity of each of the positions.

# For Further Reading

Alexander, Lawrence, and Bayles, Michael. "Hercules or Proteus? The Many Theses of Ronald Dworkin," *Social Theory and Practice* 5 (1980): 267–304.

Barry, Brian. "Circumstances of Justice and Future Generations," in Richard I. Sikora, and Brian Barry, eds., *Obligations to Future Generations* (Philadelphia: Temple University, 1978), pp. 204–48.

————. "Justice Between Generations," in Peter M. S. Hacker and Joseph Raz, eds., *Law, Morality and Society: Essays in Honor of H.L.A. Hart* (Oxford: Clarendon, 1977), pp. 268–84.

Calabresi, Guido, and Bobbitt, Philip. *Tragic Choices* (New York: Norton, 1978).

Dworkin, Ronald. *Taking Rights Seriously* (Cambridge, Mass.: Harvard University, 1978).

Gallie, W. B. "Essentially Contested Concepts," *Proceedings of the Aristotelian Society* 56 (London, 1955-56): 167–98.

Gray, John. "On the Contestability of Social and Political Concepts," *Political Theory* 5 (1977): 331–48.

Hilgers, Thomas, and Horan, Dennis, eds. *Abortion and Social Justice* (Thaxton, Va.: Sun Life, 1972).

Nozick, Robert. *Anarchy, State and Utopia* (New York: Basic Books, 1974).

Rawls, John. *A Theory of Justice* (Cambridge, Mass.: Harvard University, 1971).

Reiman, Jeffrey. *In Defense of Political Philosophy* (New York: Harper, 1972), especially pp. 17–46 for an informal elaboration of Hobbes's test.

Sumner, L. W. *Abortion and Moral Theory* (Princeton: Princeton University, 1981).

Thurow, Lester. *The Zero-Sum Society* (New York: Penguin, 1981).

Weiss, Donald. "Wollheim's Paradox," *Political Theory* 1 (May 1973): 154–70.

Wollheim, Richard. "A Paradox in the Theory of Democracy," in Peter Laslett and W.G. Runciman, eds., *Philosophy, Politics and Society,* Second Series (Oxford: Basil Blackwell, 1962).

# 6

## AGREEABLE RESOLUTIONS

### 1

Abortion is like no other issue in its capacity to enlarge our moral and political perspectives. At the center of abortion disputes is this question: How can the state regulate a moral issue when its population is polarized over the issue *and* there are no overriding arguments supporting either of the polar positions? We are clearer now about what must be addressed in any answer to this question, though still without an adequate theory of the state or of morality that can provide an answer. Let the following outline state the problems for any political resolution of abortion issues.

(1) All theories of the state accept the thought that the political system, whatever else it does, must protect its members from physical harm caused directly by others. This responsibility is the minimum requirement for any state, whatever its form or ideology. A state that does not fulfill this responsibility is no state at all. Government may be charged with more responsibilities — for example, the redistribution of wealth accepted in liberal theories; or little else — as in libertarian states that emphasize the private sector's role in distributive politics. But no state can do less.

(2) The abortion dispute has illuminated one of the ambiguous premises of this minimum responsibility — exactly who and what are the members (individuals, groups) to be protected from harm. Any political system is composed of diverse members. Single indi-

viduals, interest groups, corporate persons, institutions, even social practices—the units of a political order are often so unlike one another that no single scale can define and measure them all. But if protection from harm by others is to be the starting goal of a government (*all* government), then only those members capable of suffering harm can count as units to be protected.

(3) Several complications occur in the use of harm. There are numerous senses of harm in addition to the physical (emotional, financial, etc.). There is direct and indirect harm—for example, homicide is direct harm, pollution of the ecological system through industrial practices is indirect harm. Sometimes government policies must be zero-sum in harm calculations, where protection of some from harm must mean doing harm to others in roughly proportionate ways. Nevertheless, these complications do not discredit the paradigm cases of direct physical harm. Homicide, somehow defined, must be prohibited by the state.

(4) The central issue of the regulation of abortion practices is whether abortion is, or can be assimilated to, homicide. The paths to this central issue are marked by strong arguments against state regulation of abortion. There are first any number of rational arguments for privacy as such, including the rational paradoxes of collective choice that are illustrated at the end of Chapter 3. There are also strong arguments against government regulation of abortion practices even when the minimum test of direct physical harm is met. The right to control one's own body and the location of the unborn individual in the body of another render abortion a type of action that today is normally shielded from state regulation. But the shield cannot insulate individuals from state regulation if abortion counts as homicide. For homicide is a clear instance of those actions any state must regulate.

(5) The most cogent test to use in determining whether the state ought to regulate abortions is the capacity of the unborn individual to suffer harm. In simplest terms, one cannot harm those who cannot be harmed. The destruction of an automobile, for example, does not harm the automobile in ways that occasion government protection of automobiles. The harm is to the human who owns the automobile. Thus property laws, more disputable items, are in-

voked. (When Richard Pryor reports in his comedy routine that he "killed" his car, the report is amusing because the act is not literally a case of homicide.) Wrecking lawns, umbrellas, even computers, do not count as acts covered by the minimum responsibility of the state to protect against physical harm. If abortion were no more than the removal of a growth or appendage, then arguments for the privacy of abortion would prevail.

(6) But harm is interpreted differently by the groups opposed on abortion. Pro-life views the destruction of fetal life as homicide, on the grounds that a person is present, exists, from conception forward; and abortion harms embryonic persons by depriving them of the choice to live their lives. Pro-choice interprets harm more nearly in experiential terms. Since the physical conditions for experiencing harm include a brain and nervous system, early abortions for pro-choice do no harm because embryos lack the capacity to experience harm. Even on the minimal test for government regulation, then, the moral differences over abortion prevent a clean argument over the role of the state in abortion practices.

## 2

Imagine an individual convinced of the moral rightness of his views. He acts in accordance with values that legislate vital interests (family, way of life, etc.), not trivial matters. He is willing to universalize these values to all relevant others. He does not make special exceptions for himself when his values require him to act against immediate self-interest. And he practices what he believes (but may or may not preach) in acting out his values day in and day out. Such an individual is a standard and admirable sketch of the moral agent.

Suppose now this moral agent encounters an adversary, one who meets all of the requirements of moral agency with a contrary set of values. And suppose further that the two moral agents want to reach a collective outcome. They seek to discover and put into effect a set of rules that will govern the relations they have with each other on shared vital interests. The formation of this micro political society will likely begin with a dialogue. Each will try to persuade the other of the rightness of his own values. If the two adversaries can be seen as citizens of an idealized world where thought experiments are routinely successful, then we can imagine the theories of Dworkin and Rawls working to set the terms of the dialogue. Each may try to assume the role of Dworkin's Hercules. Or each may try to reconstruct Rawls's original position to make choices on general rather than particular interests. Neither theory (it has been argued here) can resolve abortion disputes. But both theories assume convergence—right answers for Dworkin, an appeal to moral intuitions in Rawls. Such ambitions suggest at least the use of the theories to set up a moral dialogue between the two individuals.

What might be the strategy in such a dialogue? One obvious appeal that we all use in moral argument is the facts, either old or fresh. It is unlikely that any new facts can be introduced to abortion arguments, though the data presented here on teenage pregnancies and abortion pathologies may cause some partisans to rethink their positions. Unfortunately, abortion facts, like all facts, do not in themselves create moral values. Facts must be interpreted and given value, including that most central of "facts" for partisans—when an individual human life begins. Another appeal that is wonderful in its persuasive possibilities is the use of higher moral principles to order the moral principles found in abortion disputes. But, though much evidence exists that principles higher than the right to life routinely dominate political affairs (like equality), there is not much to suggest that higher moral principles will convert either of the two individuals to the other's point of view.

An appeal to exceptions or defeats for moral rules might fare better. Here the pro-choice individual can seek an agreement to permit abortions in a variety of exceptional circumstances, when for example the woman's life is in danger, on the grounds that even the highest moral rules have limits. But even if, as seems likely, some zone for exceptions can be carved out of the dialogue, the main area of disagreement will not be touched by this appeal. Exceptions, after all, are not rules. And the rules governing each individual conflict directly, not tangentially. Indeed, after allowing for that small number of exceptions that some (not all) pro-lifers accept — life of the mother, pregnancies from rape or incest — the disagreement between the two individuals remains substantial. It appears that the only way for the two moral agents to reach an agreement is to seek a political solution that will require some conceptual restructuring of their positions and some compromise. Do not be mistaken here. As moral agents subscribing to some of the more basic principles of civilized life — life, freedom of choice — neither of the two individuals should compromise. But if each individual defines himself as a member of a political society, then different imperatives may govern. If for one brief moment a political society can be seen as a rational agent — a third party to the moral dispute — then to the representative of the political society some compromise solution is unavoidable given the polarity on the moral issue and the discovery that there is no overriding right answer to the dispute. If each of the two moral agents identifies with the political society, then some compromise must be seen as unavoidable.

In one of the more memorable exercises in conflict theory, Anatol Rapoport (1960) recognizes distinctions among fights, games, and debates. The abortion conflict has ingredients of all three types of action. It is a conflict sometimes marred by violence and indifference to rules and customs; each side is engaged in tactical and even strategic behavior in competition with the opposition; and the disagreement is characterized by strong and earnest efforts to convert the adversary through reasoned argument. If, however, there is nothing in either moral theory or biology that will produce a conclusive case for one side or the other, then the fighting and gaming can go on indefinitely, or end in a "victory" for either pro-life or pro-choice. But neither side will be able to convince the opposition through a moral dialogue without some movement in the concepts and principles currently in use.

The transformation of the two moral agents into members of a political society may be hastened if each realizes that societies are unlike individuals. Suppose, to illustrate this, that each individual is internally divided over abortion issues, where pro-life and pro-choice wage their wars on the psyches of each individual rather than in the social space between them. Suppose also that each individual comes to terms with himself, allowing after the appropriate internal struggle for either pro-life or pro-choice to dominate. In such moral battles one moral principle or the other dominates the opposing moral principle. But in the larger space of social conflict, the dominance of moral principles takes the form of individuals dominating others. This is a difference with a bite. It is one thing to resolve a moral problem by allowing one principle to dominate another, but quite another to resolve problems by allowing one individual or group to dominate another—especially if neither side has an airtight argument on behalf of its claims. This is a point either moral agent can see by hypothetically constructing a collective outcome where the opponent's point of view is in its entirety authoritative for the political society.

If the conflict between the two individuals is taken to the collective or social level, then differences between principles and programs become important. An isolated moral agent can follow rules without important amendments. But if the rationality of an action depends on how others act, then where in one's rational framework a conflict is located and how much weight to give principles are rational considerations—more decisive even than the simple following of rules. Look first at types of conflict. A pure conflict is one on which both principles and programs are opposed. For example, the conflict between a National Socialist Party member and a member of the Jewish Defense League occurs at the levels of both moral principle and practical programs. A mixed conflict is then one on which either (a) an agreement on principle is followed by disagreement on program, or (b) an agreement on program occurs with disagreement on principle. An example of (a) might be two individuals who agree on the principle of sexual equality, but disagree on whether the Equal Rights Amendment ought to be passed. An example of (b) would be two individuals who agree on a program to draft both women and men into the armed services, but one supports the program because of a principle of equal regard and the other's support is based on a principle of social utility that urges the use of all types of useful personnel in satisfying military needs.

Abortion, appearances to the contrary, is not a pure conflict. Both sides subscribe to the same basic principle respecting the integrity of all human life. They simply disagree on some of the rules that the principle generates, and on what role the principle plays in human gestation. Or, some of the rules conflict directly with each other even though the underlying principle is shared. So abortion is a mixed conflict of the type where agreement on principle is followed by disagreement on programs; and the disagreement on programs is attributable to disagreements on the weight of the principle in the special conditions of fetal development.

The collective level might also reveal to the two moral agents how principles are chronically clustered. The social realization of one principle frequently affects the successful establishment of other, perhaps equally important, principles. Consider a principle like equality, for example. It is a cluster concept covering an interesting group of ideals — equality of outcome, equality of opportunity, equal regard, and many more. Rae (1981) has demonstrated how different senses of equality compete with each other. The principle of equality also competes with other principles — liberty, in traditional democratic thought. Some recent studies have suggested conflicts between equal access to education and ideals like family influence (Green, 1982). Now if principles are located in clusters of values and related in positive and inverse ways to other principles, then the enhancement of any principle must be evaluated in terms of both the values the principle introduces and the effects the principle has on other principles. If, for example, the enforcement of equal access to education results in the abandonment of family integrity, then equal access must be weighed in terms of what it abandons as well as its own desirability as a social ideal.

Principles, it is clear by now, are unlike rules. Following Dworkin (1978), we can note that principles have more or less weight in influencing decisions, but are not valid or invalid as rules are. If two rules are in conflict, only one of the rules can be held. Exceptions to rules are established by distinct rules that mark off zones of validity. The use of self-defense, for example, defeats the rule prohibiting killing by limiting its extension. Principles, by contrast, have no clear zones of validity and invalidity. They rather supply reasons for or against decisions, but do not mandate a decision. Two principles can thus oppose one another and both be maintained, though having perhaps the effect of cancelling out each other's influence. And the idea of weight instead of validity permits the thought that having more of one principle may require less of

another. The question posed for the life principle in abortion arguments is — how much of the principle will satisfy our needs given the
reduction it brings in other principles and programs?
Notice that the structure of the abortion dialogue has changed.
Neither of the two moral agents *as individuals* need raise that question. Or, if raised, the answers are rehearsed in the moral arguments over abortion — for pro-choice, none of the principle
(because it is irrelevant for abortion); for pro-life, all of the principle is needed. But if one's moral principles are to be realized only in
the context of a society polarized over the interpretation and application of the principle, then it is rational to look closely at the effects of the principle in governing social practices. This linkage of
principle to other issues — in this case, the effects of the principle in
social conditions — is a common form of political strategy. The two
moral agents need only consider the network of allied values and
expected outcomes in trying to reach a political accommodation
with each other.
A review of facts first. Over 1.5 million abortions are performed
annually in the United States. Three-quarters of the women getting
abortions are unmarried. One-third of all abortions are secured by
teenagers. These data can be interpreted in many ways. But one
reading that is beyond dispute is that substantial numbers of
women seek and get abortions because their lives do not tolerate
pregnancy and childbirth. How a legal prohibition of abortion will
affect these women can only be a matter for speculation. Pro-life
stresses the normative effects of law, claiming that the legality of
abortions encourages abortion, illegality would discourage abortions. Certainly since *Roe* abortions have increased dramatically,
though what other factors have contributed to the increase is difficult to know. Suppose, however, that a return to a pre-*Roe* state of
affairs would cut abortions by some impressive number, say two-
thirds, so that only 500,000 abortions were performed each year,
but performed illegally. Would this type of society be morally preferable to one in which 1.5 million abortions (and more) are performed legally?
The pro-life objection to this question is immediate. The comparison is repugnant, according to pro-life, because abortion is
homicide. One does not evaluate murder in terms of the reduction

in well-being for potential and actual murderers due to homicide's proscription by law. Here, however, the logic of principles in moral decisions is telling. An individual can rationally subscribe to a rule that prohibits some action, and then measure his morality in terms of how effectively he is governed by imperatives drawn from the rule. (This is the model of moral reasoning used to organize pro-life and pro-choice positions in Chapter 2.) But a society is less easily governed by rules when individuals are divided on the rules to use and no rational argument can override one position or the other. Abortion is not viewed as homicide by pro-choice. A rational *social* policy on abortion, as distinct from the reasoning that individuals may use, then looks to the background principles that bear on abortion; for if validity cannot be established on abortion claims, at least the weight of various principles can still be used to establish an abortion practice. And the cluster efforts of principles do urge us to look at alternative social states.

A comparison of hypothetical social states, where abortion is in one legal and in the other illegal, is more plausible if the life principle itself is allowed to make the comparison. Suppose, in social state *a,* that abortion is legal and the 1.5 million abortions figure is the reality of abortion practice. Now suppose a state *b,* where abortion is illegal and a half-million abortions are performed in circumstances more hazardous to women. Say further that 5 percent of these abortions result in severe damage or death to the women having them. This is a small percentage, but it covers a large number of women—25,000 women on the hypothetical construction. Other likely features of state *b*—the problems of enforcement, the psychological effects of forced pregnancy—can be ignored on the assumption that abortion might have its own undesirable effects on women. But stated just in terms of pathologies, it is not at all clear that *b* is preferable to *a* on the life principle; for a respect for human life must also weigh the damages done by prohibiting abortions.

Remember that weighing principles in this way may not be appropriate for individual decisions. An individual committed to either pro-life or pro-choice may decide on rules prohibiting or favoring abortion, and then follow a valid norm of action that does not tolerate the adjustments in social states suggested by using principles. For pro-life, state *b* is preferable; for pro-choice, state *a* is preferable. And in each case the preferability is established by interpreting the life principle in terms of rules that apply or do not apply the principle to abortion. The rules are among the contested issues in the abortion dispute, however. So there can be no right or wrong at the collective level of decisions on abortion practices. There is only the problem of how much weight to give various principles.

The larger point here is that societies are not rational in the same way that individuals are rational. Remember again the aggregation paradox applied to abortion at the end of Chapter 3. Individuals can rationally order alternatives, but the aggregation of these orderings can fail the tests of rationality employed at the individual level. Society, put briefly, does not always perform like an individual. In settling on abortion practices, an individual can use rules that the society cannot because the consistency and validity found in individual views on abortion do not occur across the social unit. Again, and this time for different reasons, the society does not meet the rational conditions found in individual choices. Social choice on abortion must use principles instead of rules, and compare social states in terms of these principles.

But the social choice between social states *a* and *b* is not clear on the life principle. Thus it is rational to look at other principles and values to settle on abortion practices for society. The profound changes taking place in human gestation, usually offered as a consideration against abortion (as with the "slippery slope" argument), may suggest a reasonable compromise between the two moral agents. The most certain time when a human being or person is present in gestation is late in term. The least certain time is immediately after conception. True, the pro-life individual asserts personhood from fertilization forward. But the closer is the reference of pro-life arguments to conception, the more vulnerable is the pro-life position to damaging counter-arguments. These arguments stress physical anomalies of person-hood, like "twinning" (the partitioning of a fertilized ova into two or more separate embryos), and the counter-intuitive nature of claims that a small cluster of cells is morally equivalent to a sentient human being. Any discussion of abortion with pro-life advocates discloses quickly the revulsion toward late abortions, when moral intuitions (formed on our sympathetic identification with palpable human forms) converge with any number of rational tests (sentience, viability, etc.) to tell us that abortion is morally wrong. This strong combination of intuition and theory does not seem to bear so forcefully on very early stages of gestation. It is also clear that the pro-choice individual has most difficulty in justifying late abortions, more success in defending early abortions.

The cleanest compromise is a social practice that permits abortions early in term, prohibits middle and late term abortions. Such a practice can appeal to the pro-life individual if some uncertainty is permitted a place in his arguments. He can be asked to reflect again on these two revelations: that (a) contrary to his own interpretations, biology will simply not provide categorical proof of the premises needed for pro-life, and (b) those with strong and reasoned moral views believe that pro-choice is justified. Is it a certainty that the embryonic stages of human gestation are morally equivalent to all later stages of growth? In the face of the facts that the fetus lives within the body of another and lacks a brain and nervous system early in term? There are pro-life advocates who are absolutely certain of this moral equivalence. But some may be moved to recognize the possibility that the opposition has some chance to be right in that area where the moral certainty of pro-life arguments is less assured — early in term.

Individuals can still maintain a strong and singular moral view on abortion. The pro-life moral agent, however, must face the failure of the life principle to govern the adversary. This failure of persuasion creates the need to join the principle to those values of privacy and bodily integrity held by pro-choice *if* a social practice is to be achieved. The compromise union is sealed by the role of the criminal law in abortion issues. The criminal law, first, is a clumsy instrument to enforce morals. The liabilities have been well rehearsed. Enforcing morals through coercion robs individuals of that capacity to choose that has been at the center of moral action at least since Plato, and insults moral agency by protecting individuals only against themselves (Hart, 1968) — though pro-life of course sees the unborn child as protected by laws against abortion.

The main problem that the criminal law has in enforcing a

proscription of abortion, however, is found in the conditions of early gestation. Early fetal life lacks the capacity to be harmed experientially. (No brain or nervous system is present.) The harm thesis can only be applied to early abortion by interpreting harm as deprivation. Depriving potential or embryonic persons of possible lives can be viewed as immoral. A belief in teleology, while eccentric on current scientific standards, would support the condemnation of all abortions, on the ground that end-states (what an entity is to be at the completion of a process) are as important as early stages of growth. But it is beyond imagination to conceive of the criminal law as regulating potential human life. The practical problems of such regulation are only part of the difficulty. The main problem is that the scope of a potentiality principle would bring under the protective cover of the law those individuals yet to be conceived. A society that regulates conception on the same reasons that it regulates abortion fails to recognize distinctions that normally make the criminal law intelligible.

Many features of abortion favor individual choice, not state regulation. The physical intimacy and dependence of the fetus within the woman's body, the strong arguments in liberal democracy against state control of an individual's body—abortion would be an obvious item for private choice were not homicide an issue. The compromise practice that joins pro-life and pro-choice must recognize these special qualities of human gestation. On the other hand, the development of a brain and nervous system introduces the fetus to the protective cover of the law as commonly understood. So this feature of fetal life must also be recognized in a compromise. Again, the social practice best recognizing these features would allow very early abortions, deny middle and late abortions.


3


Two problems with such a compromise practice have been identified early in our discussion. The first is that of effectively enforcing rules allowing only first-trimester abortions. The second is the general inappropriateness of encoding any moral criterion on abortion in the law given the absence of principles that can resolve abortion disputes. The two problems can be sensed as soon as the compromise practice is written into law. A rewrite of the Human Life Statute that represents the critical divisions in human gestation, for example, would read like this: "For the purpose of enforcing the obligation of the States under the Fourteenth Amendment not to deprive persons of life without due process of law, human life shall be deemed to exist from a point three months after conception." A similar rewording of the Human Life Amendment also can reflect these distinctions. The paramount status of the right to life can be duly affirmed. But then the word "person" can be applied to all human beings, "including their unborn offspring at every stage of their biological development from a point three months after fertilization." The exception for the woman's life can follow suit. Medical procedures preventing the death of a pregnant woman will not be prohibited. But "this law must require every reasonable effort to be made to preserve the life and health of the unborn child from a point three months after conception."

If this language has an eerie quality to it, read again the moral and biological discussion in Chapter 2. A three-months demarcation is no more awkward (or difficult to determine) than a demarcation set at fertilization. The absence of privileged status for conception, along with the gestation of brain and nervous system later in term, makes the dividing line of three months a rational point to justify regulation of abortion. The problem is in using the law as a regulatory device. Criminal penalties for abortions after three months would be impossible to enforce, given the reality that demarcations in term are usually imperfect (depending on an informal reconstruction of when the woman's last period occurred — as recalled by the woman) or the result of medical tests that can place the fetus at risk. Also, writing a three-months demarcation into law again encodes into the legal system a test morally offensive to the substantial number of people who believe that human life begins at conception.

A compromise abortion practice thus faces the problem that reasonable rules permitting early abortions, proscribing middle and late abortions, cannot be enforced by law. At this point the distinction between principle and program is helpful. A rational abortion practice can look to preserve some part of the main principles in abortion disputes through practices that do not involve regulation by the criminal law.

Funding of abortions is the most obvious of these alternative programs. Pro-life opposes public monies for abortion on two grounds: (1) it is unfair to ask individuals to allocate a portion of their own resources to pay for a practice they view as immoral; and (2) eliminating public funds is one way that social practices can be changed without making the practices illegal. Studies have indicated that, so far, the elimination of Medicaid funds for abortions has not reduced abortion rates in any important way, though the continued absence of federal money may yet be effective. The main point, however, is that programmatic issues like funding are the types of practices on which abortion disputes can be compromised without the use of the criminal law as an instrument of enforcement.

Seen as a compromise, public funding of abortion could not be included in a rational abortion practice. There are precedents for requiring individuals to support monetarily actions they view as immoral. Those opposed to the Viet Nam war were still required to pay taxes that went, in part, to finance that war. There are also any number of arguments demonstrating that resources are never entirely private. Since, for example, the skills that individuals bring to the marketplace are developed socially (schools, neighborhoods, etc.), society has a legitimate claim on some of the economic returns from those skills. Taxes, in short, are, in principle, fair. Whether they are fair extractions for any and all social measures is of course not so certain. Opposing state regulation of early abortion is a moral point of view one can rationally assume. Demanding that those not accepting this view nevertheless support it economically is quite another thing, precedents and arguments for collective resources notwithstanding.

A compromise requires both sides to give up something of value without compromising themselves as moral persons (Kuflik, 1979). Pro-life partisans, in the proposed practice, give up the logical consequence of their moral view. Abortion is immoral to pro-life precisely because it is (on their values) homicide. Thus the moral view of pro-life requires state prohibition of abortion. If pro-life is to give up the law as an instrument of enforcement, then it is reasonable to allow other programs to enforce their moral views. The denial of public funding thus is justified in two ways: as a response to the argument that individuals ought not to be required to pay for practices they view as immoral, and as the provision of programs to substitute for the criminal law in a compromise package legalizing early abortions.

One measure accommodating pro-choice needs on funding is to assign to early abortions only those public funds that have been volunteered by individuals. Several formulae can accomplish this. One method already tried in public financing of election campaigns is a check-off on income tax returns that expresses the individual's willingness to contribute. A second check-off box can be added. It would ask each individual to designate a small sum of their income tax to provide public money for abortion (through, say, Medicaid). Those individuals morally opposed to abortion can then refuse financial support. Since the groups opposed on abortion are sizable, the pro-choice contingent should be able to support abortion funding with little difficulty.

The standard objection to any such formula is—where will it end? Should then unpopular wars be subject to such an economic referendum? What about welfare funding in general (controversial in itself to many individuals)? It is true that societies must extract taxes from all on many divisive and controversial issues. To do otherwise would make publicly funded projects impossible, especially in an era of special-interest opposition. But on the assumption that abortion is really a special issue, divisive in the sharpest of moral ways, a check-off system of tax allocations may be the only political measure available for funding needs.

Public money can be volunteered for abortion, however, only in a state where morality and politics are independent of each other in abortion practices. For if no political imperative follows from moral principles, then moral agents are voluntary players on a stage where social persuasion rather than power is the broker. The two moral agents forming a social practice are still free to convince themselves and others of the morality of their views, and to use all noncoercive devices to do so. Many mediating institutions intervene in the formation of belief, or between thought and action. The family, the neighborhood association, the church—these are the institutions that substitute for the criminal law in regulating abortion in a compromise practice. Each side in the dispute can continue to use those institutions without recourse to criminal penalties and without mandatory public funding of abortion. What pro-life and pro-choice cannot do is continue to insist on exclusive political authority for their own moral views.

4

The activists on abortion (let them have the next-to-last word here) have mixed feelings about the future of abortion politics and the complex relationships of moral rights to social needs.

*Frohock:* Let me get on to another perspective. What relationship does abortion have to recently expressed concerns over population control? Do you see any connection whatsoever? Do you, in other words, connect abortion to the rights of women, or do you see it as part of a larger picture to control the population?

*Gordon:* In the United States I see it as simply the rights of women. I know I certainly don't favor the use of abortion as a way of controlling population. I feel that we need to use contraception as a way of controlling the population, and I think that overpopulation is a real serious problem. It's the latest thing now to say that it's not a problem, that it's just a matter of unequal distribution of goods and resources, and that's absurd. We're going to have this unequal distribution of goods no matter what, especially supported by the Right to Life people, who are not known to want to distribute their goods. They mainly represent reactionary politics. So the big pro-lifers in Congress are not for sending food overseas, they want to cut food overseas, they want to cut our lunch programs. What is this business of unequal distribution? Mainly the Right-to-Lifers created that, but those of us who really care about people, even those of us who want to have a more equitable distribution of food and shelter and so on, realize that in countries like India, Egypt, Mexico, unless you have population control it's a disaster you never recover from. You think we have illegal immigrants now. Wait until thirty years from now when Mexico has 120 million instead of 60 million people, which is the current rate of growth. See what's going to happen in the United States. We won't be able to build a Berlin Wall to control the number of people who come to the United States.

*Mrs. Willke:* You can take care of population by killing certain segments of your population, but that's no answer to population. You can't use abortion as a reason on population. It's an immoral way. You can kill old people too to lower your population, or you can kill certain other segments of your population but it's not a human answer to problems.

*Frohock:* So the fact that abortion is depleting the population is not one of your mainstream arguments against abortion.

*Mrs. Willke:* No, but I think it should be something the country looks at. In the years ahead, it's going to be something that's going to have dire complications.

*Dr. Willke:* We've been below replacement level for eight years now. We are rapidly going into a time where we're not going to be able to salvage this nation in terms of replacement population. ZPG passed us eight years ago. We have a heavy overhang of old people who haven't died yet, but you measure a population growth or decline by whether the women in fertile age group reproduce themselves and they've been well below reproduction levels for over eight years. So has the entire Western world. Now what that's going to do because this population bulge of baby boom kids is going to move into the dying age in another thirty or forty years, when they do, we're going to have this tremendous overhang of old people that Reagan spoke to the other day, only two taxpayers for every Medicare patient up there. Then we're going to have a completely distorted society. The only thing that's going to happen to this nation, I believe, is a huge influx of other people's coming in, of other racial strains and I think that's going to happen and it's invigorated our nation in ages past, perhaps it's going to do that again. I don't make a judgment as to whether we should stay with the same ethnicity we have. We're merely telling you that we won't have it fifty years from now.

*Frohock:* But if that turned around and we had an expansion of population, it would not then count as a reason to liberalize abortion.

*Dr. Willke:* You don't adjust population by killing people. That's the bottom line.

---

*DeCrow:* I think it's entirely a right of the individual. Regarding population problems — I think if it's decided that there are too few or too many people a society can offer incentives. In our society we give tax deductions for each additional child, so clearly that's an incentive to have more children, although I think the United States is in general confusion. We give great financial incentives to people to buy homes rather than to rent apartments. Maybe that's not so true anymore, but in general people have been penalized for being renters. That's I think an incentive to have large families because you're out there with all that grass and space, as opposed to giving financial incentives to people who live in one-bedroom apartments in a building in the city. So there are an awful lot of things we do by our tax structure which encourages or discourages population and I don't have problems with that. I guess if I were creating the tax structure I'd give whopping tax deductions for maybe one kid and two, and then none. But I guess that's a policy decision that is made ultimately by the electorate. The population decides, theoretically, voting people. So yes, I would say abortion should always be an individual right. There are other ways to deal with population problems—by giving incentives or disincentives. Let's take a different case. Let's say we can identify Down's syndrome children. I would say that the fact that we can identify Down's syndrome children should be heavily advertised and pregnant women should be encouraged to find out if they're going to have a Down's syndrome child, but not forced to abort. I think that it would be better not to bring a Down's syndrome child into the world but I don't think we should ever force abortions. I think there are probably an awful lot of people in the society who don't know there are some genetic defects they can discover now.

---

*Frohock:* You mentioned in your reference to a pragmatic or utilitarian defense of abortion that you felt that the consequences for society of abortion would be undesirable. You mentioned something about what would happen down the road if we pursued our liberal abortion policy. What do you see down the road if we continue the Roe-Wade logic for society?

*Jackson:* First of all I'm modest as to what I think I can see, because you can be surprised, and sometimes happily surprised, and I'm not a doomsday man. I believe there's going to be a Doomsday, but I'm not a doomsday man in the normal sense of that. So I'm not sure of this, but I'd say that if you have, without considerable abatement, without real letup, a continuation of present abortion policy, then you will be further building into the people's psyche, their psychology socially, a conviction that abortion is not only thinkable, but wise in appropriate circumstances. Appropriate circumstances really turns out to be what any couple wants, or what a woman wants. That will lead far more than it already is doing towards applying the same sort of criteria to the taking of the lives of very, very little children who might be deformed, and so to the taking of life, without their real say-so, of older people, or older deformed people. I also see down the road that insofar as the abortion decision was handed down by fear, that you are putting yourself in the hands of a central authority to declare—in this case the Supreme Court—such values to you without your having input into what they're saying. I should underline *Supreme Court* here, as opposed to Congress, because in Congress we do have some say-so, but not in the same way in the Supreme Court. And I see there that you're getting into another parallel dilemma which you see in the Iron Curtain countries, whereby they can one year or one decade say we will have abortion because we think it's good economically and politically and socially, and a decade later, or two decades later, say for precisely the same reasons we will stop abortions. And regardless of what we think about abortion, you're there dealing with an imposition upon the will of everybody without their say-so of the dictates of a central committee which thinks in its wisdom that such and such is economically and otherwise good. So I think there's a trespassing upon, I see down the road a trespassing upon what we might think as private citizens, quite apart from what I think would be the brutalization of our psyches.

---

*Hughes:* . . . But life is not the question. I think I told you this. I don't think that's what it's about. It's much deeper than that. This is not the level that we're talking about. We're talking about sexuality, we're talking about reproduction, we're talking about women and men, we're talking about resources in the society—there's a lot going on. It's not just the question of life.

*Frohock:* One of the questions I always ask in these interviews is how you think the other side got their values? I've talked to both sides in the last several months and I'm impressed with the sincerity of beliefs on both sides.

*Hughes:* I think it's a different world view. I think they think that we should not control our environment, that they have almost a fatalistic point of view. For instance, they're opposed to euthanasia also. You take what God dishes out, that kind of view. Maybe some people look at suffering as good, or at least not as bad, or as what you should expect in life—very different values from the ones that I have.

*Frohock:* Suppose I ask you to isolate the single most important value that helps explain your views on abortion. We went over a cluster of them, and one of the problems I have is sorting out this cluster, on both sides. There seem to be a lot of things going on that I don't understand. If you dug really deep into your own system of values would there be anything you could isolate that would explain how it is? Would it be the individual woman having the choice? Or is it part of the whole cluster in your case also, a cluster that is difficult to sort out from the general world view?

*Hughes:* I don't think it's one thing. There's a certain ideology which I really feel is a rationalization to back up my view. I think both sides do that. I think that the feelings and the actions come first and the ideology comes second a lot of the time. I believe in the quality of life—that's important to me, not just quantity. And I view this as a world with limited resources. I want to potentiate my life skills, myself, my own resources. A lot of women I've talked to who are having abortions are upwardly mobile, hard-working, middle class—I think that plays into it. Materialism is part of it. I think some people view materialism as bad but I don't. Our culture is materialistic. If I lived in another culture I'd have different values. I think there's a certain amount of that involved.

---

*Frohock:* But to me you're suggesting almost a social revolution.

*Kisil:* It will come. It may not be in our lifetimes. It will come; it has to come. Because you see right will always win out. He gives us the free will; we do ourselves in. Then finally a change will come and He will pick us up and put it back together, and unfortunately, the hurtful part is that some people's children will get lost. We have no guarantee that our children will be on the good side, just because we think we're good. We can only hope and try, and cope with each problem as it comes. We can never give up trying. I think that unfortunately that some of the people who really want to improve things, and if things were improved you really wouldn't have teenage pregnancies and abortions—I think some of them come on too strong, like "holier than thou" and you can't preach to people. You can't go around up on a pedestal like you're so holy, and you're not. You just kind of have to hope and by your example spread some good. In the meantime, you know people aren't doing what you think is right—you have no right to judge them. You still have to take them as they are and just keep hoping people will change. I think that some of these very astringent "holier than thou" people are thwarting people from turning around. I think there is a happy medium. God didn't go around with a long face; I understand from things I read that He had quite a sense of humor. And they go around so straight and so intense and so judgmental.

## 5

Any author who tries to follow the statement above has to have a strong belief in his own ability to draw conclusions. The appropriate conclusions to draw here, however, are more like summaries.

A resolution of abortion disputes is best achieved in the form of a compromise, where (a) early abortions are permitted, (b) there is no mandatory public funding for any abortions, and (c) the criminal law is not used to regulate abortion. The obvious question that arises at this point is — how are abortions after the first trimester to be regulated in the absence of the criminal law? The obvious answer is, by means of civil law. A variety of legal devices is available to discourage almost any practice. Given that the appropriate civil laws are passed, governments can urge hospitals and clinics to confine abortions to early stages of term, using (among other devices) the positive and negative incentives that state funding *in general* provides. Also, limiting abortions to the first trimester can be joined to measures requiring resuscitation of all infants with a chance to survive. Since resuscitation measures are required currently by law, no further regulation of abortion practices is needed. First trimester abortions in any case will not (on existing medical technology) occasion resuscitation.

If these three propositions are reasonable expressions of compromise, much of the abortion dispute can be defused. But any abortion practice and its specifications in the political reality of American politics will naturally be a product of competing groups and government syntheses. No resolution formed in the abstract space of theoretical discussion can predict how abortion problems will be settled, though the arguments developed here at least call attention to some of the limits and possibilities of rational solutions.

It may be, of course, that abortion is one of those issues that vanishes, or is radically transformed, with changes in technology. The effects of technology can be seen on narrow legal issues. For example, the *Roe* decision granted states the right to restrict second-trimester abortions to hospitals on the grounds that such abortions carried higher medical risks than earlier abortions. At the time of the decision, second-trimester abortions were induced by injecting a salt solution or prostaglandins into the amniotic sac. In the years following *Roe,* however, dilation and evacuation became widely used in midterm abortions. The risks in this latter therapy are much lower than in amniotic injections. Obstetricians accordingly changed their recommendations, allowing mid-term abortions to be performed in outpatient clinics instead of requiring hospitalization for the procedure. But several states and cities continued to require hospitalization for abortions later than three months in term. In 1983 the Court addressed a number of laws and ordinances regulating access to abortion services. The Court declared unconstitutional an Akron, Ohio, hospitalization requirement, determining in doing so that women have the right to choose whether their abortions are to be performed in hospitals or not. The change in surgical procedure thus occasioned changes in the constitutionality of abortion laws.

But grander effects of technology may yet be felt on abortion practices. A perfectly safe contraceptive for both sexes may reduce, even eliminate, unwanted pregnancies if distributed widely. An Orwellian state may require consumption of a preventive substance, and then issue licenses-cum-antidotes for planned parenthood (state regulated). Or, more congenial to the liberal temperament, an abortion pill may be developed that renders abortion as private an act as birth control. That such a pill is well within current technological possibilities is undeniable. In April of 1982, a French biochemist, Dr. Etienne-Emile Baulieu of the Bicetre Hospital, announced to France's Academy of Sciences the development of a compound that inhibits the action of progesterone in women, a hormone needed to sustain pregnancy. The effect of the pill is to slough off the uterine lining, including the fertilized ovum, in bringing on a menstrual period. Barring complications (the drug may have an unwanted effect on the adrenal glands), the compound, or one like it, may be used to induce abortion once pregnancy is recognized. (*New York Times,* April 19, 1982.) The moral and economic costs of monitoring a device totally in the control of the individual woman will likely deter all sides in the abortion dispute from pressing ahead with state regulation of abortion. If early abortions have to be accepted by American society on technological grounds, it is at least comforting to know that arguments on ideals and compromise also favor them.

*Frohock:* Now suppose a pill is developed that permits the woman to abort privately, without use of clinics or hospitals in the first trimester. What would this do to the use of the criminal law as an instrument to regulate abortions?

*Hyde:* Well, that's really the same question as the IUD and you now get into the realm of enforceability. I don't believe that such proscriptions against the IUD would be enforceable. And such an after-conception pill, which is not contraception really, but would be abortifacient — I think such pills would be available whether they were criminal or not. You know it's like handgun control. They would be around. I don't like laws that can't be enforced. The surgical abortion is what I think the law can legitimately proscribe and I do not doubt that these medical and chemical compounds will be developed which will do what you just said, if they don't already. I would much prefer a contraceptive pill rather than one that terminates the conceptive from the wall of the uterus because it is my belief that fertilization as a process, when it is completed that you do have a human life there. You have a genetic package that is very special and is indeed alive, a member of the human species and if given time and nourishment will be a little boy or little girl. I deplore those things, but I doubt very much if the law would be competent to reach them and proscribe them.

*Frohock:* Do you think that we in our generation will see a time when first-term abortions might be beyond the regulation of the law because of technological developments of this type, and that the law, if there is an anti-abortion statute passed, would be concerned with middle and late term abortions?

*Hyde:* I think that's possible. I think if medical compounds that involve a minimum of prescription or treatment, that sort of thing, I think they will abound and the surgical abortion may well become a thing of the past. And if that happens, why it happens, but the furor about abortion as it now stands will not have been lost because it has a great educational value. A lot of people have never understood the physiology, never understood anything about it, are learning a great deal, particularly the lyrical treatment of conception that was contained in *Newsweek*'s January 11th [1982] issue. Absolutely lyrical.

*Frohock:* Then you don't think that members of Congress would support a measure that would make an abortion pill illegal.

*Hyde:* No, I frankly don't. That is my assessment. I don't think so. It's too close to the notion of contraception, which is a part of our society, and I don't think we could legislate against it.

Finally, abortion presents to the political theorist a lesson in state reasoning. Put in simplist terms, society is least like an individual when divided over a moral issue. The rules comfortably used by

individuals to direct their own actions on abortion issues do not
work at all to direct society; for no agreement exists on interpretations, extensions, and exceptions. A social decision on an abortion
practice must balance principles, not follow rules. A compromise
on abortion may appeal to all sides if a balance of principle is seen
as the only logic that a society can follow when moral disputes cannot be resolved by the rules of morality.

The last word in this book will be provided by neither your
author nor the partisan activists who have such strong convictions
on abortion. Instead we will listen to the thoughts of a young
woman (who will remain anonymous) who recently had an abortion. Like all who actively participate in an experience, her observations (at least to me) have that internal quality never found in formal reconstructions of experience. No comments, no analysis, will
follow. Let's just read and reflect on one individual's insights
formed from experiencing the event that is currently exercising so
many in our society. (I have changed only the names of people and
some places and deleted one paragraph late in the interview to protect her anonymity. Otherwise, except for very light edit-
ing—mainly dropping redundant, hesitating, and "like" and "you
know" phrases—the interview is printed here in its entirety.)

*Frohock:* When did you have your abortion?

*Respondent:* April Fool's Day, this year. It hasn't been too long ago. I had
to pick a landmark. It seemed to go along with the general feeling. I don't
know. I went up to Rochester. There is a doctor up there who runs a clinic.
I had it done there. I was tested at the Health Center here. I kind of got an
overview of their services too.

*Frohock:* How far along were you in term?

*Respondent:* Approximately eight weeks. I was about six when I found out.
I knew, pretty much, from about four or five weeks on, and I was home in
California visiting my parents at the time. The day I left I should have gotten the old period and I came back on the 22nd of March and it was pretty
quick, as far as finding out and taking care of it. There wasn't too much of
a decision to be made. It was a very—having contemplated what if before, I
always came up with this decision that, being single, being in school—that I
would most likely do that. There was still a lot of contemplating and won-
dering as to what the different options were and nothing else seemed to fit
as well as that as far as an answer.

*Frohock:* Was it as easy, easier or harder to go through with it than you had anticipated?

*Respondent:* Probably about the same. Friends of mine had been through it before. And I had actually gone to the hospital with one girl. She had a pretty unique experience in that she went and stayed overnight and had a surgical, a D&C, performed while she was asleep. And then the next morning I went back and got her and she managed to hide emotionally what she was going through. She really wanted to keep the child and it was there, a definite. I was a year out of high [school] and she was two years out. She was just working at a job in a hamburger place and making minimum wage and no resources at all. The man was totally out of the picture. He had moved across the country and didn't want anything to do with it. She was just in such circumstances where it would have been unreasonable to even consider keeping the child. So my friends and I put a lot of pressure on her not to keep it. Also, she just was a very immature person by nature and [we] couldn't any of us conceive of her raising a child and in fact she had a jaded outlook. One of my friends in high school had gotten pregnant at fourteen and had a baby and got support from her mother all the way through and had the child and my girlfriend kept looking at this, well she did it, I can do it. It wasn't the same circumstance. I was pretty well decided. It was still hard. It's easy to say I would have an abortion if I got pregnant, but once you're pregnant it's very difficult to come around to that conclusion. I was morning sick. Even at that point, whether it was nerves or whether it was actual physical onset was hard to say. Still you feel good 'cause you're pregnant and it's a very hard feeling to come around to doing away with it. It's a very empty feeling afterwards to realize that you no longer have that special, society deems it as a special, precious thing, and all of a sudden you're not. It's kind of a rude awakening afterwards.

*Frohock:* Did you consult with friends before making the decision or carrying through a decision you had already contemplated making?

*Respondent:* I was in a very unique situation. I lived with five people last year, four people and myself, another girl and three guys. When I was away during spring break, before spring break, and I came back, my boyfriend came and picked me up at the airport and he said to me, "Paul and Susan are getting married." Paul was one of the males who lived in the house and Susan was his girlfriend who had been hanging around the house quite frequently. The first thing that dawned on me was—Susan's pregnant. And she was. And she had decided that at all cost she would keep the child, which made it doubly difficult for me to see them going through that. My boyfriend lived in the same house. We weren't going out when we first started living there. So that additionally complicated the situation. And, as a little note on frequency of occurrence, another guy who lived in the house got his girlfriend pregnant along about the same period of time. When I went to the Health Center and the woman down there—I had mentioned Susan and she said what are you doing over there. It was funny. She was the first person I told that I was pregnant. Well, I had told her when I got home, just feeling a common ground, and even though knowing what she was going to do probably was not going to jive with my decision. It was still kind of comforting to talk to someone who was pregnant. You know, sit there and go "Don't you feel like shit?" But she was home the morning I came back from the test, so she was the first person I saw and I held out for about three days without telling my boyfriend. I was going to do it by myself and not involve him. It was a whole encompassing of different factors that just tended to affect me. I'm Catholic, which gave me a nice guilt trip on "Oh no, what you are doing is wrong." My boyfriend is very Catholic and it was—if I tell him he was going to say no. The whole thing was to keep it from him. And then it turned out he was very cooperative of my decision and agreed with it. It all worked out well.

*Frohock:* So you did consult with him?

*Respondent:* Yes, I had found out on a Thursday and finally got up the nerve to tell him on Saturday night, and proceeded to make arrangements that week.

*Frohock:* What would you have done if he had resisted?

*Respondent:* I wanted him to, I really wanted him to say no, you can't do this. It's hard to say. The thing that petrified me the most was the procedure itself, because I had heard horror stories from girlfriends of mine who had been through it, that it was extremely painful, that the whole thing was degrading. I really had a lot of fear about the procedure itself. I don't know if that, wrapped up with his resisting, would have resulted in keeping the child. I tend to think not. I tend to think our relationship may not have survived the crisis. I think I would have, for a while, I would have said yes, okay, you want to keep it, we'll keep it. But I think that reason would have held out and I would have eventually, not eventually, probably rather quickly, being that it is not good to let time pass—I think I would have stuck with the decision.

*Frohock:* Did it affect your relationship with your boyfriend?

*Respondent:* Made us a lot closer. We had just started dating three months prior. Our relationship was just kind of superficial, not really getting too much into emotions and revealing our inner selves. But that definitely made it happen and the relationship is still going rather strong. I was afraid. I really thought that it had a lot of potential, our relationship, and I was very hesitant. You hear all these rumors [that] it is never going to last. After you get pregnant, forget it. Even if he gets you through the crisis, that's it afterwards. I had a lot of fear about that too.

*Frohock:* Did you feel you had adequate counseling?

*Respondent:* I had no counseling professionally at all. When I went into the Health Center, they did tests and I sat in the waiting room. I waited eternally, probably because I was very anxious. When I got the little slip I looked at the things on it and managed to figure it out pretty much. And I knew to begin with. I was examined by the doctor, confirmed, and then she asked me if I knew what I wanted to do. I said, "Well, I think it would be an abortion." And she gave me a slip of printed out literature, I think it gave about six or seven doctors in Syracuse. Then she recommended a doctor in Rochester highly. She didn't think Planned Parenthood was a good place to go. Also the Rochester place was considerably cheaper. Like $100 cheaper than going to Planned Parenthood. She really down played Planned Parenthood, which surprised me. She said the counseling that they offer consists of three sessions you have to go through. I think the first one is a counseling session — How are you going to pay for this is the paramount question. And then you have to be confirmed pregnant even though you may already have had it confirmed. And then the third appointment is for the procedure itself. So she said that could really wear on you. And I didn't think I needed to go through three appointments. I ended up going to Rochester from that. She gave me no input at all on abortion. She didn't go into the procedure, she didn't outline any options. Just asked me what I was going to do and gave me information to support my point.

*Frohock:* Do you think if you would have had counseling from a pro-life organization that it would have made a difference?

*Respondent:* It would have made it harder emotionally, given that I know the nature of the counseling. I don't think it would have changed my mind, no.

*Frohock:* Afterwards, was it relief or regret that dominated?

*Respondent:* Immediately after walking out of the doctor's office was complete relief. A situation that had been upon me for about a month at that point was taken care of. It was resolved. Later on there were a lot of, not really feelings of regret, but feelings of guilt in one way and just being sorry the whole situation ever came about. I think if I had carried the pregnancy to term that I would have felt that way about that, too. So I don't think there is really a way to win. Just basically regret for the situation and not for going through with the abortion. Although looking back on that, I don't know if I could do it again. It's funny, because the procedure is not — there was nothing to it, to put it bluntly. Contrary to what you hear — friends of mine had said so and so did this and she was in so much pain and it was just awful. It was not awful. It was over in a matter of minutes. It's just, if you look at it logically, if I were to get pregnant again, there's nothing to it. But could I do it again is another story. Psychologically I think a lot of it is cultural. It takes a toll on you. It's hard to explain it. I was talking to my boyfriend about coming in and speaking to you. It's funny, . . . it's just like any other factor in your life that made a dent somewhere along the line. Some weeks, or some days it seems to be a big thing and then other days it seems to be nothing. So it kind of depends on what your other contributing factors are as to how you reflect on it at any given point.

*Frohock:* Did you tell your parents?

*Respondent:* My parents are divorced and are both living in California. I called my mother up later on in the week, Tuesday or Wednesday, when I finally pulled myself together enough. I spoke to my sister throughout the whole thing. My sister was very supportive and she's younger, she's two years younger, she was nineteen at the time. My sister, to my knowledge, does not even have sex yet. She's quite the opposite I guess you can say. But she was very understanding and seemed to feel that having the abortion was the right way to go. I called up my mother on the phone and given the 3,000 mile distance I told her to sit down. I said, "I have to tell you something. Get on the other phone. Sit down and relax." It's like, "What's wrong?" I said, "Nothing's wrong." And then I just had to blurt it out real quick. I was pregnant but I'm not anymore. That was my whole one liner and she's like, hang on just a minute. She just kind of pulled herself together, and went on to talk to me. Apparently she had been in the same boat and had an abortion when it was illegal, before '73. And [she] just gave me very sketchy details and said that she had to be declared by a psychologist, psychiatrist, that she couldn't deal with having another child. It was after, there are three kids in our family, after she had the three. She really didn't go into too much at all. Just to tell me that I wasn't alone and that she felt I made the best decision that I could given the point. And was everything okay, and the general mother concerns. She was very good about it. I haven't told my father. I don't think there is a need to, I don't feel a need to, and I don't think he would especially want to know. I don't know how he would feel about it. I tend to think that he would agree that I made the right decision.

*Frohock:* Would you have had an abortion if it had been illegal and you had been in your mother's position before 1973? Would that have made a difference for you?

*Respondent:* I thought about that a lot, especially on the point that if it wasn't available, people wouldn't be doing it as readily, that women still seek it out but that they wouldn't look at it as an option. And I tend to agree with that in the general sense. As far as me, I wouldn't have gone to a back-room abortionist. If there were a way, if I had known at that time that there was an option, that perhaps there was a doctor around that some people in need had referred, or if there was a safe way to do it, I would have. I may have elected to go through what my mother went through to do it legally, within an illegal framework. I really had reservations about having a child and still to this day if I were to be pregnant right now . . . I think there is a time and a place and I have very strong feelings about my freedom and am not willing to have that impeded on at this point.

*Frohock:* Would you have children at some stage in your life?

*Respondent:* One thing that I always had reservations about was having kids in general and I always thought maybe one, very well planned child at the right time. And now for some strange reason, I can't wait. It's really funny how that's changed it around for me but it's still held from the point of being pregnant to now, and if now were the right time, I would be pregnant real quick. That has been a really strange phenomenon for me.

*Frohock:* Was it the pregnancy or some kind of unworked out regret . . . what do you think is causing you to feel that way now?

*Respondent:* It was a really good feeling being pregnant. It's hard to explain. Just the fact that you are giving life and to look at it at that point. Even though you are morning sick, it still . . . there is a genuine . . . it made yourself or your body really precious. Probably something that you don't look upon every day as you bump into things, but it made you careful. You kind of view yourself in a different light. I think it was the pregnancy that is making me feel this way, not necessarily a regret. I know I can have kids now, I know I don't have any of those problems. It seems like I would be content to wait but when I think about it, it's that feeling that I guess I would be getting back. And also I am an education major and I've always had an inkling towards kids. But this has been really strange to feel this way after feeling so wishy-washy about it before. Yeah, maybe someday.

*Frohock:* Does your boyfriend have these feelings? Has he been affected in any way, that way, by the experience?

*Respondent:* Coming from a very Catholic family, I think the next question after the day we got married would be, when are we going to have a family? For him, he likes kids, but by the same token he's willing to give you the freedom that you want. So he's very workable with that, I guess you could say. He would definitely want children, I think, regardless of whether or not I had had an abortion. He would feel that way. I think both of us are a little more ready than we would have been if the situation hadn't happened.

*Frohock:* Did you see any trace of regret in him afterwards?

*Respondent:* Yes, both of us really regretted having to do it. That's probably the best way to put it. Regretting having to do what we did, but always feeling that that's what we had to do. So kind of a double justification there. He hid his feelings quite well. The one thing he said to me that really bothered me was — I started feeling I had a real conflict with killing the child, or whatever terms you want to put it in, my Catholic upbringing led me to believe I was doing. I knew he was having the same conflict but it was inevident. I stopped going to church. I never really went regularly, but I stopped altogether. I just can't deal with that too at this point. Furthermore, I feel like a big hypocrite. We've been living together. I use birth control, sometimes I don't. I've had an abortion. I feel like a hypocrite going to church. And I asked him, "How do you get away scot-free with this?" And I said, "You aren't doing it, that's it, isn't it?" And he said, "Yes. It's not me." So if it ever came time to point a finger at the one who did the abortion it would be me and not him. And it kind of bothered me that you both create the situation but the woman ends up with the real problem. I guess the man, or men, could, too, if they put themselves in that position. But it's easy not to and who would.

*Frohock:* You stopped going to church. Along about this time or earlier?

*Respondent:* I had always gone periodically and always felt that I fit in, no problem. I had had a lot of problems with Catholicism in general because of its doctrines and the way it comes out. In a way I feel alienated. But I have gone. I was going pretty regularly with him as a matter of fact. And being that that was right before Easter, we still went afterwards. I was very sensitive to any slurs that they made during the sermon about abortion, which they make a lot. Finally we were in Buffalo this summer visiting a relative of his. We went to church in the morning. In the mass they will say something like, "For all the starving children in Ethiopia, and Lord hear our prayers." And the priest said, "For all of the murdered unborn children of the world . . . ," and that was it. That hit home. I said to [my boyfriend] — and it really upset him because he would like me to go and feel the part — I said, no more. That was it, I'm sorry, I don't care if that was in

Buffalo, and I don't have to listen to that here. I said no more. And since that day, I have not gone, nor do I intend to go until I reach some kind of a resolution within myself.

*Frohock:* So you have not reached a resolution within yourself?

*Respondent:* I float it back and forth, I guess. When I read the literature on abortion, my first inclination was pro-choice — [but] it just does not even have a case. I'm sorry there's no way that they could even . . . their argument looks like a sieve with holes in it. Pro-life, I mean it's solid. They say it's life and you can't kill it. Where else do you go from there? Pro-choice always seems to be justifying itself. This, that, and the other thing. Then even the person who holds pro-choice as the highest, I mean you still talk about third trimester abortions and you still have problems with those. There is too much diversity in the camp, for one thing, and it's hard to get a rational argument together. Because I can't just tag myself as being very pro-choice, and saying above all, women have the right to decide, because I have problems with that. I definitely believe that women should be able to decide, but then again, if I was to enforce my morals, there would be conditional things placed on that. So it's really hard to say. If I talk about my own situation, I'm not really sure if I was justified in the moral sense to do what I did. To put it plainly, it was an inconvenience at the time. I'm sure that I am a very resourceful person, and my boyfriend is also. I'm sure we could have made do one way or the other. In that sense, it bothers you.

*Frohock:* Would you see yourself some point in the future receiving sacraments again?

*Respondent:* Well, if we end up getting married, it will definitely be in a Catholic church. I think I am in the process of just deciding that there are some things in my life that are none of the church's business. And that's probably the only way that I find I am going to be able to reconcile that. Just to treat them as so, and to reconcile having a belief in God, to reconcile that between myself and Him and not through an institution that thinks I am wrong or whatever. And just hope that I am, in the end, given the old heaven and hell proposition, that I come out on the longer end of the stick. It's having that ingrained in you from a child early, early on, that if you committed the ultimate boo-boo, that was it. It kind of makes you very leery.

*Frohock:* It's part of the doctrine of Catholicism that there is always the possibility of the sacrament of Penance and then, after that, Communion.

*Respondent:* I don't know if I buy that for this one. It's strange, but you have to deal with the whole realm of, first of all, was it a sin? Second of all to come out with it in confession, I can't even imagine. I think I'm still at the point of whether or not what I did is wrong. I don't think I am willing to grant the Catholic Church a sin in this case. I really don't believe it was.

*Frohock:* Would you go to Communion?

*Respondent:* I really don't know. At this point I think I removed myself. There are a lot of people who will not go to Communion unless they go to confession and receive Penance. But I think that if Larry and I were to get married, let's say this summer, and I was still at this point mentally about the whole thing, I would go through it as a ceremony, as a ceremonial thing, and treat it as such mentally, because I think that I have just put so much distance between myself and the church that it no longer carries the religious significance that it should. So that's probably how I would handle it.

*Frohock:* Do you see this ever happening to you again? Are you more careful?

*Respondent:* Definitely more careful. Without a doubt more careful. I don't think it will happen again, given the law of time, provided the relationship pans out as I think it will now. Within a year, if I were to become pregnant I would probably be ready to handle having a child. Between now and then I'm just being careful.

*Frohock:* Would abortion then in your view be a rational form of birth control?

*Respondent:* Of birth control?

*Frohock:* Yes.

*Respondent:* I don't think so.

*Frohock:* That's all I can ask. Is there anything you'd like to add?

*Respondent:* . . . I would have liked to be counseled a little bit more than I was, just to have somebody to talk to, I guess would be the thing, more than . . . is this the right decision, let's go over it, let's look at it rationally. That I didn't need. That you can do by yourself. But probably the scariest, the thing that I would like to see them do is have somebody that has been through it before who can explain. I mean to have the procedures explained on a piece of paper doesn't say much. I kept looking for something more, like a personal opinion or I don't know what. But I called the Health Center afterwards, about a week after, and I said, "Look, I want you to keep my name and my number and if anybody wants to talk about it, that asks or whatever, I'd be more than willing to sit down with them." I said I don't want to counsel as far as an opinion on what they should do. But if somebody wanted me to, I would sit down and tell them what I went through so that they could better make a decision. One of the girls that I live with now was through it. About a month after me, two months, and with a very similar experience dealing with the male, "God, I carry it all," and "Whatever happened to him," "Why doesn't he have guilt." Or I guess when they clam up about it, it's even more frustrating because you demonstrate a lot of your [feeling], as a lot of acting out. But what they say about men not understanding, I have a hard time going with that one. I think that by and large men are becoming a little more responsive now and should deserve to be treated as such. I know a lot of women's literature is just dealing with [the woman] and should focus more on the man. And I don't know, maybe it has made a greater impact on my boyfriend, her boyfriend, than they let on. I could go on forever.

*Frohock:* Do people know about your experience?

*Respondent:* My boyfriend did not want anyone to know. He didn't tell anybody. I found that I had to vocalize. I had a pretty heavy work commitment at the time, so I had to tell. . . . We had to borrow a car to drive to Rochester, which brought on another explanation. I was constantly sick, which led the other roommates to be in on it. And then my closer friends, and two professors, just for work that I was incapable of doing at the time. I had a real hard problem. And then I had a nonviolent studies class the second semester and we dealt with the Hatch Amendment and we were sitting around. There were about a dozen of us, largely male, and it was obvious that none of them had been through it, the ones that were speaking anyway, and they were all talking very right-to-life orientation, which I found strange amongst mostly sophomores, a few juniors in college, and it was the same professor that I had spoken to. After the class she said, how did you hold up on that one? Because it was just a period of two to three weeks [since] I had gone through it. I said pretty good. But it bothers me that people will talk about the subject without maybe realizing that somebody's been through it. They could be sitting right there, giving statistics. And she said to me at the time, the professor, that maybe that's the problem. Maybe enough women aren't coming out and saying yes, I have done it, so what's the big deal. By the same token—my boyfriend is a law student. He's probably going to end up in politics. Heaven knows where my future is going to take me and to have somebody dredge it up out of the past, and say, look. And you never know if 20-30 years from now it's going to be taboo. I don't think it will be. But this society could take a turn and it could really work against you. When you think about it in those terms, you have to be careful, unfortunately.

## For Further Reading

Dworkin, Ronald. *Taking Rights Seriously* (Cambridge, Mass.: Harvard University, 1978), pp. 14–80.

Green, Thomas. "The Statistical Study of Social Ideals: A Speculative Inquiry into Method," Paper presented to the Good Society discussion group, Syracuse University (April 27, 1982).

Hart, H.L.A. *Law, Liberty, and Morality* (New York: Vintage, 1963).

Kuflik, Arthur. "Morality and Compromise," in Pennock and Chapman, eds., *Compromise in Ethics, Law, and Politics: Nomos XXI* (New York: New York University, 1979), pp. 38–65.

Pennock, J. Roland, and Chapman, John W., eds. *Compromise in Ethics, Law, and Politics: Nomos XXI* (New York: New York University, 1979), especially the articles by Martin P. Golding, Theodore M. Benditt, and Arthur Kuflik.

Rae, Douglas. *Equalities* (Cambridge, Mass.: Harvard University, 1981).

Rapoport, Anatol. *Fights, Games and Debates* (Ann Arbor: University of Michigan, 1960).

Sher, George. "Subsidized Abortion: Moral Rights and Moral Compromise," *Philosophy and Public Affairs* 10 (1981): 361–72.

# BIBLIOGRAPHY

## General Studies

Allen, James Edward. *Managing Teenage Pregnancy: Access to Abortion, Contraception and Sex Education.* New York: Praeger, 1980.

Barr, Samuel Jacob. *A Woman's Choice.* New York: Rawson Associates, 1977.

Bellairs, Ruth. *Developmental Processes in Higher Vertebrates.* Coral Gables, Fla.: University of Miami, 1971.

Bok, Sissela, et al. "Case Study: The Unwanted Child: Caring for a Fetus Born Alive After an Abortion." *Hastings Center Report* 6 (October 1976): 10-15.

Bond, J. R., and Johnson, C. A. "Implementing a Permissive Policy: Hospital Abortion Services after *Roe v. Wade.*" *American Journal of Political Science* 26 (1982): 1-24.

Brady, James, and Humiston, Gerald. *General Chemistry: Principles and Structure.* New York: John Wiley and Sons, 1978.

Connery, John R. *Abortion, The Development of the Roman Catholic Perspective.* Chicago: Loyola University Press, 1977.

Cowan, Ruth B. "Women's Rights through Litigation: An Examination of the American Civil Liberties Union Women's Rights Project, 1971-1976." *Columbia Human Rights Law Review* 8 (1976): 373-412.

Deckard, Barbara. *The Women's Movement.* New York: Harper & Row, 1975.

Dellapenna, J. W. "The History of Abortion: Technology, Morality, and Law." *University of Pittsburgh Law Review* 40 (1979): 359-428.

Denes, Magda. *In Necessity and Sorrow: Life and Death in an Abortion Hospital.* New York: Basic Books, 1976.

Francke, Linda Bird. *The Ambivalence of Abortion.* New York: Random House, 1978.

Furstenberg, Frank, Jr.; Lincoln, Richard; and Menden, Jane, eds. *Teenage Sexuality, Pregnancy and Childbearing.* Philadelphia: University of Pennsylvania, 1981.

Gordon, Linda. *Woman's Body, Woman's Right.* New York: Penguin Books, 1977.

Gordon, Sol; Scales, Peter; and Everly, Kathleen. *The Sexual Adolescent.* North Scituate, Mass.: Duxbury Press, 1979.

Gould, K. H. "Family Planning and Abortion Policy in the United States." *Social Service Review* 53 (1979): 452-63.

Greenglass, Esther. *After Abortion.* Toronto: Longman Canada Ltd., 1976.

Green, Thomas. "The Statistical Study of Social Ideals: A Speculative Inquiry into Method." Paper presented to the Good Society discussion group, Syracuse University (April 27, 1982).

Hall, Robert E. *Abortions in a Changing World.* New York: Columbia University Press, 1970.

Hardin, Garrett James. *Stalking the Wild Taboo.* Second edition. Los Altos, Calif.: W. Kaufman, 1978.

Lambert, Jean. "A Conceptual Approach to Decisions about Pregnancy and Abortion." In Sheila Greeve, ed., *Feminism and Process Thought.* New York: E. Mellen Press, 1981, pp. 106-37.

Luker, Kristin. *Taking Chances.* Berkeley: University of California Press, 1975.

Manier, Edward; Liu, William; and Soloman, David, eds. *Abortion: New Directions for Policy Studies.* Notre Dame: Notre Dame University, 1977.

Matulis, Sherry. "Abortion 1954." *The Progressive* 45 (August 1981): 66.

Mohr, James C. *Abortion in America: The Origins and Evolution of National Policy, 1800-1900.* New York: Oxford University, 1978.

Nathanson, Bernard N. *Aborting America.* Garden City, N.Y.: Doubleday, 1979.

Nicholson, Jeanne Bell, and Stewart, Debra W. "Abortion Policy in 1978," *Publius* 9 (Winter 1979): 161-67.

Noonan, John. *A Private Choice: Abortion in America in the Seventies.* New York: Free Press, 1979.

Osofsky, Howard, and Osofsky, Joy. *The Abortion Experience: Psychological and Medical.* New York: Harper & Row, 1973.

Potts, Malcolm. *Abortion.* Cambridge: Cambridge University, 1977.

Ramsey, Paul. "Protecting the Unborn." *Commonweal* 50 (1974): 308-14.

Sarvis, Betty, and Rodman, Hyman. *The Abortion Controversy*. Second edition. New York: Columbia University, 1974.

Sass, Lauren R. *Abortion: Freedom of Choice and the Right to Life*. New York: Facts on File, 1978.

Sloane, Robert Bruce. *A General Guide to Abortion*. Chicago: Nelson-Hall Publishers, 1973.

Smetana, Judith G. *Concepts of Self and Morality: Women's Reasoning about Abortion*. New York: Praeger, 1982.

Sneideman, B. M. "Abortion: A Public Health and Social Policy Perspective." *New York University Review of Law and Social Change* 7 (1978): 187–213.

Veatch, Robert M. *Death, Dying, and the Biological Revolution*. New Haven, Conn.: Yale University, 1976.

Watters, Wendell W. *Compulsory Parenthood: The Truth about Abortion*. Toronto: McClelland and Stewart, 1976.

Wood, M. A., and Durham, W. C., Jr. "Counseling, Consulting, and Consent: Abortion and the Doctor Patient Relationship." *Brigham Young University Law Review* (1978): 783–845.

Zimmerman, Mary K. *Passage through Abortion: The Personal and Social Reality of Women's Experiences*. New York: Praeger, 1977.

## Ethical Issues Relating to Abortion

Abbott, Philip. "Philosophers and the Abortion Question." *Political Theory* 6 (1978): 313–35.

Algeo, Donald. "Abortion, Personhood, and Moral Rights." *Monist* 64 (1981): 543–49.

Altman, Andrew. "Abortion and the Indigent." *Journal of Social Philosophy* 11 (1980): 5–9.

Bassen, Paul. "Present Stakes and Future Prospects: The Status of Early Abortion." *Philosophy and Public Affairs* 11 (1982): 314–37.

Beauchamp, Tom L., and Walters, LeRoy, eds. *Contemporary Issues in Bioethics*. Second edition. Belmont, Calif.: Wadsworth, 1982.

Becker, Lawrence. "Human Being: The Boundaries of the Concept." *Philosophy and Public Affairs* 4 (1975): 334–59.

Bennett, Jonathan. "Whatever the Consequences." *Analysis* 26 (1966): 83–102.

Blumenfeld, Jean Beer. "Abortion and the Human Brain." *Philosophical Studies* 32 (1977): 251–68.

Boehmer, William J. "In the Absence of Proof." *Personalist* 60 (1979): 325–35.

Brody, Baruch A. *Abortion and the Sanctity of Human Life: A Philosophical View.* Cambridge, Mass.: MIT Press, 1975.

―――. "Thomson on Abortion." *Philosophy and Public Affairs* 1 (1972): 335–40.

Callahan, D. "Abortion and Medical Ethics." *American Academy of Political and Social Science, Annals* 437 (1978): 116–27.

Carrier, L. S. "Abortion and the Right to Life." *Social Theory and Practice* 3 (1975): 381–402.

Churchill, Larry R., and Siman, Jose Jorge. "Abortion and the Rhetoric of Individual Rights: Why the Abortion Debate Is Sterile." *Hastings Center Report* 12 (1982): 9–12.

Cohen, Marshall. *Rights and Wrongs of Abortion.* Princeton, N.J.: Princeton University, 1974.

Cosby, Grant. "Abortion: An Unresolved Moral Problem." *Dialogue* 17 (1978): 106–21.

Daniels, Charles B. "Abortion and Potential." *Dialogue* 18 (1979): 220–23.

Decker, Raymond. "More Christian Than Its Critics." *Commonweal* 51 (1975): 384–93.

Dinello, Daniel. "On Killing and Letting Die." *Analysis* 31 (1971): 83–86.

Englehardt, E. Tristram, Jr. "Viability and the Use of the Fetus." In Tom L. Beauchamp and Terry P. Pinkard, eds., *Ethics and Public Policy.* Englewood Cliffs, N.J.: Prentice-Hall, 1983, pp. 291–311.

Evers, Williamson M. "Rawls and Children," *Journal of Libertarian Studies* 2 (1978): 109–14.

Feinberg, Joel. "Abortion." In Tom Regan, ed., *Matters of Life and Death.* New York: Random House, 1980, pp. 183–217.

Finnis, John. "The Rights and Wrongs of Abortion." *Philosophy and Public Affairs* 2 (1973): 117–45.

Fleck, Leonard M. "Abortion, Deformed Fetuses and the Omega Pill." *Philosophical Studies* 36 (1979): 271–83.

Foot, Philippa. "The Problem of Abortion and Negative and Positive Duty: A Reply to James LeRoy Smith." *Journal of Medicine and Philosophy* 3 (1978): 253–55.

―――. "The Problem of Abortion and the Doctrine of Double Effect." *The Oxford Review* 5 (1967).

Frankena, William K. "The Ethics of Respect for Life." In Stephen Barker, ed., *Respect for Life.* Baltimore: Johns Hopkins University Press, 1976.

Freitas, Robert A., Jr. "Fetal Adoption: A Technological Solution to the Problem of Abortion Ethics." *Humanist* 40 (1980): 22–23.

Gillespie, Norman C. "Abortion and Human Rights." *Ethics* 87 (1977): 237–43.

Glover, Jonathan. *Causing Death and Saving Lives.* Harmondsworth, England: Penguin Books, 1977.

Goldman, Alan H. "Abortion and the Right to Life." *Personalist* 60 (1979): 402–6.

Goodpaster, Kenneth E. "On Being Morally Considerable." *Journal of Philosophy* 75 (1978): 308–25.

Greenwell, James R. "Abortion and Moral Safety." *Critica* 9 (December 1977): 35–48.

Hare, R. M. "Abortion and the Golden Rule." *Philosophy and Public Affairs* 4 (1975): 201–22.

Humber, James M. "Abortion, Fetal Research, and the Law." *Social Theory and Practice* 4 (1977): 127–47.

Hutchinson, D. S. "Utilitarianism and Children." *Canadian Journal of Philosophy* 12 (1982): 61–73.

Jones, Gary E. "Rights and Desires." *Ethics* 92 (1981): 52–56.

Langham, Paul. "Between Abortion and Infanticide." *Southern Journal of Philosophy* 17 (1979): 465–71.

Levy, Steven R. "Abortion and Dissenting Parents: A Dialogue." *Ethics* 90 (1980): 162–63.

Matthews, Gareth B. "Life and Death as the Arrival and Departure of the Psyche." *American Philosophical Quarterly* 16 (1979): 151–57.

McLachlan, Hugh V. "Must We Accept Either the Conservative or the Liberal View on Abortion?" *Analysis* 37 (1977): 197–204.

Montague, Phillip. "The Moral Status of Human Zygotes." *Canadian Journal of Philosophy* 8 (1978): 697–705.

Morreall, John. "Of Marsupials and Men: A Thought Experiment on Abortion." *Dialogos* 16 (1981): 7–18.

Narveson, Jan. "Tinkering and Abortion." *Dialogue* 17 (1978): 125–28.

Newman, Jay. "An Empirical Argument Against Abortion." *New Scholasticism* 51 (1977): 384–95.

Noonan, John. *The Morality of Abortion.* Cambridge, Mass.: Harvard University, 1970.

Paul, Ellen Frankel. "Self-ownership, Abortion, and Infanticide." *Journal of Medical Ethics* 5 (1979): 133–37.

Pluhar, Werner S. "Abortion and Simple Consciousness." *Journal of Philosophy* 74 (1977): 159–72.

Purdy, Laura and Tooley, Michael. "Is Abortion Murder?" In Robert L. Perkins, ed., *Abortion: Pro and Con.* Cambridge, Mass.: Schenkman Publishing Co., 1974.

Ross, Steven L. "Abortion and the Death of the Fetus." *Philosophy and Public Affairs* 11 (1982): 232–45.

Roupas, T. G. "The Value of Life." *Philosophy and Public Affairs* 7 (1978): 154–83.

Schedler, George, and Kelly, Matthew J. "Abortion and Tinkering." *Dialogue* 17 (1978): 122–25.

Sher, George. "Subsidized Abortion: Moral Rights and Moral Compromise." *Philosophy and Public Affairs* 10 (1981): 361–72.

Sherwin, Susan. "The Concept of a Person in the Context of Abortion." *Bioethics Quarterly* 3 (1981): 21–34.

Silber, T. "Abortion in Adolescence: The Ethical Dimension." *Adolescence* 15 (Spring 1980): 43–54.

Singer, Peter. *Practical Ethics.* New York: Cambridge University, 1979.

Smith, James LeRoy. "The Problem of Abortion and Negative and Positive Duty." *Journal of Medicine and Philosophy* 3 (1978): 245–52.

Sumner, L. W. *Abortion and Moral Theory.* Princeton, N.J.: Princeton University Press, 1981.

Thomson, Judith Jarvis. "A Defense of Abortion." *Philosophy and Public Affairs* 1 (1971): 47–66.

_____. "Rights and Deaths." *Philosophy and Public Affairs* 2 (1973): 146–59.

Tooley, Michael. "Abortion and Infanticide." *Philosophy and Public Affairs* 2 (1972): 37–65.

Trinkaus, Walter. "Dred Scott Revisited." *Commonweal* 51 (1975): 384–94.

Voegeli, W. J., Jr. "Critique of the Pro-Choice Argument." *The Review of Politics* 43 (1981): 560–71.

Warren, Mary Anne. "Do Potential People Have Moral Rights?" *Canadian Journal of Philosophy* 7 (1977): 275–89.

Weatherford, Roy. "Philippa Foot and the Doctrine of Double Effect." *Personalist* 60 (1979): 105–13.

Weiss, Roslyn. "The Perils of Personhood." *Ethics* 89 (1978): 66–75.

Werner, Richard. "Abortion: The Moral Status of the Unborn." *Social Theory and Practice* 3 (1974): 201–22.

_____. "Hare on Abortion." *Analysis* 36 (1976): 177–81.

Wertheimer, Roger. "Understanding the Abortion Argument." *Philosophy and Public Affairs* 1 (1971): 67–95.

Wicclair, Mark R. "The Abortion Controversy and the Claim That This Body is Mine." *Social Theory and Practice* 7 (1981): 337–46.

Zaitchik, Alan. "Viability and the Morality of Abortion." *Philosophy and Public Affairs* 10 (1981): 18–26.

## Statistical Studies

Center for Disease Control. *Abortion Surveillance 1978*. Atlanta: U.S. Dept. of Health and Human Services, November 1980.

Grimes, David A., and Cates, Willard, Jr. "Complications from Legally-Induced Abortion: A Review." *Obstetrical and Gynecological Survey* (1979): 177–191.

Guttmacher Institute. *Family Planning, Contraception, Voluntary Sterilization and Abortion*. Rockville, Md.: U.S. Dept. of H.E.W., Public Health Service, Health Services Administration, Bureau of Community Health Services, 1978.

New York State, Department of Health, State Center for Health Statistics. *Induced Abortions Recorded in New York State 1980*. Albany, N.Y., 1980.

New York Times Information Service. *Abortion: Issues and Trends*. Parsippany, N.J.: New York Times Information Service, 1978.

*Safe and Legal: Ten Years' Experience with Legal Abortion in New York State*. New York: Guttmacher Institute, 1980.

*Teenage Pregnancy: The Problem That Hasn't Gone Away*. New York: Guttmacher Institute, 1980.


## The Politics of Abortion

Crawford, Alan. *Thunder on the Right*. New York: Pantheon Books, 1980.

East, Sen. John P. "Report: The Human Life Bill–S.158." *The Human Life Review* 8 (1982): 81–112.

Francome, C. "Abortion Politics in the United States." *Political Studies* 28 (1980): 613–21.

Hansen, S. B. "State Implementation of Supreme Court Decisions: Abortion Rates Since *Roe v. Wade*." *Journal of Politics* 42 (1980): 372–95.

Hyde, Rep. Henry J. "The Human Life Bill." *The Human Life Review* 8 (1982): 6–20.

Jaffe, Frederick S., et al. *Abortion Politics: Private Morality and Public Policy*. New York: McGraw-Hill Book Co., 1981.

Langerak, Edward A. "Abortion: Listening to the Middle." *Hastings Center Report* 9 (October 1979): 24–28.

Merton, Andrew H. *Enemies of Choice: The Right-to-Life Movement and Its Threat to Abortion*. Boston: Beacon Press, 1981.

Nicholson, Jeanne Bell. "The Court, Abortion Policy and State Response: A Preliminary Analysis." *Publius* 8 (Winter 1978): 159–78.

Petchesky, R. P. "Antiabortion, Antifeminism, and the Rise of the New Right." *Feminist Studies* 7 (1981): 206–46.

Rubin, Eva R. *Abortion, Politics and the Courts: Roe v. Wade and Its Aftermath.* Westport, Conn.: Greenwood Press, 1982.

Schneider, Carl. *The Law and Politics of Abortion.* Lexington, Mass.: Lexington Books, 1980.

Segers, Mary C. "Abortion Politics and Policy: Is There a Middle Ground?" *Christianity and Crisis* 40 (1980): 21–27.

Sobran, Joseph. "The Value-Free Society." *The Human Life Review* 8 (1982): 21–29.

Sperry, Peter. "The Class Conflict over Abortion." *The Public Interest* 52 (1978): 69–84.

Steinhoff, Patricia G. *Abortion Politics: The Hawaii Experience.* Honolulu: University of Hawaii, 1977.

Tatalorich, Raymond, and Daynes, Bryan W. *The Politics of Abortion: A Study of Community Conflict in Public Policy Making.* New York: Praeger, 1981.

Vinovskis, M. A. "The Politics of Abortion in the House of Representatives in 1976." *Michigan Law Review* 77 (1979): 1790–1827.

## Attitudes Towards Abortion

Barnett, S. N., and Harris, R. J. "Recent Changes in Predictors of Abortion Attitudes." *Sociology and Social Research* 66 (1982): 320–34.

Fischer, E. H., and Farina, A. "Attitude toward Abortion and Attitude-Relevant Overt Behavior." *Social Forces* 57 (1978): 585–99.

Singh, B. K., and Leahy, P. J. "Contextual and Ideological Dimensions of Attitudes toward Discretionary Abortion." *Demography* 15 (1978): 381–88.

Tedrow, L. M., and Mahoney, E. R. "Trends in Attitudes toward Abortion: 1972–1976." *Public Opinion Quarterly* 43 (1979): 181–89.

Uslaner, Eric, and Weber, Ron. "Public Support for Pro-Choice Abortion Policies in the Nation and States." *Michigan Law Review* 77 (1979): 1772–89.

## Law and Morals

Alexander, Lawrence, and Bayles, Michael. "Hercules or Proteus? The Many Theses of Ronald Dworkin." *Social Theory and Practice* 5 (1980): 267–304.

Barry, Brian. "Circumstances of Justice and Future Generations." In Richard I. Sikora and Brian Barry, eds., *Obligations to Future Generations*. Philadelphia: Temple University, 1978, pp. 204–18.

———. "Justice between Generations." In Peter M. S. Hacker and Joseph Raz, eds., *Law, Morality and Society: Essays in Honor of H.L.A. Hart*. Oxford: Clarenden Press, 1977, pp. 268–84.

Calabresi, Guido, and Bobbitt, Philip. *Tragic Choices*. New York: Norton, 1978.

Callahan, Daniel. *Abortion: Law, Choice and Morality*. New York: Macmillan, 1970.

Care, Norman, and Trelogan, Thomas, eds. *Issues in Law and Morality*. Cleveland: Case Western Reserve, 1973.

Devlin, Patrick. *The Enforcement of Morals*. Oxford: Oxford University, 1965.

Dworkin, Ronald. *Taking Rights Seriously*. Cambridge, Mass.: Harvard University, 1978.

Feinberg, Joel. "Moral Enforcement and the Harm Principle." In Tom Beauchamp, ed., *Ethics and Public Policy*. Englewood Cliffs, N.J.: Prentice-Hall, 1975, pp. 283–96.

———. *Social Philosophy*. Englewood Cliffs, N.J.: Prentice-Hall, 1973.

Gallie, W. B. "Essentially Contested Concepts." *Proceedings of the Aristotelian Society* 56 (1955–56): 167–98.

Grassian, Victor. *Moral Reasoning: Ethical Theory and Some Contemporary Moral Problems*. Englewood Cliffs, N.J.: Prentice-Hall, 1981.

Gray, John. "On the Contestability of Social and Political Concepts." *Political Theory* 5 (1977): 331–48.

Gutman, Amy. "Moral Philosophy and Political Problems." *Political Theory* 10 (1982): 33–48.

Hart, H.L.A. "Are There Any Natural Rights?" *Philosophical Review* 64 (1955): 175–91.

———. *Law, Liberty and Morality*. New York: Vintage Books, 1963.

Hilgers, Thomas, and Horan, Dennis, eds. *Abortion and Social Justice*. Thaxton, Va.: Sun Life, 1972.

Humber, James M., and Almeder, Robert F. *Biomedical Ethics and the Law*. New York: Plenum Press, 1976.

Kuflik, Arthur. "Morality and Compromise." In Roland J. Pennock and John W. Chapman, eds., *Compromise in Ethics, Law and Politics: Nomos XXI*. New York: New York University, 1979, pp. 38–65.

Mill, John Stuart. *On Liberty*. Edited by David Spitz. New York: W. W. Norton, 1975.

Miller, Arthur S. *Social Change and Fundamental Law*. Westport, Conn.: Greenwood Press, 1979.

Nagel, Ernest. "The Enforcement of Morals." *The Humanist* 28 (1968): 20-27.

Nozick, Robert. *Anarchy, State and Utopia.* New York: Basic Books, 1974.

Pennock, J. Roland, and Chapman, John W., eds. *Compromise in Ethics, Law, and Politics: Nomos XXI.* New York: New York University, 1979.

Rae, Douglas. *Equalities.* Cambridge, Mass.: Harvard University, 1981.

Rapoport, Anatol. *Fights, Games and Debates.* Ann Arbor: University of Michigan, 1960.

Rawls, John. *A Theory of Justice.* Cambridge, Mass.: Harvard University, 1971.

Raz, Joseph. *The Authority of Law: Essays on Law and Morality.* Oxford: Clarendon Press, 1979.

Reiman, Jeffrey. *In Defense of Political Philosophy.* New York: Harper & Row, 1972.

Sen, Amartya. *Collective Choice and Social Welfare.* San Francisco: Holden-Day, 1970.

Sterba, James P. *The Demands of Justice.* Notre Dame: University of Notre Dame, 1980.

Thurow, Lester. *The Zero-Sum Society.* New York: Penguin Books, 1981.

Wardle, L. D. "The Gap between Law and Moral Order: An Examination of the Legitimacy of the Supreme Court Abortion Decisions." *Brigham Young University Law Review* (1980): 811-35.

Wasserstrom, R., ed. *Morality and the Law.* Belmont, Calif.: Wadsworth Publishing Co., 1971.

Weiss, Donald. "Wollheim's Paradox." *Political Theory* 1 (May 1973): 154-70.

Wollheim, Richard. "A Paradox in the Theory of Democracy." In Peter Laslett and W. G. Runciman, eds., *Philosophy, Politics and Society.* Second Series. Oxford: Basil Blackwell, 1962.

## Legal Issues

### General

Bennett, R. W. "Abortion and Judicial Review: Of Burdens and Benefits, Hard Cases, and Some Bad Law." *Northwestern University Law Review* 75 (1981): 978-1017.

Boyle, J. M. "That the Fetus Should Be Considered a Legal Person." *American Journal of Jurisprudence* 24 (1979): 59-71.

Bryant, M. D., Jr. "State Legislation on Abortion after *Roe v. Wade:* Selected Constitutional Issues." *American Journal of Law and Medicine* 2 (1976): 101-32.

Dembitz, N. "The Supreme Court and a Minor's Abortion Decision." *Columbia Law Review* 80 (1980): 1251-63.

Estreicher, Samuel. "Congressional Power and Constitutional Rights: Reflections on Proposed 'Human Life' Legislation." *Virginia Law Review* 68 (1982): 333-458.

Griffin, E. "Viability and Fetal Life in State Criminal Abortion Laws." *Journal of Criminal Law and Criminology* 72 (1981): 324-44.

Gunther, Gerald. *Cases and Materials on Constitutional Law.* 10th ed. Mineola, N.Y.: Foundation Press, 1980.

Horan, D. J. "Viability, Values and the Vast Cosmos." *Catholic Lawyer* 22 (1976): 1-37.

Kemp, K. A., et al. "Supreme Court and Social Change: The Case of Abortion." *Western Political Quarterly* 31 (1978): 19-31.

Moore, E. N. "Moral Sentiment in Judicial Opinions on Abortion." *Santa Clara Law Review* 15 (1975): 591-634.

Newton, Lisa H. "Abortion in the Law: An Essay on Absurdity." *Ethics* 87 (1977): 244-50.

Regan, Donald. "Rewriting *Roe v. Wade.*" *Michigan Law Review* 77 (1979): 1569-1646.

Sendor, Benjamin B. "Medical Responsibility for Fetal Survival under Roe and Doe." *Harvard Civil Rights—Civil Liberties Law Review* 10 (1975): 444-71.

Skahn, Steven L. "Abortion Laws, Religious Beliefs, and the First Amendment." *Valpariso University Law Review* 14 (1980): 487-526.

Uddo, B. J. "Human Life Bill: Protecting the Unborn through Congressional Enforcement of the Fourteenth Amendment." *Loyola Law Review* 27 (1981): 1079-97.

U.S. Congress. Senate. Committee on the Judiciary. Subcommittee on Separation of Powers. *The Human Life Bill: Hearings v. 1-2 April 23-June 18 (1981) on S.158.* 97th Cong., 1st Sess., 1981.

U.S. Congress. Senate. Committee on Labor and Human Resources. Oversight of Family Planning Programs. *Hearing March 31, 1981 on Examination of the Role of the Federal Government in Birth Control, Abortion Referral, and Sex Education Programs.* 97th Cong., 1st Sess., 1981.

Vinoskis, M. A., ed. "Symposium on the Law and Politics of Abortion." *Michigan Law Review* 77 (August 1979): 1569-1789.

Wood, M. A., and Hawkins, L. B. "State Regulation of Late Abortion and the Physician's Duty of Care to the Viable Fetus." *Missouri Law Review* 45 (1980): 394-422. .

### Funding Abortions

Ambrose, Linda. "The McRae Case: A Record of the Hyde Amendment's Impact on Religious Freedom and Health Care." *Family Planning/ Population Reporter* 7 (April 1978): 26-28.

Appleton, S. F. "Beyond the Limits of Reproductive Choice: The Contributions of the Abortion Funding Cases to Fundamental-Rights Analysis and to the Welfare Rights Thesis." *Columbia Law Review* 81 (1981): 721-58.

Cates, Willard. "The Hyde Amendment in Action." *Journal of the American Medical Association* 246, (September 4, 1981): 1109-12.

Gold, J., and Cates, W., Jr. "Restriction of Federal Funds for Abortion: 18 Months Later." *American Journal of Public Health* 69 (1979): 929-30.

Goldblatt, Ann Dudley. "Funding of Elective Abortion." In Marc D. Basson, ed., *Rights and Responsibilities in Modern Medicine.* New York: Liss, 1981, pp. 229-42.

Horan, D. J., and Marzen, T. J. "Supreme Court on Abortion Funding: The Second Time Around." *St. Louis University Law Journal* 25 (1981): 411-27.

Petitti, D. B., and Cates, W., Jr. "Restricting Medicaid Funds for Abortion: Projections of Excess Morality for Women of Childbearing Age." *American Journal of Public Health* 67 (1977): 680-82.

Sher, George. "Government Funding of Elective Abortions." In Marc D. Basson, ed., *Rights and Responsibilities in Modern Medicine.* New York: Liss, 1981, pp. 219-28.

### Case Law on Abortions and Other Moral Issues

*Anders v. Floyd,* 440 U.S. 445 (1978).
*Beal v. Doe,* 432 U.S. 438 (1977).
*Belloti v. Baird,* 443 U.S. 622 (1976).
*Brown v. Board of Education,* 347 U.S. 483 (1954).
*Colautti v. Franklin,* 439 U.S. 379 (1979).
*Commonwealth v. Kenneth Edelin,* 371 Mass. 497, 359 N.E.2d 4 (1976).
*Doe v. Bolton,* 410 U.S. 179 (1973).

*Doe v. Commonwealth's Attorney for the City of Richmond* 425 U.S. 901 (1976).

*Eisenstadt v. Baird,* 405 U.S. 438 (1972).

*Gary-Northwest Indiana Women v. Orr,* ____ U.S. ____, 49 U.S.L.W. 3806 (1981).

*H.L. v. Matheson,* 450 U.S. 398 (1981).

*Harris v. McRae,* ____ U.S. ____, 48 U.S.L.W. 4941 (1980).

*Hollenbaugh v. Carnegie Free Library,* 439 U.S. 1052 (1978).

Hyde Amendments. Pub. L. 94-439, Title II §209, 90 Stat. 1434 (1976). Pub. L. 95-205, §101, 91 Stat. 1460 (1977). Pub. L. 95-480, Title II §210, 92 Stat. 1586 (1978).

*Katzenbach v. Morgan,* 384 U.S. 641 (1966).

*Kelley v. Johnson,* 425 U.S. 238 (1976).

*Lochner v. New York,* 198 U.S. 45 (1905).

*Loving v. Virginia,* 388 U.S. 1 (1967).

*Maher v. Roe,* 432 U.S. 464 (1977).

*Miller v. California,* 413 U.S. 15 (1973).

*Minersville School District v. Gobitis,* 310 U.S. 586 (1940).

*Moore v. City of East Cleveland, Ohio,* 431 U.S. 494 (1977).

*Myer v. Nebraska,* 262 U.S. 390 (1923).

*Oregon v. Mitchell,* 400 U.S. 112 (1970).

*Parham v. J.R.,* 442 U.S. 584 (1979).

*Pierce v. Society of Sisters,* 268 U.S. 510 (1925).

*Planned Parenthood of Central Missouri v. Danforth,* 428 U.S. 52 (1976).

*Poelker v. Doe,* 432 U.S. 519 (1977).

*Roe v. Wade,* 410 U.S. 113 (1973).

*Roth v. United States,* 354 U.S. 476 (1957).

*Skinner v. Oklahoma,* 316 U.S. 535 (1942).

*West Virginia State Board of Education v. Barnette,* 319 U.S. 624 (1943).

*Whalen v. Roe,* 423 U.S. 1313 (1977).

*Zalalocki v. Redhail,* 434 U.S. 374 (1978).

# INDEX

## About the Author

FRED FROHOCK is Professor of Political Science at Syracuse University. He is the author of *The Nature of Political Inquiry, Normative Political Theory,* and *Public Policy,* and articles in the *Journal of Politics* and the *American Political Science Review* among other journals.